First Steps in Counselling

A Students' Companion for Basic Introductory Courses

3rd edition

Pete Sanders

PCCS BOOKS

Ross-on-Wye

First edition published in 1994
Second edition published in 1996
Third edition published in 2002
Reprinted 2003 twice
Reprinted in 2004

PCCS BOOKS
Llangarron
Ross-on-Wye
HR9 6PT
UK
Tel. 01989 77 07 07
www.pccs-books.co.uk

First Steps in Counselling — A Students' Companion for Basic Introductory Courses
3rd edition

ISBN 1 898059 51 9

Cover design by Denis Postle
Printed by Bath Press, Bath, UK.

Contents

Acknowledgements

The author and PCCS would like to thank the following publishers and authors for their kind permission to use the copyright material listed below.

Song Lyrics

ONCE IN A LIFETIME
Words and music by David Byrne, Chris Frantz, Tina Weymouth, Jerry Harrison and Brian Eno. © 1982 EG Music Ltd/co-publisher notice (provided by Warner Chappell Music Ltd) for the world. All Rights Reserved. © 1992 Index Music Inc/Bleu Disque Music Co Inc, USA. Warner Chappell Music Ltd, London, W1Y 3FA.

HUMAN BEHAVIOUR
Words and Music by Björk Gudmundsdottir, Nellee Hooper, Antonio Carlos Jobim © 1993 by Famous Music Corporation, Ensign Music Corporation and Warner Chappell Music Ltd. International Copyright Secured. All Rights Reserved.

I AM AFRAID
Words and music by David Couse. Reproduced by kind permission of Chrysalis Music Ltd.

BOYS DON'T CRY
The Cure. Lyrics used with kind permission from Fiction Songs Ltd, London W1P 1LB.

IF
Words and music by Roy Harper. Lyrics reproduced by kind permission of Roy Harper.

TELEVISION, THE DRUG OF THE NATION
Words by Michael Franti. Lyrics reproduced by kind permission of Guerilla Management.

FIFTEEN YEARS
Words and music by Simon Friend, Charles Heather, Mark Chadwick and Jonathan Sevink. ©1992 Universal/Empire Music Ltd, 77 Fulham Palace Road, London. Used by permission of Music Sales Ltd. All Rights Reserved. International Copyright Secured.

Poems

ALL-PURPOSE LATE TWENTIETH CENTURY CREED
Simon Rae. First published in *The Guardian* newspaper.

WHITE COMEDY
Benjamin Zephaniah (1995) from the book *Propa Propaganda* published by Bloodaxe Books.

Dedicated to the memories of
John and Joan Sanders

Foreword

Brian Thorne: Emeritus Professor of Counselling, University of East Anglia, and Co-founder of the Norwich Centre

The Third Edition of *First Steps in Counselling* has all the many merits of previous editions together with some notable and stimulating additions. For me, it remains by far the best text for those embarking on introductory courses in counselling not only because of the richness of its content but also because of its engaging style. Pete Sanders is a provocative enthusiast and his delight in his subject together with his enjoyment of debate ensure that this book contains not a single boring paragraph. This is an astonishing achievement in a subject area which all too frequently spawns books of ponderous impenetrability. *First Steps in Counselling* is immediately accessible and ensures that its readers enter into self-exploration as they are introduced to the theories and practice of the leading counselling orientations. It is the ideal companion for those who embark on what may well turn out to be a process of experiential learning with profound implications. It will help to anchor that learning by providing clear compass bearings in what can sometimes be a somewhat turbulent ocean.

The book appears six years after the second edition and Pete Sanders gives ample evidence that he is highly alert to the shifts and developments in the counselling world during recent years. He is also keenly aware of the insidious pressures of a culture which through its obsessional concern with targets, standards, accountability and cost effectiveness brings ever-escalating numbers to the counsellor's door. Seasoned practitioners and trainers will find in its pages updated material, for example, on the new ethical framework of the British Association for Counselling and Psychotherapy and a much extended section on the contexts where counselling now takes place culminating in a splendid box entitled 'Counselling Skills for Citizens'. They will also be introduced to the Independent Practitioners Network and will hear the voices of those who challenge many of the developments towards the increasing regulation and professionalisation of counselling. In short, this is not a book which is merely an admirable text for those dipping their toes for the first time into the exciting waters of the counselling experience although it is certainly that. The experience, knowledge and versatility which Pete Sanders has brought to his task offer to the reader the opportunity to engage in a highly personal way not only with the theory and practice of counselling but also with many of the questions which confront our society and culture as we enter the twenty-first century. In the deceptive guise of a manual for beginners we discover a work of considerable scholarship and no little passion for the well-being of humankind.

Norwich
July 2002

Introduction

When I started writing the first edition of this book it seemed a good idea to produce a book for students on introductory courses, since I could find precious few books (actually, none!) written for this group. I soon found out why. A very broad spectrum of people come to introductory counselling courses for a wide variety of reasons. Trying to write something that would be a useful and rewarding read for the majority proved challenging and taxing. I realise that some course participants will have no prior knowledge or experience of counselling, whilst others may have come across counselling before, or may even be doing it as a volunteer or as part of their job.

I have tried hard to pitch the book so that it is a 'catch-all' with something for everyone on introductory courses whatever their starting point. In attempting this, I realised that three things would need to be made clear; first, that the book is not trying to teach or train readers standing alone, but is intended as a supplement to a course, a 'course text' if you like. Second, that the course level aimed at is below counselling skills courses; they would need a different type of book. Finally that the key themes of the book are *information* and *self-awareness*.

The book is intended to be interactive. I hope this is self-explanatory. There are two types of 'box' in this book: a 'quotation' box with this border: ▮▮▮▮▮▮ and an 'activity' box with this border: ═══════

I am not the first to suggest that personal development is achieved via many routes and that our ideas in counselling come from many different sources. It is as if to underline this, for the benefit of beginning helpers right from the start, that I decided to include quotes from a wide range of sources. The quotes are ones that have special meaning for me and it would be a bonus if they strike a chord with some readers too.

I have felt for some time that the participants on introductory courses are a very influential group. Not only are they the seed corn for certificate and diploma courses, but even if they do not proceed any further with their counselling training, they carry away with them a view of counselling. This view of counselling will be passed on to friends, relatives, colleagues, or the person standing in the pub. These participants whose introductory course experience is their one and only contact with counselling will pass judgement on counselling on the basis of this contact. My aim with this book is to help make that judgement as well-informed and positive towards the value of counselling as possible.

None of the chapters in this book is complete. It is in the nature of helping and counselling to be a process moving towards something rather than arriving at a state of completion. I have tried to raise as many issues as possible through the examples in the book, issues which I make no attempt to resolve. It is for the course tutors (and you the reader) to decide how best to work with them.

Thanks to everyone who helped me with this book, especially Maggie, without whom I would not have written it. I am particularly grateful to the trainers at Off The Record, Tyneside circa 1972–4. They helped me take my own first steps in counselling.

Pete Sanders
July 2002

What is Counselling?

1

INTRODUCTIONS — WHO ARE YOU?

Most introductory courses in counselling begin with an activity where each person in the group has to introduce themselves to the rest of the group. Sometimes the activity is made a little more complicated and you will be asked to choose another person in the group to pair up with and talk to for a minute or two. Then you will be asked to introduce your partner to the rest of the group.

This can be quite a challenge if you're not used to speaking in groups, especially if you feel a little awkward talking about yourself. Counselling training is a challenging business, so most courses start as they mean to continue! Also, it's important for you to get to know each other reasonably well so that you can feel relaxed about talking in the group. Most of the learning in Introductory Courses happens through the process of sharing your ideas with others and listening to what they have to say. The listening bit here is important, since nearly everyone would agree that it is a skill which lies at the very heart of counselling, so the more we practise the better.

Would you like to introduce yourself now? It's just as true for this book as it is for your counselling course group — if we can form a relationship through the pages of this book, it will be all the easier for me to write and you to read. So, who are you, and how would you introduce yourself to me, what kind of information would you include?

As for me, my name is Pete Sanders. I decided to call myself 'Pete' rather than 'Peter' when I was 17 and still at school after reading a book on numerology. With my friends I worked out that according to the system in the book, 'Pete Sanders' added up to a number with better star potential than 'Peter Sanders'.

I am married to Maggie, my second wife (I am her second husband). Between us we have four children all of whom have grown up and live away from us in different parts of the world, each pursuing their own lives.

I got involved in counselling by accident when I was an undergraduate student in Newcastle-upon-Tyne in 1972. I joined a phone-in and drop-in youth counselling agency called 'Off the Record' as a volunteer and decided that I wanted to do counselling as a job. I went to Aston University and completed the Diploma in Counselling in Educational Settings Course in 1975. I went from there to work as a counsellor and lecturer in Further Education Colleges until I took voluntary redundancy in 1993 to go freelance.

'Spare' or 'leisure' time for me has become a rather curious concept since I gave up my previous job working in a college. Maggie gave up her job as a teacher at the same time and we both now work from home which means we see a lot of each other. Since writing the first edition of this book I have recently retired from practising as a counsellor, supervisor and trainer after over 25 years. I now work as a publisher of counselling books and so I have to maintain an active interest in counselling and psychotherapy in order to stay up-to-date with what's happening in the profession.

Now I've introduced myself, I'm wondering why I chose the bits of my life that I did. I deliberately put in the things that I thought you might be interested in and wanted to keep it brief so that you didn't get bored or think that I was showing off.

What about you? Did you think of 'who you are' in terms of your family and home life? Your hobbies and the things you enjoy? Or, work-related things like the job you do or whether you are in employment? Which are the most important, the most acceptable, and which would you choose to tell me? Which are the most private and which would you choose not to tell me?

How do these questions sound to you at this stage? Perhaps you feel puzzled by them, worried by them or pleased to be asked them. Counselling training tends to emphasise feelings more than other subjects, so you will find more of this as we go along.

EXPECTATIONS — WHY ARE YOU READING THIS?

There are few courses of study that do *not* start with the tutor asking some or all of the students why they have chosen to study that particular subject. There can be few books, however, which begin by asking the reader why they've chosen to read it. Something, or someone, has brought counselling and you together so-to-speak. This book is intended to be your companion on an exciting journey of discovery. When you see this symbol:

✍️   MAKE A NOTE OF YOUR OWN ANSWERS
        & EXAMPLES

On this journey you will find the answers to some important questions which will help you decide whether you really do want to pursue this interest in counselling any further. Questions such as:
  • Why am I interested in counselling?
  • What got me interested in this course?
  • What do I think counselling is?
  • What do I hope will come of it?
  • What are my fears about this course?
  • What will be expected of me — what are the

demands of counselling?
  • Will I be up to it?

It may take some time before you feel satisfied that you can answer these questions fully, but now is a good place to start. The answers will be found over the duration of your introductory course by:
  • Finding out more about *what counselling is*, and
  • Finding out more about *yourself.*

You may be wondering why finding out more about yourself and your motives is so important. Chapter 3 on *The Importance of Self-Development* will look in some detail at this issue.

DEFINITIONS OF COUNSELLING

After the introductions and getting us to ask ourselves why we've chosen to learn about counselling, it's a good idea to move on to looking at what counselling is. This question usually reveals the variety of ideas, attitudes and opinions regarding counselling, what it is, who it's for and who should be doing it. This isn't surprising since counselling has risen from almost total obscurity to become the word on nearly everyone's lips in the past thirty years. A counsellor (in the UK) and a psychiatrist (in the USA) have even been the central characters in situation comedies, but I would caution any readers who think that the media representation of counselling bears any resemblance at all to the real thing!

Over the last 30 years there have been some brave attempts to arrive at a definition, but the situation is not helped by the fact that people will keep on using the word 'counselling' to describe so many different activities!
  • In educational settings, 'counselling' is used alongside the term 'guidance', often to mean helping people find the right course or job.

  • In medical settings and the armed forces some people use 'counselling' in an old-fashioned way to mean discipline. If you have been 'counselled' it means you have been told off or warned that some misdemeanour will go on your record.

- The phrase 'debt counselling' is now used to describe the help you can get to arrange your finances by making regular payments and budgeting.

- Some agencies use the term 'counselling' to describe information and advice given on a particular topic, a healthcare issue perhaps such as family planning or safe sex.

- Many people use 'counselling' to mean any kind of helping activity that they do that hasn't got another more commonplace name like 'tutoring' in education, or 'treatment' in medicine.

- The media use the term 'counselling' to mean anything from support for contestants on 'reality TV shows' to a makeover in a lifestyle show.

So, what do you think? *Just what is counselling?* What happens to you when you see or hear the word?
- What **images** does the word conjure up for you?
- **Who** do you think of?
- What **sounds** do you hear?
- What **thoughts** come into your mind?
- What **feelings** do you have?

Where do these ideas, feelings, sounds and images come from?
- Personal experience of being counselled?
- The beliefs of friends and family?
- What you've read in the papers or seen on TV?
- Someone you know who is a counsellor?
- Books about counselling or psychology?
- Other books, e.g. novels or books about health or spiritual matters?
- The prevailing view of counselling held at your workplace?

'People become engaged in counselling when a person, occupying regularly or temporarily the role of counsellor, offers or agrees explicitly to offer time, attention and respect to another person or persons temporarily in the role of client.

The task of counselling is to give the client an opportunity to explore, discover and clarify ways of living more resourcefully and towards greater well-being.'

Counselling: Definition of Terms in Use with Expansion and Rationale. British Association for Counselling (1991).

'Counselling is an activity freely entered into by the person seeking help, it offers the opportunity to identify things for the client themselves that are troubling or perplexing. It is clearly and explicitly contracted, and the boundaries of the relationship identified. The activity itself is designed to help self-exploration and understanding. The process should help to identify thoughts, emotions and behaviours that, once accessed, may offer the client a greater sense of personal resources and self-determined change.'

Differentiation Between Advice, Guidance, Befriending, Counselling Skills and Counselling. Janice Russell, Graham Dexter and Tim Bond (1992). Advice, Guidance and Counselling Lead Body.

As you set out on this journey of discovery, it might be useful to write down your answers to these questions. It would be interesting to look at them again at the end of the course to see if, and/or how, your views have changed.

```
        COUNSELLING IS

BEING HEARD  CARED-FOR  TRAGEDY
WARMTH    CONFIDENTIALITY    LOVE
   EQUAL       NON-JUDGEMENTAL
NOT TOLD WHAT TO DO        HONESTY
TWO-WAY      FLEXIBLE      SUPPORT
  ONLY FOR PEOPLE WITH PROBLEMS
GRIEF     FRIENDSHIP     NO LIMITS
TIME FOR ME   HELP  CO-OPERATION
EMERGENCY  CRYING  BEREAVEMENT
     A  GENUINE  RELATIONSHIP

  ✍...........  .............  .............
```

The flip-chart above shows some possible responses from a hypothetical training group on an introductory course (the blank spaces leave room for your ideas). How do they compare with the thoughts and feelings you came up with? Each phrase says something about a person's view of counselling, what it is and what it means to them. Let's look at some in a little more detail to find out what people mean by these words.

BEING HEARD
Means being **really heard**. It feels as though the other person is **really interested** in me, and is trying to **understand**.

WARMTH
This is when I feel **welcomed** by someone. As if they're pleased to see me and **really mean it**. It seems as though they genuinely like me.

CONFIDENTIALITY
This is very important if I'm to feel safe. I must be sure that the other person **isn't going to tell anyone else** about what I've said, or even that I've been to see them, in case it's embarrassing.

BEING EQUAL
I like to feel I'm on an equal footing with the other person. So that they're **not acting in a superior way** like an 'expert' or have any power over me.

NON-JUDGEMENTAL
I don't like the feeling of being judged or told off. Some people make me feel as though I've done wrong by the way they speak to me. I prefer to **feel accepted** as a person, then I feel safe.

IT'S ONLY FOR PEOPLE WITH PROBLEMS
Counselling is for people with problems, e.g. marriage guidance. I don't have problems so I don't need to see a counsellor.

NO LIMITS
If I go to a counsellor I should be able to talk about **anything at all** that I think is important.

CRYING
It's OK to cry when you're upset, e.g. if someone close to you has died. Counselling should help you **express your feelings**.

RELATIONSHIP
Counselling is a helping *relationship*, a caring *relationship*. It's about what happens **between two people**. Most counsellors believe this is a central pillar of counselling. Some counsellors (this is explained in Chapter 2: *Where do Ideas in Counselling Come From?*) do not see the relationship as important as the techniques the counsellor teaches the client to use.

Having looked in more detail at some of the meanings behind the 'key words' on the flipchart, do you agree or disagree? (Remember that these are the fictitious views of an imaginary group.)

I have found it helpful to look at counselling in comparison to other helping roles and activities to see where the boundaries are between counselling and the rest of everyday life. Most of us are familiar with the roles of Parent, Friend and Doctor. By this I mean that we have experience of being a patient visiting the doctor, of being a son or daughter and of being someone's friend. What do we want from people in these roles and what do we try to offer when we are in these roles? They are all helpers of one sort or another, so it's clear that helping comes in many different colours. You could also try other helping roles such as teacher, nurse, priest, etc., if you are wanting to practise counselling skills in conjunction with your work. *Here are three more flipcharts with ideas from our hypothetical group:*

PARENT

EVER-OPEN POCKET   SENSITIVE

SENSE OF HUMOUR   TOUGH LOVE

UNSELFISH   ENCOURAGING

DISCIPLINE   TEACHING SELF-CONTROL

PROTECTING   GUIDANCE

UNCONDITIONAL LOVE   FORGIVENESS

GENEROUS WITH TIME   ALWAYS THERE

ASKING FOR AND VALUING
YOUR CHILD'S OPINION

....

DOCTOR

HAS PROFESSIONAL
KNOWLEDGE AND EXPERTISE

RESPECTFUL   NOT INTIMIDATING

SEES ME AS A PERSON PRIVATE

AVAILABLE WHEN I WANT

USER FRIENDLY   TRUSTWORTHY

COMMUNICATION SKILLS   SAFE

WON'T LAUGH AT ME WHEN I
TAKE MY CLOTHES OFF

....

FRIEND

ON YOUR SIDE + WILL STAND UP FOR YOU

HONESTY   SPEAKS UP FOR YOU

LOYALTY   BEING A GOOD COMPANION

FALL OUT + MAKE UP AGAIN   RELIABLE

LENDS MONEY   COMMITTED   SHARING

ALWAYS AVAILABLE   SPARES TIME

RESPECTFUL OF YOUR PRIVACY

YOUR BEST FRIEND WILL TELL YOU

....

How do your thoughts about these helping roles fit in with the flipcharts above? These roles represent the ways of helping and caring that are commonplace in our culture and that we've probably grown up with. Our ideas about good caring tell us a lot about ourselves and it seems as though there might be some common themes about helping which are shared by these roles. This activity also helps us understand where counselling-style helping begins and ends, where it overlaps with other helping activities and where it's different. These limits are called *boundaries*.

BOUNDARIES BETWEEN COUNSELLING AND OTHER WAYS OF HELPING

Boundaries help define an activity by creating a **space** within which the activity can take place. 'Space' brings to mind *my* space, *safe* space, *open* space, *sacred* space, the client's space. In order to make the counselling space safe for the client we protect it with boundaries. These boundaries will keep certain non-counselling or worldly things out and certain counselling-style helping things in.

As can be seen in the panel below, some ways of helping are role- or context-specific. It would not be appropriate for a counsellor to lend clients money or be constantly available for them. Just to make things more complicated, if you work as a volunteer in a helping agency, you will also have to get to grips with the policies of your agency when it comes to boundaries. For example, you might not be allowed to tell a client your surname, yet you might be allowed to lend them money to get home on the bus. These different boundaries are always context-specific, in other words the context in which the helping takes place will bring its own sensible rules regarding how helpers conduct themselves with clients. Some of these agency rules will be informed by whether-or-not 'counselling' is taking place. Or whether the volunteers are using 'counselling skills' or whether the volunteers are offering what I call 'basic helping' or others might call 'listening' or 'support'.

I hope you can now appreciate why making distinctions between types of helping is important. The boundary between what counselling is and

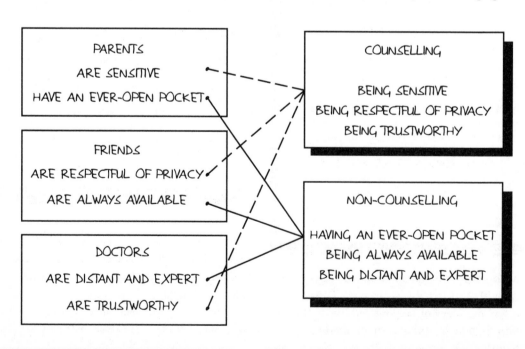

Counselling and Non-Counselling Ways of Helping

Some ways of helping in our culture are fine as counselling ways of helping. On the other hand, some perfectly good ways of helping as a friend, parent, or doctor would be no good as counselling ways of helping. For example, taking some items from our flipcharts on page 5:

PARENTS
ARE SENSITIVE
HAVE AN EVER-OPEN POCKET

FRIENDS
ARE RESPECTFUL OF PRIVACY
ARE ALWAYS AVAILABLE

DOCTORS
ARE DISTANT AND EXPERT
ARE TRUSTWORTHY

COUNSELLING
BEING SENSITIVE
BEING RESPECTFUL OF PRIVACY
BEING TRUSTWORTHY

NON-COUNSELLING
HAVING AN EVER-OPEN POCKET
BEING ALWAYS AVAILABLE
BEING DISTANT AND EXPERT

> The wise ruler says:
> I take no action and the people are transformed of themselves;
> I prefer stillness and the people are rectified of themselves;
> I do not interfere and the people prosper of themselves;
> I am free from desire and the people of themselves become simple like
> the uncarved block.
>
> Lao Tzu: *Tao te Ching*, LXXIII,179.
>
> 'Look here,' Furii said. 'I never promised you a rose-garden. I never promised you
> perfect justice . . . and I never promised you peace or happiness. My help is so that you
> can be free to fight for all these things. The only reality I offer is challenge, and being
> well is being free to accept it or not at whatever level you are capable. I never promise
> lies, and the rose-garden world of perfection is a lie — and a bore too!'
>
> Hannah Green: *I Never Promised You a Rose Garden*, p. 101.

what it is not has been, and is currently, the subject of serious debate. The debate is held by just about everyone involved in counselling, including organisations and professional associations. One section of the counselling profession is intent on eventually agreeing a set of competencies for counselling so that qualifications in counselling can be standardised. One of their first tasks is to identify what counselling is and how it is different from other forms of helping such as befriending, guidance, advice, etc.

BRITISH ASSOCIATION FOR COUNSELLING AND PSYCHOTHERAPY

The professional organisation representing the largest number of counsellors and therapists is the *British Association for Counselling and Psychotherapy*. It was established in the mid-1970s as the *British Association for Counselling* (BAC) with just a few hundred members, steadily growing until in 2000 it changed its name to the *British Association for Counselling and Psychotherapy* (BACP) and its members now number over 20,000.

BACP is interested in the distinction between *using counselling skills* and *being a counsellor* for a number of reasons. BACP would like to assure prospective clients that someone claiming to be a counsellor has a minimum level of qualifications and experience. At the same time, BACP know that many people offer helping relationships in a variety of settings and contexts. The type of helping is counselling-like, but the person doing the helping would not call themselves a counsellor. The BACP have developed a framework over the years to help clients, other non-counselling professionals and the public at large understand the different types of helping that are available. We will look at these in later chapters.

Also, in Chapter 9: *Counselling Contexts and Connections*, we will look at the new 'profession' of counselling and there will be more on the role of the BACP there.

BASIC HELPING

In the previous editions of this book I used the phrase 'helping in a counselling way' to describe the type of *informed helping* we might aspire to on completion of a 20–30 hour Introduction to Counselling course. Because this is a cumbersome phrase to fit into sentences, I now prefer to use the term 'basic helping'.

This basic helping will incorporate an awareness of what theories of helping there might be without necessarily *knowing* them in any detail. Allied to this will be an awareness of helping and counselling skills, but not the ability to offer a good range of them. In addition, this basic helping includes an awareness of the goals of counselling and the ethical framework within which professional counsellors work. Finally, we will be aware of the central role of self-development in the effective and responsible training of counsellors, together with the requirement for adequate support and supervision.

As a result of this new and developing awareness our ability as a helper at the most basic level will be improved. We will also be able to confidently assure ourselves, our relatives, friends, colleagues and others that we may try to help, that counselling is a responsible, skilled and useful helping activity whenever they might be in distress. This is basic helping. In Chapter 14 we will briefly review the learning on your basic introductory course and see where you might want to go next in the development of your helping skills.

BEING A BETTER PARENT, FRIEND, NEIGHBOUR AND CITIZEN

There are many reasons why people embark upon basic helping training. Whatever the reasons for starting, there may well be some side benefits that you might not have signed-up for. Since the skills and attitudes central to basic helping are also central to good human relationships, you will find that an introductory course is quite likely to enhance your qualities as a parent, friend, neighbour or even citizen. As we work through the values, qualities and skills of good helping, you will see how these build up to being a more fulfilled person and

---

Definitions of Non-Counselling Helping

Guidance

To offer a confidential, accountable service which helps the client to develop self-awareness. To enable the client to be aware of and have access to accurate, appropriate information on available opportunities in order to make informed choices. The client is offered opportunities to explore relevant concerns and to develop decision-making skills. The activity is designed to help the management of transition appropriate to the client's needs and wishes.

Advice

Advising enables the client to solve problems and make decisions by offering accurate, current and appropriate information. It seeks to widen the client's choice by informing them of their rights, options and possible action programmes.

Befriending

To provide on-going quality support to distressed individuals for an indeterminate period of time. The activity should enable appropriate, realistic and healthy coping skills to be developed in a warm and trusting relationship. Befriending is intended to lessen the person's sense of social or personal isolation.

Differentiation Between Advice, Guidance, Befriending, Counselling Skills and Counselling. Janice Russell, Graham Dexter, Tim Bond (1992). Advice, Guidance and Counselling Lead Body.

responsible citizen. You may find that you feel more able and prepared to help a friend or neighbour in their grief when someone dies, or in making a difficult life decision.

BASIC HELPING IN A VOLUNTARY AGENCY

One of the most popular ways to share your basic helping is through voluntary work. You will see more about this and who might benefit in Chapter 10. Many people in the course group will already be volunteers in a helping agency. Some will have already participated in some agency-specific helping training. What you will find in this book is intended to back up and add to the training you will receive from your agency. If some of the things you read in this book appear to conflict with agency policy, that is not bad news. There are lots of different views in counselling and basic helping, and by exploring these different views through discussion you will learn much more. Discuss any differences you find in your course group and with your agency trainers.

USING COUNSELLING SKILLS

Counselling skills can be used by anyone either as a separate set of techniques or, more usually, as a set of skills either integrated with, or alongside, an already well-established set of professional or 'people' skills. In such a case we might find:

- a nurse using counselling skills when he listens to a patient or comforts grieving relatives.

- a teacher using counselling skills when she is told by a school pupil that he is being bullied.

- a manager using counselling skills when an employee tells her that he is thinking of quitting work to look after an ageing parent.

- a person working at home to bring up children might use counselling skills to comfort a neighbour when their spouse is made redundant.

- a colleague listening really well in order to resolve a disagreement in a meeting.

You might have chosen to attend a basic counselling course to help you in a similar setting at your place of work or in the community. We will look at *who counselling is for* in more detail in Chapter 10.

My own definition of counselling skills is:

'Counselling skills are interpersonal communication skills derived from the study of therapeutic change in human beings, used in a manner consistent with the goals and values of the established ethics of the profession of the practitioner in question. In addition, the user of counselling skills will find that their own professional skills are enhanced by the process.'
Pete Sanders: *An Incomplete Guide to Using Counselling Skills on the Telephone, (Revised 2nd edition),* p. 18.

COUNSELLING

There are many different ways of understanding the nature of counselling. It can be seen as:

- a **counselling approach** to people, i.e. a way of *understanding or looking* at caring for and helping our fellow humans,
- a set of **counselling skills**, i.e. some ways of *behaving* in a caring way,
- a set of **counselling goals** or caring and helping *aims* which we are hoping to achieve.

Some other ways of helping may share some of these features, but not all. When you have all three of the above, then you have counselling.

Helping in a counselling way may share a counselling approach to helping and some of the goals, for example. When using counselling skills, we may share the counselling skills but have a different approach and different goals, e.g. using counselling skills in a nursing setting to achieve nursing goals.

A slightly different way of looking at the problem is to see the definition of counselling as dependent upon the *boundaries of the activity,* the *qualities of the relationship*, and the *aims or functions of the activity*.

The essential **boundaries** of counselling are:
- That it is practised by someone designated as a counsellor.
- That the counsellor be appropriately trained to be able to practise to an acceptable standard.
- That the counsellor abides by a code of ethics and practice (see Chapter 7).
- That the client knows that the service being offered by the counsellor is counselling.

One of the key differences between counselling and using counselling skills is that the counsellor is bound by a code of ethics and practice, and carries a set of professional responsibilities. When using counselling skills, you are also governed by another set of ethical principles and professional responsibilities, e.g. nursing or teaching.

The essential **qualities** of the relationship are:
- That the counsellor shows deep respect for the client.
- The counsellor and client will agree on what the relationship will set out to achieve and how it will seek to achieve it.
- That the client will feel safe enough to be challenged.
- That the client will feel valued as a person.
- The counsellor does not judge the client.

Another of the key differences between counselling and the use of counselling skills, is that the counsellor and client will make an agreement regarding what the client wants from the counsellor and what the counsellor is prepared to offer.

The **aims** or **functions** of counselling are:
- That the client will feel empowered (i.e. have a greater sense of personal autonomy).
- The client has a greater sense of self-understanding.
- To enable the client to live in a more 'satisfying and resourceful way'. (See Russell et al., 1992.)
- That the client has a greater sense of well-being.

- That the above 'gains' should be enduring.

Hopefully the elements of the definitions above will find agreement amongst a wide range of counsellors. As you can see from the various quotations in the bold edged boxes, there is a general convergence of views on what counselling actually is, albeit expressed in slightly different ways.

How do the various definitions and elements of definitions we have looked at compare with your own ideas?

WHAT COUNSELLING IS NOT
As this introductory chapter has progressed, we have looked both at what counselling is and what counselling is not.

Counselling is not:
> Being a friend.
> Caring in a parental way.
> 'Treating' or 'healing' someone like a doctor.
> Instructing or teaching.
> Advising.
> Giving guidance.
> Just using counselling skills.

Sometimes we can find counselling difficult to do well and when we begin to find it difficult we tend to revert back to a way of helping which is more familiar to us.
- The chances are that *you* will prefer to help in a particular way or style. Perhaps because of your job, or maybe because of your personality, you tend to help in a *'teaching'* style or a *'parental'* style or a *'friendly'* style etc.

Others take the view that counselling is potentially a very 'natural' helping style for us as long as we can *stop* trying to do something else like taking control of the situation, thinking we know best, or judging the person we are trying to help.

    • What tendencies do you have to rescue, judge or take control when you are trying to help in a counselling way?

Throughout your basic introductory course you will get feedback from your fellow students and tutors. Some of this feedback might concern what they experience of your natural style of helping. It will be useful to take note of this so that you can identify those occasions when you feel most tempted to stop a counselling style and revert to your natural style. When this happens you have a choice between two styles of helping, both useful under different circumstances. How should this choice be exercised?

• Your children might generally prefer you to help them in a parent-like way rather than be a counsellor.

    Would it be appropriate to offer them counselling-style helping under some circumstances?

• People in a client role might prefer you to help them in a counselling way.

    Would it be appropriate to offer them help in a parental style, teaching style, friendly style or healing style under some circumstances?

Each way of helping is fine under the right circumstances. Counselling, using counselling skills and helping in a counselling way are no better or worse than other ways of helping, just different and suited to certain circumstances. People seeking help have the right to ask for a helping style that suits them; however, we are under no obligation to provide a helping style that we don't feel comfortable with.

There are few of us for whom a counselling way of helping is easy the first time we try to do it, even though we think it is 'right' for us because it is in harmony with our values. We need to practise and work at it on a number of levels: our self-

awareness, our knowledge and our skills. The remaining chapters in the book look in more detail at each of these at a level appropriate to an introductory course.

As a final note on definitions, at its 1996 Annual General Meeting the BAC resolved to formulate a definition of counselling. The Association acknowledged the difficulty of the task, i.e. defining counselling so as to capture the special nature of the helping activity without excluding anyone from the practice of counselling.

COUNSELLING OR PSYCHOTHERAPY?

I have made some effort to come to some helpful definitions in this first chapter, but the truth is that the whole area of professional counselling and psychotherapy is still rather ill-defined in this country. One of the most frequently asked questions is 'What is the difference between counselling and psychotherapy?' Worse still from a public relations point of view, I cannot say that there is an answer on which most professionals can agree.

The British Association for Counselling (BAC) had a keynote speech by Brian Thorne at its 1992 Annual Conference with the title 'Psychotherapy and Counselling: The Quest for Differences' — see *Counselling*, Vol.3, No.4, December 1992 — and he wrote again on this topic in 1999 (Thorne, 1999). At the 1993 Annual General Meeting, the BAC debated whether it should embrace the word 'psychotherapy' in its title (remember that the BAC changed its name in 2000 to **The British Association for Counselling and Psychotherapy**). So you can see that, whilst in professional circles it is a matter for debate, some would say that the debate is really about professional status or even control of the psychological side of the helping professions.

The 'old' BAC Code of Ethics and Practice says on the subject:

    'It is not possible to make a generally accepted distinction between counselling and psychotherapy. There are well-founded traditions which use the terms interchangeably and others which distinguish them.' (para 3.3.)

Clearly this doesn't help if a definitive answer is what you want. It simply means what it says, that for years some groups of professionals have been saying that counselling and psychotherapy are the same whilst other groups of professionals have been saying they're different.

Do you think there are any differences between counselling and psychotherapy? What general impression do you get from media, publicity, friends, family and personal experience? Maybe you think you are not qualified to answer?

In his 1992 paper Brian Thorne looks at possible grounds for distinction including:
- The type of problem: psychotherapy is for deeper-seated problems.
- The type of treatment: psychotherapy uses the dynamics of the relationship between therapist and client.
- Duration of treatment: psychotherapy lasts for a longer time than counselling.
- The setting: psychotherapy takes place in medical settings, counselling in educational settings.

He concludes that there are no grounds for maintaining any difference in usage of the terms 'counselling' and 'psychotherapy'. He emphasises the need to clear up any confusion for the sake of our clients (in my terms, for public relations purposes). Counselling, psychotherapy, call it what you like, has a valuable contribution to make to our quality of life in the twenty-first century and confusion over names and titles will only serve to keep valuable skills away from the people whom they are most likely to benefit. He reiterated these conclusions in 1999.

If I am Helping in a Counselling Way

I am **informed** by:
counselling aims,
counselling skills,
counselling boundaries,
counselling and *counselling skills* ethics.

I will:
have *my own* aims,
use *my own* helping skills,
use *my own* boundaries,
be guided by *my own* ethics.

If I am Helping in a Counselling Way in a Voluntary Agency

I will also:
• know and work according to *agency* policies and protocols.

I am also **informed** by: the aims *of the agency.*

If I am Using Counselling Skills

I will **practise**:
• *counselling skills*
— within *counselling skills* ethics,
• other *professional skills* (e.g. nursing, teaching)
— within other *professional ethics* (e.g. nursing).

I am **informed** by: counselling aims, counselling boundaries.

If I am a Counsellor

• I will **practise** *counselling* skills.
• I will **keep** *counselling* boundaries.
• I will **have** *counselling* aims and goals.
• I am **governed by** *counselling* ethics.

Where do Ideas in Counselling Come From?

2

When I wrote the first edition of this book there was much debate amongst counsellor trainers regarding the blend of ingredients in training. Just how much skills, theory and so on, make the perfect training course? On a basic introductory course, the debate was whether to have theory at all. My view then was expressed in this chapter, the title of which should give the game away; it's a thinly disguised *Counselling Theory* chapter. I think that now, in the new millennium, the debate is old hat. It is universally accepted that an awareness of the theories of helping is essential. Otherwise basic helping would simply be a collection of the best ideas the helper can come up with at the time.

When I first started helping as a volunteer at 'Off the Record' in Newcastle-upon-Tyne the training consisted of around three months of weekly meetings in which we discussed ourselves and did some role plays of 'problem' situations. At no time did anyone mention 'theory' or *where ideas in counselling come from*. Of course, it may have been assumed that, as a psychology undergraduate, I knew it all anyway. (This was not true, since my psychology degree didn't even have a section on 'personality'.) When I asked one of the trainers for more information, it was suggested that I read 'On Becoming a Person' by Carl Rogers. (I misheard the title and spent several hours approaching puzzled bookshop assistants asking if they knew 'I Am Becoming a Person'!)

Later I was thrilled to discover that someone had been thinking about helping skills in such a systematic yet approachable way. Then I discovered that Carl Rogers wasn't the only person to have thought deeply about human psychological distress. Indeed there were several approaches, theories and systems. Each one making claims to be successful and a new one seemed to be added to the list every week!

I decided to try to unravel this tangle of ideas, claims and counter claims. I discovered that the roots of the ideas can be traced as far back as you have the resources and energy to go. From centuries-old ancient philosophies and cultures, through to current ideas in our own white European

'Like most psychologists, I appreciate the breath of fresh air which Freud introduced into the musty dry-as-dust atmosphere of nineteenth-century academic psychology. The brilliance of his mind has opened doors which no one now would wish to close again, and his keen insight has given us a storehouse of theories and hypotheses which will keep researchers busy for years to come.'

H. J. Eysenck: *Uses and Abuses of Psychology*, p. 241.

culture. A summary of the more recent landmarks would go back around 100 years to the work of Sigmund Freud. But first I want to look at some of the popular ideas we share about helping today, starting with the language we use.

Look down the following list of words. They are all ones we may associate with counselling, listening to and helping this person. Which ones are most likely to come to mind when you think about helping?

- Empathy
- Manipulative
- Positive thinking
- Genuine
- Hidden meaning
- Client-centred
- Unconscious
- Making plans
- Non-interpretative
- Symbols
- Non-judgemental
- Getting it in perspective
- Different people
  with problems need
  different sorts of help.
- Behaviour
- Defences
- Active listening
- Goals
- Non-directive
- Problem-solving
- Dreams
- Logical thinking
- Irrational beliefs
- Step-by-step
- Avoidance
- Homework

All of these words can be traced to the five fundamental and very influential approaches to the psychology of human mental distress covered in this chapter. You may be familiar with many of the ideas which are reflected in these approaches. We make certain assumptions about effective helping in our culture which again are reflected in these approaches to human psychology. Each approach has its founders and many more recent approaches to helping have been directly or indirectly influenced by these schools of thought.

The founders of the approaches didn't invent these ideas out of thin air. Each is a product of a person in a social context at a moment in history. Each had their own influences from which they

Defences, Dreams
Hidden meaning
Manipulative
Unconscious
Symbols, Avoidance

Active listening
Non-directive
Non-judgemental
Empathy, Genuine
Client-centred
Non-interpretative

Behaviour
Homework
Goals
Step-by-step
Making plans

Irrational beliefs
Homework
Positive thinking
Making plans
Logical thinking

Different people and
problems need different
sorts of help
Getting it in perspective
Problem-solving

Psychodynamic Approaches
Several contemporary approaches can all be traced back to the original work of Sigmund Freud (1856–1939), founder of *Psychoanalysis*.

No contemporary psychologist or psychotherapist could claim not to be influenced by the work of Freud. Many schools of therapy grew more directly out of his work, sometimes founded by Freud's ex-students or associates, including C.G. Jung, Wilhelm Reich, Melanie Klein, D.W. Winnicott. Modern counselling approaches influenced by Freud include *Transactional Analysis*.

Humanistic Approaches
Developed by a group of American psychologists in the 1950s. In counselling terms, the most influential was Carl Rogers (1902–1987), founder of the *Person-Centred Approach*.

Other influential humanistic psychologists, contemporaries of Rogers, include Abraham Maslow and Rollo May. Rogers' ideas have had a very wide influence in counselling and psychology. Many modern approaches to helping and education now incorporate his ideas or claim to be person- or student- 'centred'.

Behavioural Approaches
Modern psychological approaches based on scientific learning theories of Russian psychologist I.P. Pavlov (1849–1946) and American psychologists J.B. Watson (1878–1958) and B.F. Skinner, founders of *Behaviourism*.

Skinner (more so than Watson) is another highly influential psychologist whose work has touched many modern ideas. 'Behaviour Therapy' became popular in the 1970s after Joseph Wolpé refined the work of the early Behaviourists. Elements of learning theories can be found in most modern counselling approaches since all psychologists would acknowledge the role of learning processes of some sort in human development.

Cognitive Approaches
Emphasising the central role of thoughts in mental processes, cognitive approaches were developed by Aaron Beck and Albert Ellis, founder of *Rational Emotive Behaviour Therapy*.

Beck and Ellis separately developed cognitive approaches to mental distress and change. Cognitive approaches have influenced the development of time-limited helping work which enjoys some support in healthcare settings. Other cognitive approaches have had an impact upon the treatment of severely disturbed people with enduring mental health problems.

Integrative Approaches
The quest to blend components of different therapeutic approaches has enjoyed varying success since the mid-1970s, popularised by Gerard Egan, founder of *Developmental Eclecticism*.

At the forefront of the development of integrative approaches were Egan and Arnold Lazarus with his 'Multimodal Therapy'. In recent years models (some without names) have been developed by Richard Nelson-Jones, Munroe and Manthei and Gary Hermansson. All living in Australasia, the new epicentre of integrative development.

borrowed, sometimes acknowledged, sometimes not. The real picture of where ideas come from is, of course, much more complicated than this. It is probably impossible to understand the origin of ideas fully, but fun to try.

This short introduction to the history of the ideas behind modern counselling will look first at the three foundation-stones of counselling theory, psychoanalysis, behavioural psychology and humanistic psychology. These are sometimes referred to as the first, second and third force in psychology respectively. These terms were coined by an American psychologist in arrogant fashion, rather like the way Americans refer to their national baseball championship as the 'World Series'. It is important to realise that these ideas are probably not new, and it is certain that there have been very sophisticated ideas about healing mental distress in many great and lesser civilisations throughout the ages from China to Africa. Many of these ideas do keep cropping up in modern thinking.

In addition to looking at these 'three forces' in psychology, we will look at a couple of slightly more recently developed ideas in counselling, namely the notion that our *thoughts* are important in shaping our feelings (called the *cognitive* approach) and the idea that the best way of helping is to blend together or *integrate* the best of each approach (called *integrative* counselling).

I will be asking you to discover your *own* ideas about helping and to look at how these fit in with the approaches covered in the book. At this stage in your learning as a helper it is useful to know how your own ideas fit in with classical theories. If you decide to progress to developing and using counselling skills, or to counselling proper, such an appreciation of your own and other people's ideas is *essential*.

You may be reading this and thinking that you don't have any ideas about helping other than 'common sense'. Do not be too hasty to dismiss common sense, since it is the helping approach used by the vast majority of the human race. Your own version of common sense will be a blend of personal experience of being helped, things you've learned from your parents, guardians, priests and teachers, the impact of literature, films, etc. on your thinking and . . . well, you complete the rest:

What experiences, events and people have determined your views on helping?
- What sort of helping did you get from your parents when you needed it?
- Did you get help from teachers at school?
- How have you tried to help friends, relatives and colleagues?
- What books have you read that have influenced your ideas about helping others?
- What ideas about helping others do you get from the newspapers you read and the TV you watch?
- What other influences on your ideas about helping can you list?

THE PROBLEM WITH MOST COUNSELLING THEORIES

It will not take you long to work out, as you read through the next few pages, that each of the 'theories' or approaches I am going to cover was developed and presented by a white man from northern Europe or North America. This is a serious problem since ideas that people have, spring from the culture in which they live. The ideas that white men can think up are limited by their whiteness and their maleness (and in the case of the theorists covered here, by their privileged, educated status).

We have to ask ourselves whether it is reasonable to believe that white, middle-class, educated men are the only people with anything useful to say about helping and counselling, and the answer is, of course, no. We now realise that the ideas that have guided our thinking about counselling for the last 100 or so years are, for the most part, androcentric (centred around male ways of thinking and doing things) and ethnocentric (centred around the culture and race of the theorist, i.e. white culture).

I have already suggested that the men whose ideas have shaped contemporary helping and counselling were and are products of their time. We can, then, reasonably expect the ideas to reflect and be shaped by the cultural biases and mores that prevailed. In my view it would, for example, be unfair to criticise Freud for coming up with a helping system based on the expert knowledge of the therapist, since society in Northern Europe in the late 1800s revolved around the experts who held knowledge (and therefore power), such as priests, judges and physicians.

It would be less forgivable for someone to base a twenty-first century theory of helping on the powerful 'expert' knowledge of the helper, since Northern European/American culture is now much more 'customer-centred'. Doctors are now much more likely to ask patients if they have any idea why they are ill and few priests still claim to have direct links with gods.

The effect of basing a helping approach on theory that is so culturally narrow, that only supports the status quo, is that it simply absorbs and passes on any institutionalised discrimination and oppression that is a feature of that culture. So to different extents, all of the theories are presenting very narrow views of people — namely psychologies based on being white, being a man, being able-bodied, being educated, etc. Black people, women, gay men, lesbians and disabled people all ask *'Where do I fit in to this theory?'* and *'Where is my psychology in this?'* You will find more material on prejudice and oppression in Chapter 4.

For the moment I am suggesting that you read about the ideas which have shaped helping in our culture on the following pages with some questions in your head:
- How do these ideas measure up to *your* views on:
  - The nature of human beings?

- The causes of human distress?
- The nature of helping?
[Don't be afraid of having your own ideas — remember the activity on page 16 — let your own experience and your common sense be your guides.]

- Can you find *yourself* in the ideas. In other words, if you are gay, black, a woman, disabled or non-European, do the ideas at least account for your experience?

- To what extent are these ideas still relevant to helping today in our 1990s culture?

- You might find it useful to make notes as you go along.

In addition to the chapter on *Prejudice, Oppression and Counselling* you will find more material related to the current topic in Chapter 9: *Counselling Contexts and Connections*.

WHY IS THEORY IMPORTANT AT THIS STAGE?
Helping is a skilled and responsible activity. Anyone wanting to improve their helping capacity needs to look at three aspects which contribute to their final performance as a helper:

- Theories -
- Skills -
- The personality of the helper -

A quick look at the contents page will reveal that each of these three aspects is represented in this book.

You may have thought that you know nothing about the theoretical origins of counselling before you started reading this chapter. I hope that pages 13 to 15 have shown that theory is not always something we get from books. Theories about how and why humans behave as we do are all around us in our culture. From the small, micro culture of our family and its myths to the large, macro-culture of white Anglo-America we get ideas about the way humans are. As I suggested before, ideas don't come out of thin air. Freud, Rogers, Skinner and others were all influenced by their respective cultures.

If I was to answer the question in the chapter title as briefly as possible, I would say 'Ideas in counselling come firstly from our own personal theories and secondly from books on counselling.' The aim of this section is twofold. Firstly to help you think about your personal ideas about human behaviour. Secondly to help you identify the possible origins of these ideas. You can then find and understand your starting point on theory in terms of ideas in contemporary psychology.

I am fascinated by theories, who thought them up and the circumstances under which they came to think them up. Add to that my belief that helpers should always be ready to explain what they are doing in terms a little more elegant than 'Just listening', 'Being caring' or 'Letting the client let off steam', and you will understand why I've included this chapter in an introductory book. I like to know a little about the main players in the theoretical field, so I've included some short biographical sketches of Freud, Rogers, Skinner, Ellis and Egan on pages 34–38.

I will start by introducing a framework with which we will evaluate ideas. It has a superficial appearance of complexity, but I hope you will find it entertaining.

On the next page you will find a series of scales on which we might have opinions about human personality and behaviour. Do you think, for example, that we learn to be 'who we are' or that our personality is largely inborn, the result of hereditary factors? Do you think that we have conscious free will and can make emancipated decisions about how we act, or is our behaviour determined by unconscious motives beyond our knowledge and control?

If you go through the scales noting your position on each, we will move on to looking at how each of the major approaches fares on the scales. Then we will be able to find out where we fundamentally agree and disagree with each approach. It is common for people to find that their personal views are reflected by a mixture of ideas from each approach.

The idea for these scales comes from Hjeller, L.A. and Ziegler, D.J., *Personality Theories — Basic Assumptions, Research and Applications.* McGraw-Hill, (1981).

'Life is, and we are, far bigger and more vital than the ultimately flimsy, hero-worshipping thought systems and prized ingots of intellectual property with which we weigh ourselves down. Institutions institutionalise us. Core theoretical models infantilize and zoologize us and our clients — that is, deny us our autonomy, cage, shrink and dehumanise us. At least, that's my theory — for now!'

Colin Feltham, 'Against and beyond core theoretical models' p. 191. (In House and Totton 1997)

'Thus psychotherapists ignore the fact that we do not really know what goes on in anyone else's mind, that people are very suggestible and that we do not understand how some of them manage to get better. These facts are disguised by a variety of elaborate conjectures about mental processes which are presented as hard data.'

Katharine Mair, 'The myth of therapist expertise', p 88. (In House and Totton, 1997)

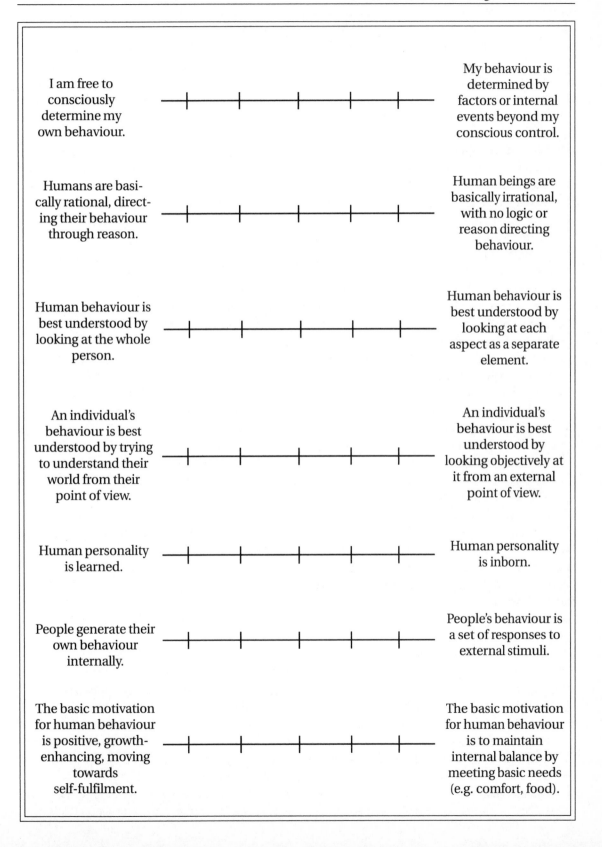

I am free to consciously determine my own behaviour. |—+—+—+—+—+—| My behaviour is determined by factors or internal events beyond my conscious control.

Humans are basically rational, directing their behaviour through reason. |—+—+—+—+—+—| Human beings are basically irrational, with no logic or reason directing behaviour.

Human behaviour is best understood by looking at the whole person. |—+—+—+—+—+—| Human behaviour is best understood by looking at each aspect as a separate element.

An individual's behaviour is best understood by trying to understand their world from their point of view. |—+—+—+—+—+—| An individual's behaviour is best understood by looking objectively at it from an external point of view.

Human personality is learned. |—+—+—+—+—+—| Human personality is inborn.

People generate their own behaviour internally. |—+—+—+—+—+—| People's behaviour is a set of responses to external stimuli.

The basic motivation for human behaviour is positive, growth-enhancing, moving towards self-fulfilment. |—+—+—+—+—+—| The basic motivation for human behaviour is to maintain internal balance by meeting basic needs (e.g. comfort, food).

Psychoanalysis (Freud)

THE NATURE OF MENTAL ACTIVITY

Freud believed mental activity existed in three domains:

- *Unconscious* or beyond our awareness and inaccessible. An individual cannot gain access to her unconscious because it always remains hidden from her conscious mind. Hidden and inaccessible though it is, unconscious mental activity motivates much of our daily actions. The unconscious makes itself known through symbols, for example in dreams, which our conscious mind needs help in interpreting. Only through the process of psychoanalysis can this be revealed. The mental processes in the unconscious domain are chaotic and bizarre, obeying no laws of logic

- *Pre-conscious* activities are those which although unconscious can be drawn into awareness through memory. Anything out of our immediate awareness which can be recalled, such as telephone numbers, postcodes, names, etc. are pre-conscious.

- *Conscious* mental activity, fairly obviously, is the domain of full awareness. All thoughts and feelings of which I am aware are conscious. The conscious domain is governed by logical processes obeying the laws of reason.

Freud believed that everything we do and think has a 'goal'. There is no such thing as an accident or chance event. This is where the phrase 'Freudian Slips' comes from — indicating that our slips of the tongue are by no means accidental.

STRUCTURE OF PERSONALITY

Freud divided human personality into three distinct structures or areas:

- *Id* This is part of the personality that we are born with. Freud described the id as a seething cauldron of instincts and desires which seek gratification at all costs. Id processes are unconscious, therefore chaotic and are ultimately pleasure- and comfort-seeking. The id has no values, morals or concept of right and wrong.

Its workings are most clearly seen in the behaviour of a new-born baby. Freud called the inborn energy of the id the life energy or *libido* and he believed that it was largely sexual in nature.

- *Super-ego* This is the conscience, the internalised parent part of the personality. Freud believed that the super-ego formed when the child identifies with the same-sex parent, changing 'You mustn't do this' to 'I mustn't do this' so internalising rules, morals, notions of right and wrong, sex roles, etc. The development of the super-ego is basically a learning process. The strength of the super-ego is accounted for by the fact that it develops at a very early age (around five years old) when young children are very vulnerable and impressionable.

- *Ego* The ego develops through childhood, first as a mediator between the chaotic id and the outside world. The ego works out the consequences of behaviour aimed at satisfying the id and checks the id impulses based on reality. Later the ego has to appease the demands of the super-ego, so its task becomes a delicate balancing act. The ego is only fully developed at maturity. A properly adjusted adult is governed by the ego, balancing the 'I want it now!' demands of the id against the 'You mustn't do this you naughty boy!' admonishments of the super-ego.

The ego maintains control by using defence mechanisms which are unconscious. They help protect us from the demands of the id, often by simply avoiding the issue.

PSYCHODYNAMIC APPROACHES

The modern generic name for approaches based on Freud's theory is 'psychodynamic'. Nowadays, only the traditional psychoanalysts hold the more rigid ideas, such as the *unknowable* unconscious, strictly. Many psychodynamic therapists will, for example, incorporate in to their practice the *instrumental* (see Chapter 5) use of, for example, empathy and positive regard for their clients.

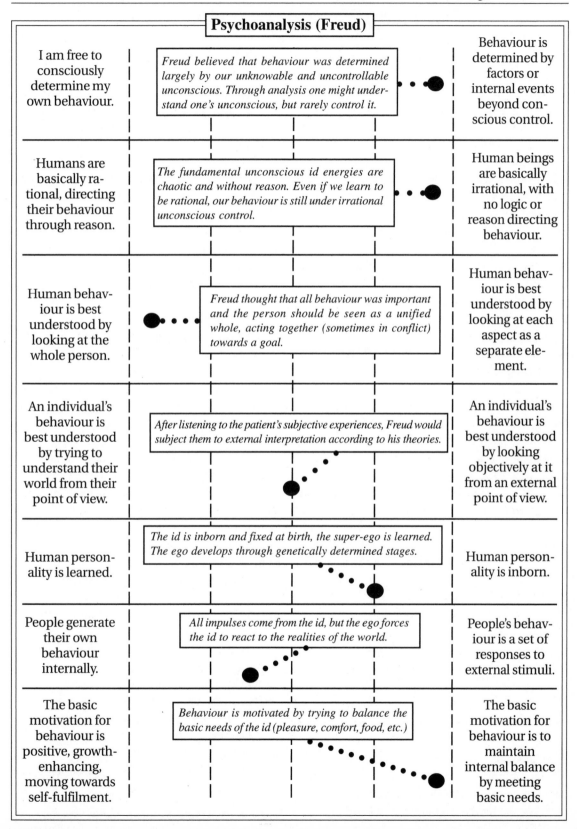

Psychoanalysis (Freud)

I am free to consciously determine my own behaviour.

Freud believed that behaviour was determined largely by our unknowable and uncontrollable unconscious. Through analysis one might understand one's unconscious, but rarely control it.

Behaviour is determined by factors or internal events beyond conscious control.

Humans are basically rational, directing their behaviour through reason.

The fundamental unconscious id energies are chaotic and without reason. Even if we learn to be rational, our behaviour is still under irrational unconscious control.

Human beings are basically irrational, with no logic or reason directing behaviour.

Human behaviour is best understood by looking at the whole person.

Freud thought that all behaviour was important and the person should be seen as a unified whole, acting together (sometimes in conflict) towards a goal.

Human behaviour is best understood by looking at each aspect as a separate element.

An individual's behaviour is best understood by trying to understand their world from their point of view.

After listening to the patient's subjective experiences, Freud would subject them to external interpretation according to his theories.

An individual's behaviour is best understood by looking objectively at it from an external point of view.

Human personality is learned.

The id is inborn and fixed at birth, the super-ego is learned. The ego develops through genetically determined stages.

Human personality is inborn.

People generate their own behaviour internally.

All impulses come from the id, but the ego forces the id to react to the realities of the world.

People's behaviour is a set of responses to external stimuli.

The basic motivation for behaviour is positive, growth-enhancing, moving towards self-fulfilment.

Behaviour is motivated by trying to balance the basic needs of the id (pleasure, comfort, food, etc.)

The basic motivation for behaviour is to maintain internal balance by meeting basic needs.

Humanistic Approaches (Maslow & Rogers)

The views developed by several American psychologists (Maslow, Rogers, May) in the 1950s constitute what has become known as *humanistic psychology*. Whilst there are some differences between their ideas, there is an overwhelming agreement about key themes. Rogers is best known for his theories as they relate to the practice of counselling and psychotherapy, and it is his ideas I will use as the basis for evaluation on the framework opposite. However, in order to build a well-rounded picture, I will begin with some of Maslow's ideas.

Humanistic theories of personality maintain that humans are motivated by the uniquely human need to expand their frontiers and to realise as much of their potential as possible. These theories emphasise 'growth motives' and so contrast with both psychoanalytical and behavioural approaches which highlight the reduction of biological needs.

According to Maslow, the motive to develop one's basic potential can take precedence over other motives including, occasionally, those related to biological needs. Maslow called this striving to achieve personal potential 'self-actualisation'. He saw it as a pyramid of needs with the needs at each level having to be met before the next level can be approached meaningfully. We are always striving for self-improvement according to Maslow, and this goes beyond the simple meeting of our basic needs.

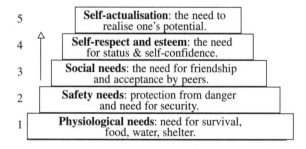

Carl Rogers' work concerning the process of change in therapy and education is based on the following fundamental propositions:
• That the fundamental underpinning or 'core'

of human personality is constructive and forward-moving.
• That humans have this instinctive movement towards achieving their full potential in a constructive way, which he calls being 'fully functioning'.
• That this movement towards fulfilling one's potential (actualisation) includes the organism's capacity for self-healing (including psychological healing).
• That if the counsellor can provide the right conditions, then this self-fulfilling, self-healing process can flourish.
• That the right conditions are primarily when there is a complete absence of threat to the individual (see below).
• That the best vantage point from which to understand another person's behaviour is from their subjective viewpoint.
• That people respond better if they experience the helper as a genuine ('real') person, rather than someone in the role of 'expert'.

It is easy to see why Carl Rogers called his approach *Person-Centred*, since the client is the centre of the helping process in the sense that helping is seen as activating the self-healing process located in the client themselves by providing basic or *'core'* helping *conditions*. It is a respectful, non-threatening method, letting the client direct the process themselves through the wisdom of their self-healing tendencies.

In 1957 Rogers detailed the six conditions that are necessary for therapeutic change. These are:
• that the helper makes psychological contact with the person to be helped
• that the client is vulnerable or anxious
• that the helper is congruent or genuine
• that the helper experiences non-judgemental warmth or acceptance towards the client
• that the helper experiences empathy
• that the client receives the empathy, UPR and genuineness of the helper

These are covered in more detail in Chapter 5.

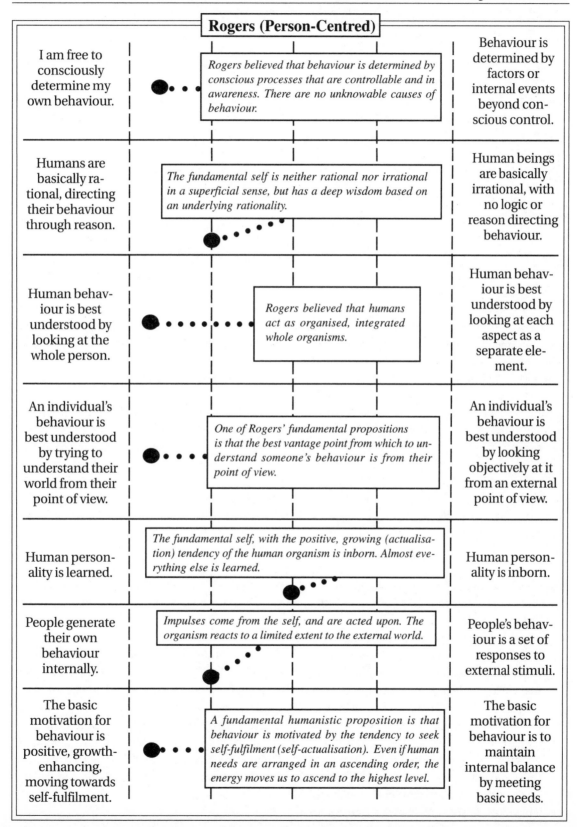

Rogers (Person-Centred)

I am free to consciously determine my own behaviour.	*Rogers believed that behaviour is determined by conscious processes that are controllable and in awareness. There are no unknowable causes of behaviour.*	Behaviour is determined by factors or internal events beyond conscious control.
Humans are basically rational, directing their behaviour through reason.	*The fundamental self is neither rational nor irrational in a superficial sense, but has a deep wisdom based on an underlying rationality.*	Human beings are basically irrational, with no logic or reason directing behaviour.
Human behaviour is best understood by looking at the whole person.	*Rogers believed that humans act as organised, integrated whole organisms.*	Human behaviour is best understood by looking at each aspect as a separate element.
An individual's behaviour is best understood by trying to understand their world from their point of view.	*One of Rogers' fundamental propositions is that the best vantage point from which to understand someone's behaviour is from their point of view.*	An individual's behaviour is best understood by looking objectively at it from an external point of view.
Human personality is learned.	*The fundamental self, with the positive, growing (actualisation) tendency of the human organism is inborn. Almost everything else is learned.*	Human personality is inborn.
People generate their own behaviour internally.	*Impulses come from the self, and are acted upon. The organism reacts to a limited extent to the external world.*	People's behaviour is a set of responses to external stimuli.
The basic motivation for behaviour is positive, growth-enhancing, moving towards self-fulfilment.	*A fundamental humanistic proposition is that behaviour is motivated by the tendency to seek self-fulfilment (self-actualisation). Even if human needs are arranged in an ascending order, the energy moves us to ascend to the highest level.*	The basic motivation for behaviour is to maintain internal balance by meeting basic needs.

Behavioural Approaches (Skinner)

Academic psychology has made a patchy contribution to theories of helping and counselling. What often happens is that psychotherapists and counsellors call upon the findings of academic psychology to support their ideas, usually integrating several diverse findings to try to form a coherent therapeutic approach. As they do this they often leave out any academic findings that do not support their approach. This way of doing things is not limited to one of the counselling approaches — they all do it to a greater or lesser extent.

The behavioural approaches, more than any other theory, uses academic psychology as its starting point. Much of modern psychology owes a great deal, at least in part, to the work of early behaviourists. Behaviourism grew in the early 1900s to all but dominate American psychology in the middle of the century. J. B. Watson and B. F. Skinner working separately and on different learning processes founded the movement which Skinner hoped would set humans free from the shackles of their existence by developing a technology of change and making it available to everyone — science to set the common man free. Armed with an understanding of learning processes, humankind would take control of their destiny.

The basic principles of behaviourism are:
- Apparently complex behaviour is a collection of more simple elements which can be understood in terms of basic learning principles.
- Learning, or the acquisition of new responses, requires reward. Ignoring unwanted behaviours leads to their 'extinction' or disappearance. (Punishment suppresses the expression of responses but doesn't eliminate them.)
- Human personality is acquired entirely through learning, i.e. human personality is a collection of favourite or most used responses based on those that have brought success in the past.
- Behaviour is a set of responses where internal stimuli such as hunger, thirst, etc., are paired with external stimuli such as the sight of food, drink, etc., in variously complex ways. Behaviour is therefore seen as being directed towards a specific goal.
- Whatever has been learned can be unlearned and modified through the application of learning principles.

These rather harsh and uncompromising views of the early behaviourists have been tempered in recent years by the incorporation of more 'human' factors such as thinking processes (e.g. positive thinking), attitudes and emotions, etc. The nature of the learning processes themselves has been broadened to include more 'soft' processes such as learning by observation and learning without obvious physiological reinforcement (i.e. getting food or drink as a 'reward').

Some of these basic principles were marshalled into therapeutic methods by therapists such as Joseph Wolpé who refined a step-by-step method of overcoming irrational fears (phobias) by presenting people with more and more fear-provoking stimuli whilst they were relaxed (called systematic desensitisation). Similar efforts led to systems of reward where tokens were given to (for example) patients in mental hospitals for 'good' behaviour (perhaps related to their individual treatment plan) which they could exchange for privileges such as tobacco (called token economy systems).

Behavioural approaches identify a clear goal which is achieved by repeated rewarded practice, often in small steps leading to the desired change. They are built on the idea that human difficulties and distress can be overcome by unlearning (or 'extinguishing') unproductive ways of thinking, feeling and behaving, then learning better, more fulfilling ways of behaving, thinking and feeling.

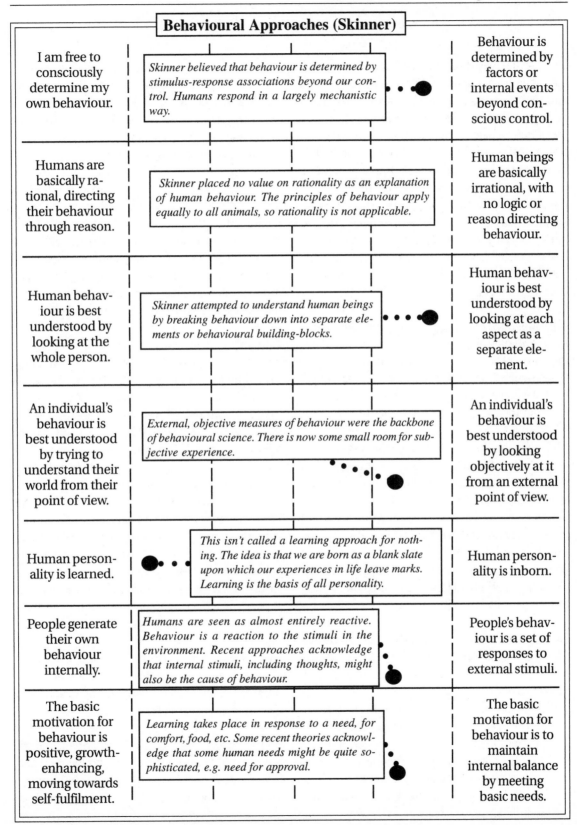

Behavioural Approaches (Skinner)

I am free to consciously determine my own behaviour.	*Skinner believed that behaviour is determined by stimulus-response associations beyond our control. Humans respond in a largely mechanistic way.*	Behaviour is determined by factors or internal events beyond conscious control.
Humans are basically rational, directing their behaviour through reason.	*Skinner placed no value on rationality as an explanation of human behaviour. The principles of behaviour apply equally to all animals, so rationality is not applicable.*	Human beings are basically irrational, with no logic or reason directing behaviour.
Human behaviour is best understood by looking at the whole person.	*Skinner attempted to understand human beings by breaking behaviour down into separate elements or behavioural building-blocks.*	Human behaviour is best understood by looking at each aspect as a separate element.
An individual's behaviour is best understood by trying to understand their world from their point of view.	*External, objective measures of behaviour were the backbone of behavioural science. There is now some small room for subjective experience.*	An individual's behaviour is best understood by looking objectively at it from an external point of view.
Human personality is learned.	*This isn't called a learning approach for nothing. The idea is that we are born as a blank slate upon which our experiences in life leave marks. Learning is the basis of all personality.*	Human personality is inborn.
People generate their own behaviour internally.	*Humans are seen as almost entirely reactive. Behaviour is a reaction to the stimuli in the environment. Recent approaches acknowledge that internal stimuli, including thoughts, might also be the cause of behaviour.*	People's behaviour is a set of responses to external stimuli.
The basic motivation for behaviour is positive, growth-enhancing, moving towards self-fulfilment.	*Learning takes place in response to a need, for comfort, food, etc. Some recent theories acknowledge that some human needs might be quite sophisticated, e.g. need for approval.*	The basic motivation for behaviour is to maintain internal balance by meeting basic needs.

Cognitive Approaches — REBT (Ellis)

The widespread emphasis on feelings in counselling was challenged by both Aaron T. Beck and Albert Ellis in the 1960s and 70s. Ellis developed Rational Emotive Therapy, or RET, later changing the name of his therapeutic approach to Rational Emotive *Behaviour* Therapy or REBT. These approaches are now known as cognitive behavioural approaches — *cognition* is the psychological term for thinking. The literature suggests that Ellis and Beck (both originally trained in Psychoanalysis) developed their ideas more-or-less in parallel, and I have chosen to look in more detail at Ellis because his ideas are easily put in everyday language.

Ellis suggested that thoughts are important factors in determining feelings and that in fact it is our thoughts that are at the centre of human disturbance. In particular Ellis suggested that it is the beliefs we have about ourselves and the world that shape our emotional and behavioural reactions.

This isn't so different from any other set of ideas about human functioning, since most approaches put beliefs about ourselves and the world pretty much at the heart of things. Ellis went on to suggest that there were two basic types of belief we could have, *rational* and *irrational*. In Ellis' terms, rational beliefs were those which promoted personal fulfilment and irrational ones were self-defeating or ideas that frustrated our natural efforts to lead personally fulfilling lives.

He then went on roughly to list types of irrational thinking and the consequences of holding irrational beliefs. For example, he suggested that human beings have a tendency to:
- Make mountains out of molehills, or in Ellis' terms, *awfulize*. This means, for example, taking an event or experience which may be mildly distressing and believing that it is a catastrophe or the end of the world.
- Personalising events in the world — thinking that things are done specifically to get at us,

e.g. believing that the traffic warden singled me out for a parking ticket, rather than thinking that she was just doing her job.
- Overgeneralise by, for example, thinking that something bad will always happen when it has just happened once or twice.

Many readers will, I am sure, recognise these as unhelpful ways of thinking, and may be able to identify such thought patterns in their own lives. Perhaps because such beliefs *are* widely held is one of the reasons behind the popularity of REBT and the other cognitive approaches. The question is, how can an awareness of these unhelpful beliefs be turned into an active and effective helping method?

Ellis maintained that because these thoughts or *cognitions* were essentially intellectual events, they should be tackled at that level. He proposed that the best way to defeat these ideas was for the helper to argue with the person being helped, or *refute* the irrational ideas until the person being helped sees the error of their ways. This may seem a little brusque for a *helping* method and indeed, these ideas about helping — and the method developed from these ideas — are very different from the other ideas we have looked at so far. According to Ellis, helping is not about *pleasing* the person being helped, or being *nice* to them. The best form of helping is to be brutally honest without any gentle let-downs, frills or apologies. To argue with the person you are trying to help so that they see how irrational their ideas are, is the kindest thing to do.

After successful Rational Emotive Behaviour Therapy, Ellis believes that the client will have a 'therapist in their head' who can carry on the battle against irrational beliefs.

Ellis and Beck disagree on the importance of the *relationship* between the client and the therapist. Ellis thought that it was *not* helpful to be warm towards the client, since this might help reinforce the client's irrational behaviour.

Ellis — (REBT)

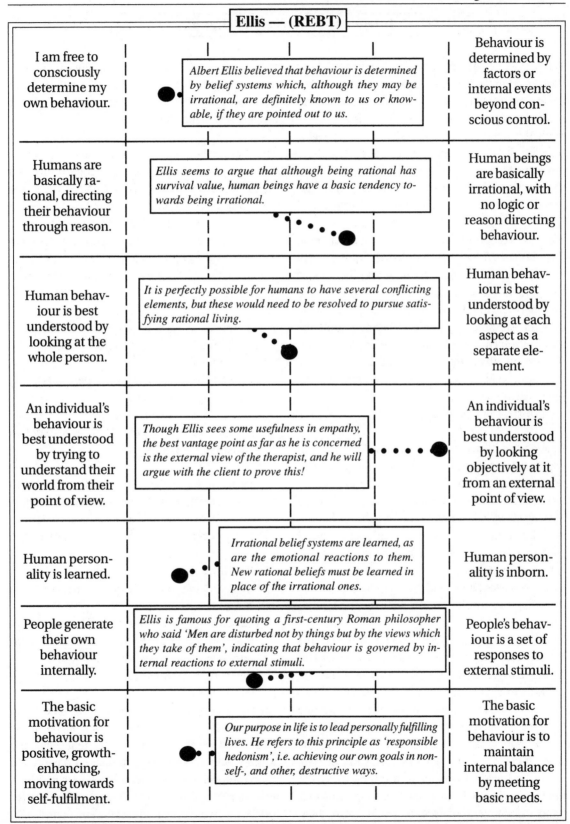

I am free to consciously determine my own behaviour.	*Albert Ellis believed that behaviour is determined by belief systems which, although they may be irrational, are definitely known to us or knowable, if they are pointed out to us.*	Behaviour is determined by factors or internal events beyond conscious control.
Humans are basically rational, directing their behaviour through reason.	*Ellis seems to argue that although being rational has survival value, human beings have a basic tendency towards being irrational.*	Human beings are basically irrational, with no logic or reason directing behaviour.
Human behaviour is best understood by looking at the whole person.	*It is perfectly possible for humans to have several conflicting elements, but these would need to be resolved to pursue satisfying rational living.*	Human behaviour is best understood by looking at each aspect as a separate element.
An individual's behaviour is best understood by trying to understand their world from their point of view.	*Though Ellis sees some usefulness in empathy, the best vantage point as far as he is concerned is the external view of the therapist, and he will argue with the client to prove this!*	An individual's behaviour is best understood by looking objectively at it from an external point of view.
Human personality is learned.	*Irrational belief systems are learned, as are the emotional reactions to them. New rational beliefs must be learned in place of the irrational ones.*	Human personality is inborn.
People generate their own behaviour internally.	*Ellis is famous for quoting a first-century Roman philosopher who said 'Men are disturbed not by things but by the views which they take of them', indicating that behaviour is governed by internal reactions to external stimuli.*	People's behaviour is a set of responses to external stimuli.
The basic motivation for behaviour is positive, growth-enhancing, moving towards self-fulfilment.	*Our purpose in life is to lead personally fulfilling lives. He refers to this principle as 'responsible hedonism', i.e. achieving our own goals in non-self-, and other, destructive ways.*	The basic motivation for behaviour is to maintain internal balance by meeting basic needs.

Integrative Approaches (Egan)

With several approaches to helping being developed in the 50s and 60s some helpers began asking the question *'Which, if any, has the **correct** theory and practice for helping people in distress?'* With each approach making claims to be the 'right' one, or the most effective, a vigorous debate developed amongst devotees of each approach. In the midst of the claims and counter claims the current trend towards integration was forged.

The first edition of Gerard Egan's popular book *The Skilled Helper* was published in 1975. He turned away from constructing grand theories of the person and concentrated on looking at the process of helping itself. He described what he thought were the key skills of helping someone with a problem by selecting what he believed to be the most effective elements of other approaches, thus he assembled a number of techniques to be practised in a series of stages, i.e. that you followed a set of steps in a particular order.

Egan did not propose a personality theory, but suggested that human problems were acquired and perpetuated by a number of internal and external factors. The internal factors, he suggested, were deficits in 'skills' (e.g. of problem-solving, having self-defeating attitudes, etc.) and the external factors were mainly destructive social or interpersonal 'systems' (e.g. families, social conditions, etc.). It made sense, then, to help people 'manage' their problems in a skills-centred way.

This idea that psychological helping (still regarded by some as the exclusive domain of medically qualified psychiatrists) could be reduced to a series of skills or techniques, was inspirational to some and contentious nonsense to others. On the one hand it continued the trend, started by Carl Rogers, to see helping as an activity that is not 'expert' based. On the other hand, it offended some helpers who saw Egan's approach as stripping away the human *qualities* of helping and replacing them with handy, de-humanised *techniques*. Helpers, then,

were to become skilled technicians in Egan's model. Egan took this idea from behavioural psychology, where the whole process could be broken down into steps.

This was the beginning of the equally contentious idea that psychological change (counselling and therapy) could be *manualised*. In other words the steps could be written down cook-book style in a manual and the technician-helper would simply carry them out in the right order. Central to this approach is the ability to assess or diagnose what the problem is, in order to apply the right 'treatment'.

The contribution made by Egan and other integrative pioneers has forced helpers to think hard about what they are doing and why. Key questions are:
- Is it possible to know what the 'best' bits of the various approaches are?

- Can they be put together to form a seamless and effective helping style?

- Is it necessary to have a theory of personality to help understand why a person is asking for help and to give some idea of what must be done in order to get some relief from their suffering?

- Why have the techniques been assembled in this particular way? (Is there a theory?)

- Is a sequence of techniques sufficient for anything other than the most basic levels of helping, or as Egan termed it later *'Problem management'*? (Egan, 1982.)

For many people wishing to improve their basic helping skills, Egan's approach has proved to be simple and useable. However, for many wishing to graduate to counselling 'proper' it has proved to be insubstantial. Egan's work is looked at in a little more detail in Chapter 5 and suggestions for further reading can be found at the end of the book.

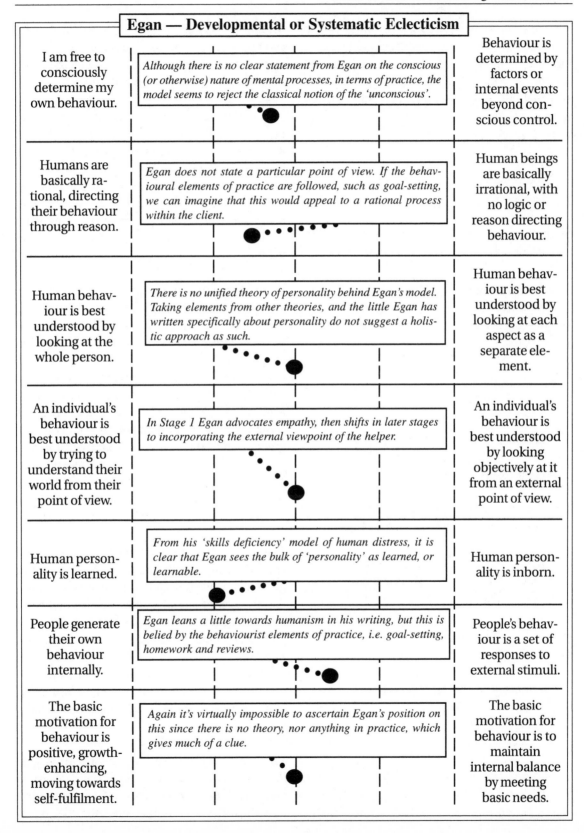

Egan — Developmental or Systematic Eclecticism

I am free to consciously determine my own behaviour.	*Although there is no clear statement from Egan on the conscious (or otherwise) nature of mental processes, in terms of practice, the model seems to reject the classical notion of the 'unconscious'.*	Behaviour is determined by factors or internal events beyond conscious control.
Humans are basically rational, directing their behaviour through reason.	*Egan does not state a particular point of view. If the behavioural elements of practice are followed, such as goal-setting, we can imagine that this would appeal to a rational process within the client.*	Human beings are basically irrational, with no logic or reason directing behaviour.
Human behaviour is best understood by looking at the whole person.	*There is no unified theory of personality behind Egan's model. Taking elements from other theories, and the little Egan has written specifically about personality do not suggest a holistic approach as such.*	Human behaviour is best understood by looking at each aspect as a separate element.
An individual's behaviour is best understood by trying to understand their world from their point of view.	*In Stage 1 Egan advocates empathy, then shifts in later stages to incorporating the external viewpoint of the helper.*	An individual's behaviour is best understood by looking objectively at it from an external point of view.
Human personality is learned.	*From his 'skills deficiency' model of human distress, it is clear that Egan sees the bulk of 'personality' as learned, or learnable.*	Human personality is inborn.
People generate their own behaviour internally.	*Egan leans a little towards humanism in his writing, but this is belied by the behaviourist elements of practice, i.e. goal-setting, homework and reviews.*	People's behaviour is a set of responses to external stimuli.
The basic motivation for behaviour is positive, growth-enhancing, moving towards self-fulfilment.	*Again it's virtually impossible to ascertain Egan's position on this since there is no theory, nor anything in practice, which gives much of a clue.*	The basic motivation for behaviour is to maintain internal balance by meeting basic needs.

Now re-examine the five panels on pages 14 and 15 to see how the words listed there are linked to the five approaches to human behaviour and helping. It is clear that the following words are attributable to psychodynamic approaches and the work of Freud.

Defences   Unconscious
Dreams   Symbols
Hidden meaning   Avoidance
Manipulative

Similarly, the following words are attributable to humanistic approaches and the work of Rogers.

Active listening   Genuine
Non-directive   Client-centred
Non-judgemental   Non-interpretative
Empathy

Also, the following words are attributable to behavioural approaches and the work of Skinner.

Behaviour   Step-by-step
Goals   Homework
Making plans

Likewise, the following words are attributable to cognitive approaches and the work of Ellis.

Irrational beliefs Logical thinking
Homework   Making plans
Positive thinking

Finally, the following words are attributable to eclectic approaches and the work of Egan.

Different people and problems need
different sorts of help
Getting it in perspective
Problem-solving

I hope you can now see how the language of helping has roots in the theories of helping. The words we use are clues to the ideas we hold about helping, helpers and those we are hoping to help, and now you may be able (to some small extent) to trace backwards from the words you use to the theories and the underlying philosophy.

I want to be clear, however, that I am not suggesting that you decide what approach suits you best at this stage. It is too early to 'nail your colours to the mast' in the theories-of-helping sense. It is simply a moment to learn about where the ideas in counselling come from and how, even without being trained in psychology, or even knowing about it, our own ideas have been affected by these theories.

If you decide to continue training in counselling, you will soon have to decide what approach to follow. You have to decide whether you want to practice counselling as a 'pure' approach or as an integration of ideas, ways and methods. This is an inescapable decision, and you can't do both. If you will be continuing in your studies to intermediate level or 'counselling skills' level, you will find that some courses offer 'pure' or mono-theoretical training and others offer 'integrative' training. There will be some input from other theories on both kinds of course, but the core of the training will be person-centred, psychodynamic or whatever on the 'pure' style of course.

THERE ARE THREE POINTS TO THIS CHAPTER
One is to help identify the origin of ideas, not to give a comprehensive introduction to these theories. At this level of learning about helping and basic counselling skills, it would not be appropriate to go into any more detail than I do here. There are suggestions for further reading at the end of the book for those readers who are intending to progress to higher level counselling skills training in one approach, or those who have developed a special interest.

The second is to give you an opportunity to discover which of the approaches is most in harmony with your own views. Over the years I have heard many trainees describe the joy of

How they work — in a nutshell

Psychodynamic Approaches

Inborn instincts are the foundations upon which childhood experiences build our personality.

Our true motives are unconscious and hidden from us because the instincts and urges are taboo.

Our unconscious only lets itself be known to us indirectly through symbolic events like dreams or behaviour.

Using their knowledge and skill, the therapist interprets our experiences and behaviour (e.g. dreams) to unveil our unconscious motives, giving us an opportunity to be free of these unconscious controls.

Humanistic Approaches

All human beings have an inbuilt capacity to grow and achieve their full potential.

This is called actualisation.

If the actualising tendency can be harnessed, human beings can solve their own problems and heal their own psychological hurts.

Actualisation will happen quite naturally if we have the right conditions for it.

The therapist provides these conditions in which we can explore our own experiences. This will help strengthen our self-structure and our tendency towards actualisation.

How they work — in a nutshell

Behavioural Approaches

We are born as 'blank slates'. Human personality, in fact everything we are, is learned.

Behaviour is the objectively observable manifestation of our personality, although thoughts and feelings are important.

Learning leads to only a relatively permanent change, so what can be learned can be unlearned.

We can unlearn behaviour, thoughts and feelings which cause us distress and replace them by learning 'good' ways of thinking, feeling and behaving.

The therapist helps us identify our aims and goals then designs learning programmes that will achieve the desired goal if we follow them.

Cognitive Approaches

We are happiest when the things we do help us achieve personally meaningful goals.

We have a tendency to think in ways that prevent us from leading fulfilling lives. These ways of thinking are 'irrational'.

These irrational beliefs cause unpleasant feelings about the things that happen to us in life because our feelings are controlled by our thoughts. We then adjust our behaviour to fit this pattern.

We can unlearn these irrational ways of thinking and learn rational beliefs which will lead to pleasant feelings and help us achieve our goal of fulfilment.

The therapist helps us identify our irrational beliefs by arguing with us, putting forward logical reasons showing us how to change.

How they work — in a nutshell

Integrative Approaches

People suffer from a wide range of psychological distress and disturbance caused by a lack of personal skills and being caught in destructive social systems.

No one approach could possibly be flexible enough to be helpful to all, or even the majority of, people.

The best idea is to take the 'most effective' bits of a number of approaches so that the widest range of problems can be tackled.

The helper learns techniques from many approaches with a view to applying these elements to help people learn better problem-solving skills.

The helper might either apply skills and techniques in a set sequence or select from a range of skills according to the problem and the person.

learning about a counselling approach which really resonates with their own life-path as like 'coming home'. If you are on a basic introductory course, or beginning your introduction to counselling through independent study, I hope that you will be able to find your 'home' by working through this chapter.

Finally, I wanted to explain that ideas about helping do not, as I have said elsewhere in this chapter, come out of thin air. You will see that these ideas are all around us in our culture. The ideas and language in our twenty-first-century culture owes much to psychoanalysis, humanistic, behavioural and cognitive psychology, so, more particularly, does the vocabulary of helping.

WHERE DO YOU AND YOUR IDEAS FIT IN? YOU MIGHT LIKE TO MAKE A NOTE OF YOUR VIEWS

As you proceed in training, your helping style will be a mixture of your own deeply held views and new theories that you learn along the way. On the next couple of pages you will find very brief summaries of each approach — but, when I graduated from O-level chemistry to A-level chemistry the teacher disconcerted me somewhat by saying that much of what we had learned thus far in chemistry was wrong! The point he was making was that in order to make the ideas understandable to us, they had been simplified to the point of being inaccurate. Having tried to write about quite 'big' theories of personality and helping along with their philosophical roots, I know just what he meant! It's not that I had to simplify the ideas as much as try to squeeze it all into a few pages. I am sure that I have not done justice to the complexities of each theory or approach, but I do hope I have been able to give a flavour of each without too much prejudice.

This chapter concludes with a look at the lives of the founders of each approach to give us a personal dimension to their ideas. In my view it is clear that, in each case, they were or are passionate about their beliefs, they 'lived their ideas' and also that their personalities are to a greater or lesser extent reflected in the approaches which they developed. This section reminds us that, in addition to the social conditions and cultural background from which these men have come, their personal lives and personalities have an effect too.

Finally, I would return to my previous point that all of these theories are the products of men, developed largely at the expense of women and black and gay psychologies. You could still ask 'Why have you not included any of the Feminist Counselling literature or the work of Anna Freud, Melanie Klein or Karen Horney?' My answer is that I have chosen the theories here that I believe represent the foundation-stones of contemporary helping theory.

I'm sure you will not be surprised to learn that history isn't quite as simple as I have portrayed it in these simple sketches. For example a little digging around reveals that Carl Rogers credits the work of a social worker (a woman) called Jesse Taft, and his ideas were clearly influenced by the psychoanalyst Karen Horney. These 'schools' of counselling and psychotherapy have complicated histories which you would do well to look at in detail should you continue your studies to diploma level and beyond. For the moment I will just say that we cannot change the past, but we can learn from it and make a different future.

> 'All theory is autobiographical . . . in the history of ideas, every choice has personal motives . . . The main human problem is: How to lead an honorable life.'
>
> John Shlien: *Untitled and Uneasy* 1994.

BIOGRAPHICAL SKETCHES
(PSYCHOLOGISTS ARE PEOPLE TOO)

Sigmund Freud

Freud was born in Moravia, then part of the Austro-Hungarian Empire. When he was four years old, his family moved to Vienna where he lived until the last year of his life, 1939, which he spent in London having fled from the Nazis.

In 1873, Freud began his studies at the University of Vienna where his original interest was medicine and he conducted some important research on the anatomy and physiology of the nervous system. In 1885 Freud went to Paris to study under Charcot who was experimenting with hypnosis in the treatment of hysteria. (Hysteria is when a person shows apparent physical symptoms such as blindness or paralysis without any physical cause. The condition also has the apparent purpose of gaining attention, e.g. hysterical paralysis of my writing arm before my exams!)

On returning to Vienna, Freud continued to use hypnosis in his treatment of patients during which time he learned that, under hypnosis, people were able to 'reach down' below their ordinary consciousness and recall old, painful memories. Freud identified links between these memories with the present mental troubles his patients were experiencing.

From the case studies of his patients, from dedicated self-analysis over a period of 50 years (he set apart half an hour at the end of each day for this), and from discussions with his teachers and contemporaries, Freud developed his theories of psychoanalysis. His early theories place a strong emphasis on the role of sexual energy or drive in the development and structure of the personality. It would seem, for example, that during the informal discussion of a case Charcot suggested that the only thing that would surely benefit the patient was an active sex-life, of which she was deprived. Freud was deeply impressed by this and returned to Vienna with a deepening conviction regarding the role of sex in human psychology.

His work has attracted criticism since the late 60s from many quarters including feminists who contend that his basic ideas are anti-women. He believed that anything other than heterosexual penetrative sex was a 'deviation' from the natural, biological function of adult sex. It was a symptom of the sexual energy stuck in an infantile stage of development and therefore a suitable subject for treatment. Such views have been used for years to make the oppression of gays and women legitimate, by appearing to give academic or scientific credibility to prejudices.

Whatever our views might be regarding the role of sex in our lives, it is clear that Freud's contribution to psychology has been incorporated into our culture even though we may not now realise it. Many people accept that the unconscious mind exists and that it directs our behaviour, hidden from view. We talk of Freudian slips, interpret each other's dreams and speculate about the 'real meaning' of a colleague's absence from work on the day his appraisal is due. Although it might be argued that people had similar notions before Freud, the way we incorporate such ideas into our everyday lives today must be credited to Sigmund Freud.

Burrhus Frederick Skinner

Skinner was born in 1904 in Susquehenna, Pennsylvania into what has been described as a warm, stable family environment. In addition he notes that learning was esteemed, discipline prevailed (though never physical punishment), and rewards were given when deserved.

During his childhood, Skinner devoted much time and energy to building a variety of contraptions ranging from sledges and trolleys through to a device that would not allow him to leave his bedroom without hanging up his pyjamas! It has

been suggested that this early fascination with mechanics was an indication of his later interest in modifying observable behaviour — also done in a somewhat mechanical way.

He majored in English at College and spent two years attempting to be a writer, during which time he found that he had little to write about. However, at the same time he became progressively more interested in psychology through the works of early behaviourists such as Watson. He went to Harvard University in 1928 to study Psychology.

In order to update himself on the emerging field of behavioural psychology he set himself a rigorous schedule of study involving an early rise, study before breakfast, his usual working day, then study until bedtime with breaks of no more than 15 minutes — a routine he maintained for two years.

Like other innovators Skinner 'lived' his belief in behavioural principles, even using a controlled environment (referred to as a 'baby box') in the raising of his daughter. Similarities have been drawn between this device and the eponymous 'Skinner boxes' he developed to train rats and pigeons to press levers for food.

If Watson is seen as the 'father of behaviourism', then Skinner took the initial ideas and moulded them into a comprehensive scientific perspective. He has produced a large amount of published work and made a massive contribution to contemporary culture. Through his rudimentary attempts to help people with their problems using learning processes, he inspired a rejuvenation of interest in *behaviour therapy* and, indirectly, the new popular cognitive approaches.

He was always ready to give a clear account of behavioural philosophy and psychology and he engaged in vigorous debate in print, at scientific conventions and on film with many whose views he challenged (including Carl Rogers). He remained a dignified and respected figure throughout, held in high esteem by those who crossed swords with him.

His ideas have been particularly influential in education, an area which he felt passionately about. His assertion that punishment does not help us get rid of unwanted behaviour, and the idea that learning should be a process of small steps to ensure almost continuous reward for inevitable success have given rise to changes in classrooms all over the world. He developed the first (what now seem to us to be very rudimentary) programmed learning devices in which students progressed through set steps, revisiting the same problem until they had successfully conquered it. These were the forerunners of all present-day computerised, interactive learning programmes.

Carl Ransom Rogers

Rogers was born in rural Illinois in 1902. A shy and quiet child, he went to the University of Wisconsin to study agriculture. Rather than pursue agriculture he decided to join the Christian ministry and went to Union Theological Seminary in New York City shortly after marrying his childhood friend Helen Elliot.

He soon took up the study of psychology at Teachers' College, Columbia University after becoming disillusioned with the more rigid doctrines of the church. He worked with children and their families for 12 years in Rochester, New York and during this time began to develop his ideas about the individual's capacity for self-help and the role of the counsellor as co-worker rather than expert in the helping process.

He continued to develop his theory through the 1950s after publishing *Client Centred Therapy* in 1951. Particularly concerned to validate his ideas through research, he made a huge contribution to research in psychotherapy throughout his life, inspiring thousands of projects in the 60s, 70s and 80s to evaluate the effectiveness of counselling and psychotherapy. Rogers himself undertook one of the largest studies into the use of psychotherapy with schizophrenic patients whilst at Wisconsin in the 60s.

He then settled in La Jolla, California where he founded the *Center for Studies of the Person* with like-minded colleagues. He continued to expand his breadth of vision beyond counselling and psychotherapy to relationships, education, politics and world peace until his death in 1987. His particular contribution to contemporary culture was to put the individual, their experience and self-healing potential at the heart of the effective change process. This was a serious challenge to mainstream psychology at the time, which was busy trying to convince the world that psychologists were the 'experts' on human behaviour. Rogers railed against the destructive effect of incongruence, facades and roles. He believed passionately that the helper or therapist should be *themselves*, or the healthy change process would falter and fail. It has proved difficult for trainees and qualified counsellors alike to accept just how damned hard it is for us to be truly ourselves in a healing way.

Honoured by the American Psychological Association with their first Distinguished Scientific Contribution Award and twice voted 'The Most

'... if I am willing to take that one hour in and for itself ... I myself am the remedy at this moment, if there is any, and I can no longer escape my responsibility ...

Here is just one hour to be lived through as it goes, one hour of present immediate relationship, however limited, with another human being who has brought himself to the point of asking for help. If somehow this single contact proves to have value for the applicant, how does this happen?'

Jesse Taft: *The Dynamics of Therapy in a Controlled Relationship*, p. 11.

Influential American Psychologist', Rogers never stopped being controversial in his views, which have now been incorporated into our culture in many ways. Not only do psychologists talk about being person- or client-centred, but education now talks about being 'student-centred' and even industry and commerce want to be 'customer-centred', but many Person-Centred Counsellors are not happy with the ways in which these ideas have been superficially interpreted and appropriated for shallow purposes. Many in the twenty-first century are attracted to the basic humanity of this approach.

One favourite criticism of his approach made by behaviourists is that Person-Centred Counselling only works because when the counsellor is understanding, genuine and warm towards her clients she is doing nothing more than teaching them to do the same and so they become understanding, genuine and warm themselves. If this is a criticism of the approach, I for one can't think of a better way to get things wrong!

Albert Ellis

Born in Pittsburgh, Pennsylvania in 1913, Albert Ellis does not believe that his background and upbringing affected his life as a psychotherapist. He said *'That notion belongs to the "psychoanalytic bag", and fortunately I am no longer suffocating in that particular bag'* (Ellis, 1991). However, I will let the reader decide.

One of three children, he moved at the age of four with his family to New York where he has lived ever since. His childhood was set with challenges described by Yankura and Dryden (1994) as:

'Benign' Parental Neglect: He hardly ever saw his father (literally for about five minutes a day) and how his mother showed no interest in her children. He looked after his brother and sister and they survived by effort and good fortune.

Poor Health in Childhood: Ellis suffered a series of health problems, being hospitalised some

eight times around the ages 5–7. Add to this the infrequent visits from his mother or father (see above) and the true nature of this deprived childhood begins to be revealed.

Shyness and Social Avoidance: By his own description he was very shy and introverted, avoiding any kind of public exposure at school, or with girls where he lived. He developed elaborate strategies to avoid any situation which might cause him anxiety.

He met these challenges in various ways from learning to manipulate his mother to get what he wanted through to trying to chat up girls he didn't know to prove to himself that getting rejected wasn't the end of the world.

He planned a short career in accounting to fund his dream of becoming a famous author, but was denied this goal by the Great Depression. After repeated failures to get any of his writings published he began graduate psychology training at age 28.

His areas of special interest were sex, family and marital therapy, but these interests were not supported by the psychology department at Columbia University New York, so he moved to the rival institution, Teachers' College to complete his training. This he managed even though he still had to abandon his sex research due to pressure from faculty. He initially worked in private practice and then as a clinical psychologist, when he gained substantial clinical experience and published research. Unusually for someone with no medical training, he received psychoanalytic training and then proceeded to try to reform the psychoanalytic movement which he shortly abandoned.

Throughout the 1950s Ellis had been developing his ideas which grew into RET in the latter part of that decade. From the late 1950s onwards the story of RET is the story of Ellis' unstinting efforts to refine and develop the theory and practice of rational living and its therapeutic applications in the form of RET. Along the way he founded the Institute for Rational Living in 1959 (now called the Institute for Rational Emotive Therapy) and later changed the title of his approach to Rational Emotive Behaviour Therapy to acknowledge the role of behaviour both in the theoretical constructs and practical applications of the approach.

Albert Ellis has had an enduring impact upon contemporary helping and continues to drive REBT theory and practice with undiminished energy.

Gerard Egan

It is, I think, telling that the psychologist about whom there is little if any biographical information published should be Gerard Egan. His writing is functional and instructive rather than inspirational or transcendent; rather like the approach he has developed. He seems to have little time for gurus and has not himself been the subject of great biographical attention which is sometimes the making of a guru. It is also interesting that the theorist with least to say about spiritual connections in counselling is, in fact, an ordained priest.

I had some difficulty locating biographical information on Gerard Egan to begin with. I even resorted to trying to get some information from

Reshaping life! People who can say that have never understood a thing about life — they have never felt its breath, its heart — however much they have seen or done. They look on it as a lump of raw material which needs to be processed by them, to be ennobled by their touch. But life is never a material, a substance to be moulded. If you want to know, life is the principle of self-renewal, it is constantly renewing and remaking and changing and transfiguring itself, it is infinitely beyond your or my theories about it.

Boris Pasternak: *Doctor Zhivago*, p. 282.

the Internet and World Wide Web, to be greeted by a very chatty man from New Zealand who announced on my screen *'Hello! I am Gerard Egan.'* Needless to say he was not the Gerard Egan I was seeking. I was saved by the August 1996 edition of *Counselling* which contained a rare interview with Egan by Adrian Coles.

The third of four boys, Gerard Egan has spent most of his life in Chicago; his parents were born in Ireland and emigrated to the USA on their honeymoon. He describes his mother as having a '. . . kind of pragmatic approach to life.' (Coles, 1996). He was brought up in a community where school and church were tough and demanding, with family and community social life being easy-going. After high school he spent nine years in a Jesuit seminary, took Latin and Greek as an undergraduate then obtained an MA in Philosophy. He changed his views about religion and education as he passed through graduate school, believing himself to be too conformist in his early years, soberly reflecting on the narrow, restrictive nature of the education he himself received. When teaching philosophy, he became interested in psychology, returned to college and studied for a PhD in clinical psychology which he then taught for 12 years. It was during this period that the germs of his skills-centred, problem management approach to helping started to grow.

He began to think that the problems experienced by people were more to do with external factors, i.e. the social settings they were living in (family, work, culture) rather than internal factors such as having a 'twisted psyche' as he put it in the Coles interview. Accordingly he developed a model of helping based on a helper skilled in assisting the development of problem-solving capacities and opportunity-development strategies in the client. This approach currently underpins many skills-training courses in the UK but is not always acknowledged as the source of the structure of their counselling practice — there is no doubt that at the level of basic helping, Egan's ideas have been influential in the UK.

The Importance of Self-Development

3

When planning this chapter, I considered calling it 'The Importance of Self-Awareness'. After all, self-awareness is at the centre of developing as a counsellor. Then I realised that essential though self-awareness is, it's just not enough. It wouldn't be sufficient to sit back after a while with a satisfied smile and say, 'That's it, I'm self-aware now!' The emphasis for counsellors is on a continuing *process of improvement* not arriving at a given *state of awareness*. Ongoing self-development is so important to being a good counsellor that it is built into the ethical frameworks for all of the major professional bodies. Counsellors are *required* to continually pursue self-development, however experienced they are or however highly qualified. At the very beginning of learning about a counselling style of helping, knowing and understanding yourself better is the first step in this process.

In his book *Practical Counselling and Helping Skills* (1993), Richard Nelson-Jones suggests that we could benefit from considering several areas of ourselves as a starting point for self-awareness before we begin counselling, including our:

- Motives for helping.
- Capacity to feel.
- Sense of worth.
- Fears.
- Sexuality.
- Values and ethics.
- Culture and awareness of other cultures.
- Race and attitudes to race.
- Social class and attitudes to class.

'All they had in them was themselves but they would keep going until they found what was in them to find.'

Russell Hoban: *Turtle Diary*, p. 170.

'What may appear as coincidences are not coincidences at all but simply the working out of the pattern which you started with your own weaving.'

Claude Bristol: *The Magic of Believing*.

The prospect of beginning a journey of self-exploration may seem daunting; many of us feel a strong urge to run a mile in the opposite direction whenever anyone mentions self-awareness. How do you feel about the prospect of looking at yourself, your motives, your fears, your sexuality, etc.?

Looking at the list of self-awareness topics opposite, how do you feel about exploring any or all of them?

- How would you go about the task of exploring or becoming more aware of, for example, your *capacity to feel* or your *sexuality*?

- Would you like to do this self-exploration alone, in a pair with one other person, or in a small group?

- With friends, family or strangers?

Whenever we think about developing greater self-awareness, we might have several feelings such as

Excitement
'Great I can't wait to get started!'

Fear
'Oh no, what dreadful things will I uncover?'

Relief
'At last, I've been meaning to do this for ages!'

What about you? Do you have any hopes or fears about self-development such as 'Leave well alone, all this thinking isn't good for you'? When you see this symbol:

✍ MAKE A NOTE OF YOUR ANSWERS & EXAMPLES

These feelings often come in conflicting bundles. It's difficult to shake off the notion that self-exploration is *risky*. We think we might get hurt or

that, in some vague way, it might not be good for us. 'Better leave well alone, you never know what you might discover, and above all else don't do it with people around because it will make you vulnerable.' I can clearly remember being told as an adolescent that I was too introspective and that I thought too much and too deeply for my own good!

The idea of opening up, sharing our thoughts and fears may well seem odd or dangerous to many people. Many jobs are very distressing — nursing, social work, emergency services and so on. People working in such jobs have traditionally built up defences to the distress. They have to 'toughen up' and become hardened to the terrible sights and sounds and haunting thoughts they endure on a daily basis. It is often part of the workplace ethos in such jobs that you just get on with the job and don't talk about it.

[Counselling and basic helping is different. Even working as a volunteer you may see and hear very

---

The Johari Window

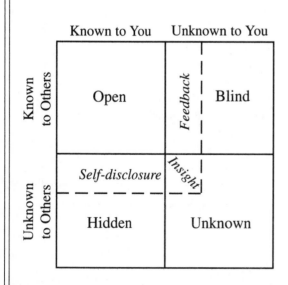

Self-awareness can be 'mapped out' using a Johari Window:
- **Open** area is your open, conscious, public behaviour, known to you and others.
- **Blind** area is where others can see things about you that you cannot see yourself.
- **Hidden** area represents things we know about ourselves which we do not reveal to others.
- **Unknown** area includes feelings, thoughts and motives within you that are known to neither yourself nor others.

The open area is expanded by talking honestly about ourselves (*self-disclosure*) and listening to *feedback from others*.

'It costs so much to be a full human being that there are very few who have the love and courage to pay the price. One has to abandon altogether the search for security and reach out to the risk of living with both arms. One has to embrace life like a lover.'

Morris West: *Shoes of The Fisherman.*

'And you may find yourself living in a shotgun shack
And you may find yourself in another part of the world
And you may find yourself behind the wheel of a large automobile
And you may find yourself in a beautiful house, with a beautiful wife
And you may ask yourself — Well . . . how did I get here?'

Once In A Lifetime: Talking Heads, words and music by David Byrne, Chris Franz, Tina Weymouth, Jerry Harrison and Brian Eno.

distressing things, but you are not expected to clam up and deal with it yourself. We will look at how counsellors deal with these issues in Chapter 8 **Support and Supervision in Counselling**.]

Although we feel most at risk when we contemplate baring our soul to others, it is, paradoxically, from the genuine responses of others that we stand to learn something about ourselves. By talking about ourselves as honestly as we can in a *safe* environment and listening to the feedback from others, we can check whether the view we have of ourselves is the one received by others. In addition we may discover some of the hidden motives that may have been influencing our attitudes and behaviour all along. This new self-awareness may make it possible for us to change, if we choose. This prospect of change may also bring new challenges.

It would seem, then, that the right environment is required before self-exploration feels safe. This process that we go through in training is similar to the process that a client might go through in counselling. We can now appreciate how vulnerable and frightened anyone seeking help might feel because we have experienced our own

High Challenge

Too scary, we get too frightened, defensive or hostile.	*The right balance for active participation in self-exploration. Exciting stuff!*

Low Support   **High Support**

Too dull, we become bored, disinterested and lose heart.	*Too comfortable and cosy, we don't get much work done.*

Low Challenge

fears and joys on our own road to self-discovery. The conditions which lead us to feel safe enough to disclose some previously private feelings, are also similar to the conditions talked about by Carl Rogers (see Chapter 5), namely, empathy, non-judgemental warmth and genuineness or congruence.

In training, even on an introductory course, we need to be aware of an extra ingredient which will help us move towards greater self-awareness. That ingredient is the balance between feeling supported and feeling challenged. This balance point is different for everyone, and in a group we all share the responsibility for trying to get the balance right. If some of the issues in this book seem too low or too high in challenge, what can you do to increase the challenge for yourself, or increase the support you need to help you meet the challenge?

🖎

It is important to understand challenge. Too much challenge and we close down to learning, too little and we get bored.

GIVING AND RECEIVING CONSTRUCTIVE AND EFFECTIVE FEEDBACK

Giving and receiving feedback are two of the most important activities or processes in training in counselling and counselling skills. Feedback is both verbal communication (the words we say) and non-verbal communication (our actions, facial expressions and posture). It is through receiving feedback that we get an opportunity to see ourselves as others see us. It helps us become more aware of our behaviour — what we do and how we do it.

Giving feedback

We can tell people how we see them.
We can tell people our feelings about the way they are.

Receiving feedback

Others can tell us how they see us.
Other people can tell us their feelings about the way we are.

Both giving and receiving feedback can feel quite scary. What others think of us may not be in accord with our image of ourselves. This can be hurtful, flattering or simply puzzling. Whichever it is, I find feedback either exciting or uncomfortable to give or receive — a little like playing the children's game of *'truth, dare, kiss or promise'*.

When others receive your feedback, they may also be feeling uncertain, uncomfortable or scared. Your impressions may well not fit in with *their* views of *themselves*. For these reasons, feedback needs to be thoughtful and given sensitively, not hastily, without thinking or like a 'bull in a china shop'.

You might be asked to give feedback to others on some personal issues on your course, such as whether you found the other person helpful, caring, sensitive and why. You may find the prospect of this daunting, but it requires no more than developing a sensitivity to other people's needs which is at the heart of good counselling. Here are some ground rules for giving feedback:

- All of your observations of another person will include both positive and negative elements. Try to include both positive and negative observations in your feedback. Avoid saying just negative things — or all positive things — to the other person.

- What you are picking up is the behaviour of the other person. Comment on the other person's behaviour rather than give your impression of the person, i.e. 'Your voice had a very harsh quality', rather than 'You are very harsh.'

- Stick to describing *what* you see or feel rather than either *making a judgement* about it or saying *why* it's happening, i.e. 'Your shouting frightened me'. rather than 'Shouting is a terrible thing to do, you do it because you are inadequate.'

- Try to give feedback on something that the other person can do something about, rather than something beyond their control.

- Speak for yourself not others, say 'I think . . .' or 'I feel . . .', rather than 'Everybody thinks . . .' or 'It's clear to everyone . . .' or 'I'm sure nobody knows . . .'

- Give feedback about specific instances or behaviours rather than generalising, i.e. 'When you did this . . . I felt threatened.' rather than 'You threaten me' or 'You are threatening'.

The things you say about other people when giving feedback will nearly always say as much about you as they do about the other person. Be prepared to receive feedback on your feedback! It might be, for example, that you always give positive feedback — maybe you can't bear to hurt other people's feelings. Or perhaps you tend to give predominantly negative feedback — maybe you think that people will only learn if you point out their mistakes.

Carl Rogers (see Chapter 2) thought that people learn best when they feel safe. Most counselling courses are organised on this principle. It is important that you feel safe enough to give honest feedback and that you feel safe enough to listen to feedback without feeling got at. The processes of giving and receiving feedback require a feeling of safety if they are to be of any real use.

PERSONAL MOTIVES
Examining motives is a good thing to do whatever the activity in question. When considering involvement in counselling it is, at some stage, essential to look at *why* you want to be a helper. It is crucial for us to be as sure as we can be that our motives for offering to help someone will not distort the helping we can give so that it ends up being unhelpful or even damaging. Although we cannot hope to examine *all* motives here, we can look at a couple.

As an extreme example, there have been cases in the news recently where people working in children's homes have been found guilty of sexual abuse of the children in their care. It would seem that their motives for wanting to work with children were questionable.

Of course it would be stupid to suggest that we do not serve our own needs at some levels when we choose to volunteer or work as a helper. The question is, do our motives get in the way of our ability to offer constructive help, or do they facilitate our offering constructive help? Do these motives add to or take away from our helpfulness? For example:

• the central issue of *emotional pain* in my life can be the focus of helpful or harmful motives:

Helpful: If I have worked through a past traumatic event, I may have gained personal strength from the experience and also may be more sensitive to others suffering trauma.

Harmful: I may be over-sensitive to certain issues because my emotional pain is unresolved from a recent trauma. I might also be trying to resolve my own trauma through contact with clients, rather than trying to help the client.

• The central issue of *wanting to help others* can be the focus of helpful or harmful motives:

Helpful: Expressing an unselfish concern for others as helping behaviour can be seen as similar to the core condition of warmth or valuing others.

Harmful: If I require others to be dependent upon my help so that I can be seen as a 'good guy', I am distorting helping relationships to meet my own needs.

It is interesting to discover that there are certain safeguards that professional counsellors can make to guard against questionable motives and these are looked at in Chapters 7 and 8 on Ethics and Supervision respectively. Although a professional code of ethics and supervision of counselling practice are not strictly applicable to those interested in learning about a counselling way of helping on an Introduction to Counselling course, the principles of getting support for yourself and helping in an ethical way should be at the heart of everyone's helping activities. We will look at the new BACP ethical framework in Chapter 7 and how it might relate to basic helping.

> '. . . it is his own hurt that gives the measure of his power to heal.'

Jung, C.G.: *The Practice of Psychotherapy*, par 239.

> 'The therapist is ultimately not there to treat the patient but, via a circuitous and well-concealed route, to treat or protect or comfort himself.'

Thomas Maeder: *Children of Psychiatrists and Other Psychotherapists*, p. 77.

> 'One would rather have a really suitable person for doing this kind of work than an ill person made less ill by the analysis that is part of the psychoanalytic training.'

Winnicott, D.W.: *Therapeutic Consultations in Child Psychiatry*, p. 1.

Personal values

Another of the many possible foci for personal development during a basic counselling course is the area of conflicting values. This might come up in four ways:

- Conflicts between different sets of values within myself.

- Conflicts between my values and my behaviour.

- Conflicts between my values and the values of the person I am in a helping relationship with.

- Conflicts between my values and the values of counselling (whatever I understand them to be).

As someone interested in helping others it is necessary for me to become aware of the values that I bring to the helping relationship since my own strongly held values may distort the help I am hoping to give. It is another tricky balancing act to try and offer genuine help in some areas of life without influencing a person's values by subtle means or maybe by disclosing my own values. You may not intend to influence the other person's values, but it is possible that the other person might see you as a role model or copy you in an effort to get relief from their distress.

In terms of the core conditions discussed in Chapter 5, it is a matter of being simultaneously non-judgementally warm *and* genuine towards a person with whom you feel there is a conflict of values. [You will discover that this in not an easy thing to do.]

Similarly, if I have a conflict between two values or a conflict between my values and my behaviour, this incongruence will almost surely be picked up by the person I am trying to help, possibly making me seem ingenuine or false. For example, I might find myself saying one thing and doing another — imagine what message that would send to the person whom you are trying to help. Examination of my personal values is therefore essential before I can be an effective helper.

Personal values, however, change as a result of life, new experiences, the passage of time or even doing an Introduction to Counselling course. Although we might examine our personal values now, there's every chance that they might have changed by the time this book is finished. If I'm serious about being a helper, I must monitor my personal values to see how I change and develop. It might help to make a note now and then look back at the end of this course to see if, and/or how, your values change.

It is likely that there will be no formal time on your course where the named task is to examine your personal values. This does not mean that you will not be aware of your personal values and the personal values of others practically every time you attend a course meeting. It is inevitable that you will have checked out other people's values during class discussions and exercises and also during coffee-breaks. This is a natural part of 'sizing people up', figuring out who our friends are going to be, who might support us, and who will be for us or against us. It is a perpetual social process.

Since you have decided to participate in this course and get a better understanding of human behaviour, you might take some time to reflect on the class discussions and coffee-breaks to see what you think they reveal about you. How have your values shone through the things you have said and done?

Later in this chapter, I will look at the importance of keeping a Personal Journal whilst you are doing your training. It will be the ideal place to record your observations about your values and the conflicts that you discover, both within yourself and between your own values and those of other people.

COUNSELLING VALUES

Returning briefly to the five models of helping we overviewed in Chapter 2, you will realise that each one carries with it a set of attitudes about human beings and change. The very fact that you are on a counselling course means that your values probably include the notion that helping people is a good thing. Some people, however, believe that helping others makes them weak and dependent — where do you stand on this?

If we look to the 'core' conditions for effective helping proposed by Carl Rogers — empathy, non-judgemental warmth and genuineness (see Chapter 5 for details) — we find that the core conditions are more than just the foundations of good counselling and relationship skills. They suggest that in order to be effective helpers we need a certain set of attitudes and values as well.

Discussion points on personal values:

How do you react to the following statements?

Suicide and self-harm are wrong. If someone told me they were going to harm or kill themselves, I would do my utmost to stop them.

I could not listen to someone using sexist or racist language, I would tell them that it was wrong and to stop doing it. To listen without comment is to condone it.

I just couldn't sit in the same room as a child abuser. I would want to kill them!

I help people to make them happy. I would always try to end a session on a positive note.

I believe that there is nothing wrong with being gay, but I feel uncomfortable when gay people of my sex come too close to me.

I can't work out what my position on abortion is. I keep changing my mind. If I have an unwanted pregnancy, I suppose I'll work it out then.

For some of these issues, there are no 'right' or 'wrong' stands to take. Counsellors, as a group, don't have a 'position' on suicide, or abortion. These are personal values regarding human life. However, there are some 'counselling values' which are generally held, e.g. counselling isn't about making people happy or cheering them up. Also, if you have conflicts between your values and your behaviour, then the process of personal development should help you resolve these before you start offering your help to others.

Discussion points on counselling values:

How do you react to the following statements?

•People need help in understanding the hidden meanings in their lives.

•People need to be offered a range of solutions to problems so that they can choose an appropriate one for themselves.

•People should have control over their own destiny.

•People have no right to make immoral or antisocial choices in counselling.

•We should take responsibility for the consequences of our actions, praise ourselves when we do good, admonish ourselves when we do bad, not praise or seek forgiveness from God.

•All people are equal and therefore are equally deserving of my help, regardless of who they are or what they have done.

These discussion points have been chosen to represent issues on which there is no 'party-line'. Counselling values may well conflict with your personal spiritual and political values.

Will this conflict distort, or get in the way of, your helping capacity?

Will being open to these conflicts through a commitment to personal development enhance your helping capacity?

What other value-conflicts can you identify?

These 'hidden' helping values may be:

• Completely new ideas to us.

• Familiar but different from the ones we are used to.

• Ones with which we totally and enthusiastically agree.

• Values with which we disagree in part or have difficulty in accepting.

• Attitudes with which we basically agree but have difficulty in genuinely displaying.

When we begin to learn about helping we might think that counselling is value-free, or perhaps transparent to values or culture. After all, helping is just helping, isn't it? People wanting help is natural, and people offering help to each other is natural. Consider the following examples of possible values that may be implicit in counselling processes:

• Change is a good thing.

• Change involves struggle and pain.

• People are basically good underneath the surface.

• Co-operation between equals is the best way to structure helping relationships.

• People are best helped by someone who has had a very similar experience or problem.

• People are not born bad, they're made bad by the world and can therefore be helped to change.

• Some people are beyond helping.

• People are basically weak and vulnerable and need to be protected.

• In order to be helped to change you've got to want to change.

• Counselling is for people with problems.

What do think the values implicit in *your* helping might be?

FEELINGS

That counselling is about, or involves the expression of, 'feelings' might seem obvious to many. Even though it's obvious, the prospect of *working* with feelings in some way, can *stimulate* many feelings in us. It's possibly the realisation that feelings beget feelings that makes some of us so anxious about looking too deeply at feelings. We might meet feelings or *emotions* in the following ways on a basic counselling course:

• *Listening* to someone talking about their feelings or emotions, i.e. they might tell us how angry they are.

• *Witnessing* someone express their feelings strongly, i.e. they might cry inconsolably in front of us.

• *Thinking* or *talking* about our own feelings or emotions, i.e. being reminded of how angry we were.

• *Expressing* our own feelings or emotions, i.e. feeling sad and crying on our own account, perhaps remembering some loss we have suffered.

Our general reaction to the expression of feelings and emotions will depend upon our values and beliefs about emotions. We will have acquired these values and beliefs from past personal experiences and from the views passed on to us from our upbringing and culture.

So, the famous British 'stiff upper lip' and 'passionate Latin temperament' are examples of ideas about cultural influences. Statements like 'she's got her mother's red hair, so she'll have her mother's fiery temper' might indicate family influences. Emotional expression is also linked to sex-role stereotyping. Women are supposed to be more open and free in expressing their feelings than men, who are supposed to 'keep it all in'. Like me, you might think that these stereotypes are too rigid and simple to be applicable in everyday life. But then I ask myself why it is my wife who feels more able to cry than me when we go to watch a sad film?

Helping someone by listening accurately and sensitively to them means being sensitive to their whole person, including their feelings. I need to be able to respond to another person's whole range of expression, not have any blind spots caused by my own fear of expressing my own feelings.

What are your emotional blind spots? Are you afraid of feelings?

'I would say I'm sorry
If I thought that it would change your mind
But I know that this time
I've said too much
Been too unkind

I try to laugh about it
Cover it all up with lies
I try and laugh about it
Hiding the tears in my eyes
'Cos boys don't cry'

Boys Don't Cry: The Cure. Words by Robert Smith.

'One way of putting this . . . is that if I can form a helping relationship to myself — if I can be sensitively aware of and acceptant toward my own feelings — then the likelihood is so great that I can form a helping relationship toward another.

Carl Rogers: *On Becoming a Person*, p. 51.

THINKING AND UNDERSTANDING

There is so much emphasis put on feelings that some people believe helping in a counselling way is *all* about feelings and there is no room for thinking at all. Psychologists call our thought processes 'cognitions' and it is from this word that we get the title 'Cognitive Therapy' (see Chapter 2). There are a few approaches to change that put a high value on our thought processes by looking at how we keep ourselves unhappy by saying irrational things to ourselves such as:

- 'I'm unattractive, so no one will ever love me and I will be unhappy for the rest of my life.'

- 'I daren't speak out in the group because everyone will see that I'm stupid and I will get so embarrassed that I'll blush and it would be the end of the world.'

Although we know that these thoughts are daft we have difficulty in trying to change them. We still behave as though they were true, for example, by never talking in a group. These patterns of thought can be really troublesome to many people and we need to be able to enter into their world of thoughts in order to understand.

The way I *understand* and *think* about my world is obviously important to me so when you are helping me I want you to see, accept and value my thoughts and understandings, not try to tell me that feelings are the only important bits of me. It is important to value your own thinking if you are to genuinely trust and value the thought processes of the person you are helping.

My personal psychology is a mixture of thoughts, feelings and sensations. Although I might feel unbalanced, i.e. that my mind is dominated by thoughts or that I am overwhelmed by feelings, it is not helpful if you, my helper, thinks that my problem is *just* about feelings, or *just* about thoughts. A healthy mental life is a balance — harmony — between thoughts, feelings, sensations and the meanings I attach to them. A good helper will be able to help me explore all aspects of my mental and physical life without bias or preference.

PERSONAL CHANGE

On the previous page we looked at counselling values and the possibility that change is a good thing. Whether or not you view change as a *good* thing, one thing is certain — counselling and helping is inextricably interwoven with personal change.

Mapping changes in our lives

This grid will be different for each person, e.g. someone with restricted mobility might put learning to ride a bike in a different place.

Where on the grid would you put the change events in your life over the past 12 months?

High personal content

Changing your name

Moving house

Small change ——————————————— **Big change**

Learning to ride a bike

Can any big change have a low personal content?

Low personal content

One way of thinking about change is to see it on a continuum, from big changes to small changes, and a continuum from high personal content to low personal content. Make a list of the changes that you have gone through in the past year. Then rate them in terms of whether they are big or small, and whether they involve a high or low personal content:

✍

Take a look at the grid on the previous page to see how you might arrange your change events according to whether they were big or small, high or low personal content.

Psychologists researching the effects of change believe that change and coping with it is very stressful to human beings. I'm sure this will not come as news to anyone! However, you may be surprised to see the top ten most stressful life events include moving house, divorce, bereavement and giving birth — consider whether they involve change, and where on our grid on page 48 they might fall.

Interestingly enough, psychologists also view learning as change because when we learn something new we have to re-arrange all of our previous knowledge to make room for (and make sense of) the new information. Learning that Father Christmas doesn't exist certainly made me review my experience in the light of new information. It was also very painful.

The idea that learning new things is painful is not a new one. Every time we learn something new we have to let go of an old view of things. What evidence is there in your life for these notions of change and learning?

✍

Change is involved at many levels when thinking about helping in a counselling way:

• People ask for help because they want change: in simple terms they want to feel settled, happier and problem-free.

• People come to counselling because the want something to change: in simple terms they want to feel better. Or perhaps they are wanting to cope with an unwelcome change such as a bereavement.

• During training, even on an introductory course we want change: we want to know more about helping in a counselling way and we might want to be better at it. Or perhaps we want to change some aspect of ourselves to become a better helper.

In order to cope with change we need support; both clients and those learning about counselling. Our personal reaction to change will affect the way we are able to help others cope with it. This is why, as people interested in helping, we must seek to understand our own thoughts, feelings and behaviour about change.

• If we are afraid of change or believe that change is a bad thing or have unhelpful ways of reacting to change in our own lives, we may distort the helping we offer clients, since change is often what they've come for.

> '. . . the more I am willing to be myself in all this complexity of life and the more I am willing to understand and accept the realities in myself and in the other person, the more change seems to have been stirred up. It is a very paradoxical thing — that to the degree that each one of us is willing to be himself, then he finds not only himself changing; but he finds that other people to whom he relates are also changing.'
>
> Carl Rogers: On *Becoming A Person*, p. 22.

Change in everyday life

Learning a new fact
Learning a new skill
Going to school
Puberty
Leaving your childhood home
Discovering your sexuality
Becoming a parent
'Marriage' — or deciding to stick
with one partner
Separation or 'divorce'
Being ill
Moving house
Getting a job
Losing a job
Joining a counselling course
Being bereaved
Going to live in another country

Which changes do we choose to make?

What feelings arise from such change?

Which changes are we forced to make?

What do we need to support us during change?

It is clear that change is common in our everyday lives and that it can be accompanied by strong feelings. These feelings can be negative or positive, however. Some ways of looking at change emphasise the transition from one state to another and suggest that our strong feelings are associated with the loss of the old (grief) and the shock of the new. It can be helpful to take a moment to consider change in your life and what it means to you.

In the Chinese language the same character stands for both 'crisis' and 'opportunity'

Rather than see change as a threat, it is possible to see positive aspects in change. In business it is fashionable to look at the prospect of change in terms of *Strengths, Weaknesses, Opportunities and Threats.* By considering these elements of a change situation it is possible to see what can be gained from it.

'On our farm we have a row of maple trees that illustrate the mysterious process of adaption. Many years ago these trees were used as fence posts for the stringing of barbed wire around the pasture. Now, fifty or sixty years later, it is possible to look at those trees and observe the way the life process shows itself in adaptation. In some places the trees fought against the barbed wire as a hostile agent, and here the trees have long and ugly scars that deface the bark and inner structure of the trees. In other places, the barbed wire has been accepted and incorporated into the life of the tree. Where this happened, the barbed wire left no mark on the tree, and all that shows is the wire entering on one side and exiting at the other.

It is natural to wonder what makes the difference in the quality of a tree's response to injury. What was there in some trees that made them injure themselves by fighting against injury? What made it possible for other trees to be able to incorporate the injuring object and become master of the barbed wire rather than its victim?'

Edgar N. Jackson: *The Many Faces of Grief,* pp. 123–4.

'Can you find a wholeness that includes pain and a readiness to suffer?'

The Religious Society of Friends: *Questions and Counsel.*

'Our futile effort at control impedes the flow we might otherwise have in our lives. Once we get out of our own way, we can become ourselves.'

Marilyn Ferguson: *The Aquarian Conspiracy.*

'Life is worth living. Not because there is nothing else, but because of what we each may give one another; pain, joy, anguish, peace. It's not an easy journey. You may even call it an adventure. It doesn't matter about the problems, the contradictions. In our hearts we understand everything. We understand it's the struggle that counts.'

Ann Oakley: *Taking it like a Woman,* p. 204.

'Multiple and converging sources of evidence indicate that the person of the psychotherapist is inextricably intertwined with the outcome of psychotherapy. There is a dawning recognition . . . that the therapist him- or herself is the focal process of change.'

Dryden, W. and Spurling, L. (Eds): *On Becoming a Psychotherapist,* p. 215.

'Ever since I
Was a small child
I cannot sleep at night
Without the light on

I am afraid to laugh out loud
Or to stand out of the crowd
I am scared of loving you
I am afraid of losing you
I am afraid to lose control
I am afraid of growing old
I am afraid to die
But it's something I must do

It's not that I'm not strong
It's just that I'm not strong enough for you
It's not that I'm not brave
It's just that I'm not brave enough for two.'

I Am Afraid: A House, words by David
Couse.

'if you ever get close to a human
and human behaviour
be ready to get confused

there's definitely no logic
to human behaviour
but yet so irresistible

there's no map
to human behaviour'

Human Behaviour: Bjork, words and music
by Gudmundsdottir, Hooper and Jobim.

'Therapy training programs and their
teachers are merely the whetstones on
which the novice therapists hone their
instruments. Those instruments are the
selves of the therapists.'

Ned Gaylin: *Family, Self and Psychotherapy:
A person-centred perspective,* p. 131.

KEEPING A PERSONAL JOURNAL

Many courses, from basic introductions right up
to diploma level and beyond, ask participants to
keep personal journals to document their
experiences during the life of the course in some
way. Courses vary in their requirements, but most
agree that keeping a personal journal can be a
powerful aid in the process of personal
development. Sometimes the keeping of a personal
journal can be part of the course assessment.

If your course does require you to keep a personal
journal, you will receive any assistance necessary
from the course tutors. If the process seems too
vague for you, perhaps you could make that the
subject of your first journal entry before asking
the tutors for more guidance.

If you are not required to keep a personal journal,
I would strongly suggest that you do. Both as a
trainer and a participant, I have found personal
journals to be useful, challenging, awkward,
contentious and moving in equal measure.
(Sometimes all at the same time!)

For some people who never previously kept
journals or diaries, the requirement of having to
write one for a counselling course can be an
irritation or burden. For others it is the start of a
rewarding activity that lasts a lifetime. Counsellors
sometimes find it very useful to keep a personal
journal of their client work, quite separately from
a professional log, or notes, of their counselling. A
personal journal can be a great help in supervision.

The next page is an extract from a personal journal
kept by me when I attended a Person-Centred
Expressive Therapy Institute intensive 12-day
residential course. I include it not as an example of
good practice or model for journal-keeping, but to
give an idea of what *I* made out of journal-keeping
on that occasion. It *is* personal, and records some
significant personal struggles of my own. (I wrote
the original diagonally across the page.)

January 10th

Day 2 of the Expressive Therapy course and my second 'journal' entry. Although I feel I am writing this mainly out of duty, I do feel quite keen to see what happens as I set pen to paper. Should I give an account of today or just pick up on any- thing that has moved me? We started today with movement, as we will do each day, at 7:30am before breakfast. I have been re-acquainted with my lack of exercise my movement has become very restricted. I think it may be a metaphor for my whole life, since I know I am capable of a wider range in relationships, at work, in play etc. than I currently display. Why is that? How can I loosen up in life? I thought I would find the free movement stuff difficult, awkward and embarrassing. It has turned out to be easier and more enjoyable than my typically conservative expectations. Expressing myself freely by moving around is still difficult for me. I feel stupid, exposed, vulnerable. Maybe people will laugh at me? The whole group movement directed by Shellee was brilliant. Just very moving . . . nearly everyone was crying, me too . . . simple meeting connecting . . . and all the things I can't, don't or won't do in everyday life. I think I was crying for myself and all of the lost opportunities to make connections with people like this. Natalie did a counselling demonstration today which was interesting and, I was impressed. She asked the group to take part at one point which I thought was great. I am constantly impressed by her genuineness (in a technical sense) when she is facilitating the group or counselling an individual. She never lets an opportunity go by without letting us know what she is feeling. She does it in a way that doesn't intrude, direct or push. I must get a handle on it since I would like to be able to do it too. It's a way powerful tool . . .

January 11th 11pm.

I have real difficulty in understanding D sometimes. I can't get a handle on why — she seems so airy (in the elemental sense of the word) so delicate, so 'other-worldly' that the contact we make is like the landing of a butterfly on my hardest, most insensitive skin. She and I seem to be from different planets. I think she senses this too, but I don't know for sure, and this is further testimony to our unconnectedness. I shrink from raising the issue for fear of it exploding like a dandelion clock in a puff of wind. She is like a fragile fluttering bird and I fear that she could hurt me.

'Our deepest fear is not that we are inadequate. Our deepest fear is that we are powerful beyond measure. It is our light, not our darkness that most frightens us. We ask ourselves, "Who am I to be brilliant, gorgeous, talented, fabulous?" Actually, who are you not to be? You are a child of God. Your playing small doesn't serve the world. There's nothing enlightened about shrinking so that other people won't feel insecure around you. We were all meant to shine, as children do.'

Return to Love: *Reflections on a Course in Miracles* by Marianne Williamson

'Here now is another, more literal theory of anxiety (that which cripples), with no packaging. It is a major anxiety, traumatic in the instant of its experience, at any age, and with long remaining consequences of fear that it might be re-experienced. Anxiety, "massive and terrible", is the result of embarrassment. More accurately, fear of embarrassment. Perhaps eventually, fear of that fear. . .

. . .Most shocking to me was the confession of a Vietnam veteran, who said that he was "too embarrassed not to kill"! He had been with other soldiers who destroyed a village. He was afraid that if he did not join in the murder, they would laugh at him, feel scorn for him. Terrible, is it not, to murder because you fear being embarrassed if you do not follow the crowd?'

John Shlien: *Embarrassment Anxiety: A literalist theory.* pp. 102–3.

Prejudice, Oppression and Counselling

4

When we concentrate so much on the individual and their needs as we do in counselling, we can sometimes lose a certain perspective. That perspective is the one which gives us a glimpse of the real world and the forces active within it that affect us as individuals. The real world that I see is often harsh and brutal with many inequalities. I don't want to lose the harsh 'edge' to this view by wearing rose-coloured spectacles.

Sometimes the world of counselling and helping can be a little like a pair of rose-coloured glasses, through which I see people making choices about their lives in the safety of a helping relationship. The truth is, of course, that the real world gives me, a white, middle-class, able-bodied, heterosexual man with a university education, many more opportunities and choices than anyone else. Can a counselling way of helping make any headway against prejudice and oppression?

We should always be aware of what helping in a counselling way can realistically achieve. There is a tendency for us to get too enthusiastic about the possibilities and very soon we start to believe that counselling can be a cure for everything. On the other hand, some people think that counselling, with its concentration on the individual person, fails to take into account important social processes. Then, rather than being part of the cure, counselling is seen as part of the disease, since a counselling way of helping can appear to say:

'Let's talk about why you are depressed — it'll get better if you share your troubles.'

However, talking won't get this person a job and decent housing or stop the racial abuse. It is important that helpers and counsellors do not turn away and walk on the other side of the street whenever prejudice and oppression raise their heads.

If basic helping — a counselling way of helping — gives us the privilege of being let into, and understanding, another person's world, we should be prepared to face up to the unpleasant truth that sometimes we (yes, uncomfortably, me too) may be part of the problem.

My purpose in spending time considering prejudice and oppression in an introductory book is to acknowledge that the roots of prejudice and oppression are very deep and we simply cannot start too soon to understand our own attitudes and how we turn them into behaviour. If we put such a premium on self-awareness then we must surely want to become aware of our prejudices and if we are so keen on self-development, then we must surely try to live our lives in a way that doesn't oppress others.

Many books and courses concentrate on culture and race as the focus of their work on prejudice and oppression. In this book, I am simply going to set the process in motion by looking in more general terms at differences between people, e.g. differences in colour, class, gender, religion, culture, sexual orientation or whatever, and how we often translate those differences into prejudices.

In recent years some people have become

concerned about the effects of global commerce on the 'third world'. It is interesting that many people refer to oppressed groups as 'minorities', e.g. 'ethnic minorities'. I read a quote some years ago but can never remember who said it. It brought home to me the parochial nature of such terms. Although I can't remember who said it, it helped me put oppression into a bigger picture:

'There is only one minority: rich white men.'

PREJUDICE

Prejudice has been defined as: 'an attitude that predisposes a person to think, feel, perceive and act in favourable or unfavourable ways towards a group or its individual members' (Secord and Backman, 1974). This means that our views and beliefs will reveal themselves in the way we show preferential treatment towards, e.g. ourselves and 'our group' and in the way we try to disadvantage others and 'their group'.

If we wish to help in a counselling way, we must do something to become aware of our prejudices so that we can understand the way they will affect our helping relationships. We will see in Chapter 5 how important it is to be able to be respectful, warm and accepting towards the person you are trying to help, whilst also being genuine. This is clearly going to be difficult if you harbour prejudices towards people.

Most of us who are drawn towards helping others like to think that we are a prejudice-free zone. It might come as a surprise to learn that this is not the case. However open-minded we like to think we are, we will have prejudices directing our behaviour. As a white man, I can only think as a white man with all of the views, perspectives and prejudices of a white man.

In some circumstances we tend to focus on the similarities between people, the things that bind us together as humans. Under other circumstances we emphasise the differences. A counselling way of helping tries to capture the positive elements of both similarities and differences — whilst

celebrating everyone's uniqueness and their individual qualities, we also want to respect the rights of that person as a human being — to be treated as an equal, with dignity.

What comes into your mind when you think about the word 'prejudice'?

PREJUDICE

FRIGHTENED   DIFFERENT

HURT   NOT ALLOWED IN HERE

BLIND   NOT LIKE ME   WEIRD

I DON'T LIKE THEM   FEAR

EVIL   NOT NORMAL   INVISIBLE

I'M NOT PREJUDICED BUT...

PREJUDGMENT   UNFAIR

INSULARITY   BAD INFLUENCE

LOTS OF MY FRIENDS ARE...

CATEGORISATION   PIGEONHOLING

EVERYTHING IN BLACK AND WHITE

✍ ....

The flipchart above illustrates the views of our hypothetical group that we first met in Chapter 1. When you think about this hypothetical group, who do you picture: a mixed group of men, women, black, white, gay, straight? In your mind's eye, who is missing? Did your imaginary group have no black people, no men? What does your mental picture say about your prejudices?

Prejudice revolves around a negative view of difference — the differences between you and me. When you see this symbol:

✍ MAKE A NOTE OF YOUR OPINIONS ↓ EXAMPLES

The sort of dimensions on which we judge these differences include:

Race/Ethnicity
Nationality
Religion
Class
Gender
Sexual orientation
Age
Dis/ability
Any other dimensions you can think of

What is it in your experience about these dimensions of difference that cause so much prejudice? What do you think?

Let's look at a few statements to find out where we stand in relation to some of these issues. The questions are sometimes deliberately contentious to get us thinking about our prejudices. We may find that powerful feelings accompany our views on these issues. These feelings are signals that the issues are connected to deeply held views which may be difficult to confront and change. The process must start, however, with raising our awareness. When looking at these statements, try to stay with your first, gut reaction.

- Private clubs should have the right to exclude people on the grounds of gender, disability, race, colour or religion.

- If black people really wanted to get on in life, they would stay on at school and work harder.

- Women have made no real progress in getting equal treatment in recent years.

- I saw a woman breastfeeding her child in the cafe yesterday. It shouldn't be allowed.

- All children should speak English at school.

- I would be very happy if my son or daughter told me they were gay.

- Other people's religious rituals are daft — fancy not eating milk and beef together, or not using a toilet that faces east!

- There's plenty of jobs if you go looking for them, the dole is just for scroungers who don't want to work.

- Everybody over the age of 55 should be made to retire to make more jobs for the younger people.

What are your reactions to these statements? Do you disagree and feel angry about them or agree passionately?

POWER

A counselling way of helping is based on a recognition that all humans are equal. It may seem strange, therefore, to look at power in counselling relationships. We may feel uncomfortable when it is suggested that we have power *over* other people in a helping situation and it would be convenient to think that we are equal to all those we are trying to help but, on one basic dimension, there is an inequality — *they* are asking *us* for help.

In some jobs in the 'helping professions' power vested in roles is very real. This includes the power to control access to services, or funds. The power to take children away from their parents and put them into care or the power to say who is mad and who is sane. If you have ever been in the position of having to ask for help from a statutory service, you will appreciate just how powerless you can feel and just how powerful the social workers or nurses appear to be.

As a volunteer in a helping agency, you may feel as though you have little or no power in this regard, but someone coming to you for help is likely to see you as a powerful, sane person in control of your life. You may also have valuable information which would be of help to them. Infirmation which you could give . . . or withhold.

There are certain factors which shift our sense of power in relation to others; some factors shift it up and some factors shift it down (in the UK, in general):

Being between the ages of 25–45
Being middle or upper class
Being white
Being English-speaking
Being articulate
Being educated
Being a counsellor
Being employed
Being able bodied
Being tall
Being 'attractive'
Being a man

Factors which shift power up.

Being black
Being young
Being a woman
Being old
Being short
Being a client
Being uneducated
Being unemployed
Being working class
Stuttering and stammering
Having a strong regional accent
Not speaking English well
Being a victim (of violence, abuse, etc.)

Factors which shift power down.

Are there any other factors in your experience that have had the effect of giving you more power or less power?

Differences in power between counsellor and client may have a number of effects. We need to be aware of potential power and status differences in our helping relationships so that they do not get in the way of us offering help.

• Some people are uncomfortable about asking for help unless the helper is seen as equal, i.e. they want a companion or someone to help in a co-operative way.

• Some people are uncomfortable about asking for help unless the helper is more powerful or higher status, i.e. they want help from an expert whom they think will give them good quality help.

• As a helper do you think your helping is only effective if you and your client see each other as equals?

• Some women do not want to receive help from a man.

• Men from some cultures would not ask for help from a woman.

What specific examples of power differences can you come up with that might give rise to problems in helping relationships?

OPPRESSION

This is one of those words that I think I *know* the meaning of, but I really don't *understand* it. As I mentioned before, I must be one of the least oppressed people around. I looked in the dictionary for a definition and read that oppression is 'prolonged cruel or unjust treatment or control'. Other words come to mind — what do you think of when the word 'oppression' is mentioned?

> 'People frequently ask me, "Are you Carl Rogers' daughter?" It has taken women's groups like these to raise my consciousness to give the appropriate answer to that question which is
> "Yes, I'm the daughter of Helen and Carl Rogers."'
>
> Natalie Rogers: *Emerging Woman*, p. 170.

```
OPPRESSION

ABUSE    HARASS      DO DOWN
MISTREAT   SUPPRESS   DICTATOR
TORTURE     PAIN      TORMENT
PERSECUTE   DISCRIMINATE AGAINST
     STOP US GETTING JOBS
     GLASS CEILING   SEGREGATION
HARDSHIP  SLAVERY  OVERPOWER
APARTHEID  MEN OPPRESS WOMEN
SUBTLE, UNSPOKEN SECRET CODE
NO JOBS, NO HOUSING      GHETTO
INEQUALITY-EQUAL RIGHTS FOR ALL

☜ ..........    .............    .............
```

Above is a flipchart with the thoughts of our imaginary group. How did you get on — and how did you feel? Did you think that oppression has nothing to do with you? Perhaps like me you feel fortunate or in some way protected from oppression? This doesn't mean that we should or can do nothing. I wish I could remember who it was that said 'If you're not part of the solution — you're part of the problem'. This phrase seems to catch the feeling exactly and asks me what *I* am doing about *my* attitudes and behaviour.

A good starting place is to understand yourself better in terms of what gives you your own identity and realise that this gives you certain viewpoints and perceptions. So to return for a moment to the list of 'power factors' on page 58, how do these factors contribute to your sense of identity — i.e. your race, colour, religion, physical stature, gender, education, class, physical ability and status, etc? Asking such questions can be a painful process, so I would not recommend you get too deep without support. Perhaps you could try it with a friend or someone else on your introductory course.

As a white, middle-class, able-bodied, non-gay

male, I have a set of perceptions which are particular to that group. I cannot see into the worlds of disabled people, women or black people with ease, if at all. It is difficult or impossible for me to understand and insulting of me to claim to be able to, but I can *try*. If I am sensitive and humble in the trying, then I may be experienced as empathic.

After trying to understand your own position and prejudices better, it can help to try to give oppression some personal meaning:

- Think about a time when you have experienced oppression yourself. (You may have difficulty in admitting to being oppressed, but most people have been oppressed at some time in their lives; perhaps because of your nationality, religion, accent or during childhood.)

- What were your thoughts and feelings at the time?

- What did you want to do about it for yourself?

- Did your oppressors realise that they were oppressing you?

- What did you want the person or people responsible to do about it?

This last question is important since it seems reasonable to find out what an oppressed person wants from you that would help — and to listen very carefully. And secondly if all else fails, we could fall back on the old proverb: 'Do as you would be done by'.

Finally, let's not assume that because everyone may have experienced oppression at some time in their lives, this means that we can ignore the issue since it all somehow cancels out. There are many inequalities built into the system in this and most countries. These inequalities oppress both individuals and groups, restricting their freedom to live fulfilling lives. This institutional oppression

'There are several natural reactions on the part of white Americans which are of no help whatsoever: "I can understand your bitterness because I've been oppressed too"; "Yes, yes, I can understand how you feel, but I have never personally been a part of your oppression. It is the white society which has oppressed you." Whites who are effective seem to learn two attitudes — one toward self and one toward the minority members. The first is the realisation and ownership of the fact that "I think white." For men trying to deal with women's rage, it may be helpful for the man to recognise "I think male." In spite of all our efforts to seem unprejudiced, we actually carry within us many prejudices.'

Carl Rogers: *On Personal Power.* p. 204.

is familiar to all of those with some of the negative factors listed on page 58. Systems are staffed by and voted for by individuals, so we all have a role in maintaining such institutional oppression. We could do well to ask ourselves whether we do anything to oppose oppression when we get the opportunity.

LANGUAGE

One way in which the system oppresses people is in the way language is used to devalue people, to exclude and invalidate their experience. There has been a lot of publicity recently concerning PC or *Political Correctness* and the issue of language. My own view is that since, as a counsellor I try to choose my words with care, I am careful to not contribute to the continuing oppression of others by using offensive or demeaning language.

The current 'backlash' against so-called *Politically Correct* language just diverts attention away from the real issue. If we are to be respectful towards each other in helping relationships, this must surely include the language we use. Who in the twenty-first century would say 'n****r' other than someone with racist intent? Our language is a window to the attitudes we hold, so first of all note the words you use, then wonder whether you might find them offensive if used to describe you.

Language can be used in oppressive ways other than being racist or sexist (either intentionally or unintentionally). Language can be used to oppress others by excluding them. This is done by, for example, educated people to exclude the uneducated and by professional people to exclude the non-professionals. Both the words used (vocabulary) and the way they are used in sentences (grammar) can be used to prevent others understanding you, and therefore making them feel left out and inferior. As counselling moves towards greater professionalism, it is important that we do not fall into the trap of excluding people with the language we use.

It has been argued that counsellors (and the profession of counselling) do this by their use of jargon. One way counselling may exclude working-class people or those from different ethnic backgrounds is by using language that only educated middle-class *counsellors* can understand. What do you make of the following words and phrases?

- Boundaries
- Empathy
- Personal limits
- Defence Mechanisms
- Personal Growth
- Client
- Counselling Skills
- Sharing

- Do you think they are jargon words that may exclude people from understanding the world of counselling?

- What other words would you add to the list?

- Try to explain helping in a counselling way without any of the above words, just using everyday language.

white comedy

I waz whitemailed
By a white witch,
Wid white magic
An white lies,
Branded a white sheep
I slaved as a whitesmith
Near a white spot
Where I suffered whitewater fever.
Whitelisted as a whiteleg
I waz in de white book
As a master of white art,
It waz like white death.

People called me white jack
Some hailed me as a white wog,
So I joined de white watch
Trained as a white guard
Lived off the white economy.
Caught an beaten by de white shirts
I was condemned to a white mass.
Don't worry,
I shall be writing to de Black House.

Benjamin Zephaniah, 1995

WHAT ELSE CAN I DO?

There are many subtle ways in which we are all racist, sexist, ageist, failing to see the value in other people because of their religion, class or whatever. One way is to think that there are no differences. If I say, 'I'm not racist, I treat everyone the same!' I am failing to acknowledge the important *differences* between people which give each of us our identity. A useful phrase which sprung from the women's movement in the seventies was 'different but equal' meaning that women do not want to be seen as the same as men at all (and black people do not want to be seen as the same as white) but as different with valid, useful differences worth celebrating.

If we think that everyone is the same, we are racist and sexist, since we are denying the culture, religion, history and biology that makes us different. Does the organisation you work for reflect the community which it serves? How much effort do you personally put in to find out about different cultures?

Actions speak louder than words, and, if you get involved, you will learn about the issues through reading, meeting people and making friends.

- If you work for an organisation:
  - Familiarise yourself with the equal opportunities policy and help monitor the way it is implemented.
  - If there is no equal opportunities policy could you propose one and work with any oppressed groups to write it?

- What can you do to get to understand the issues better?
  - Have you got a list of contacts for local

groups for women, gays, lesbians, different ethnic communities, disabled, etc.?

• Have you made contact with any for literature, to meet with the staff, to discuss their services?

• Have you sought out any specific training or personal development opportunity on race, sexuality, oppression, power?

• Make an effort to learn about different cultural and religious groups in your community:

• Most agencies, hospital wards and colleges 'celebrate' Christmas. What message does this give to the users of your service?

• Do you know when the religious festivals of other ethnic groups are?

• Does your organisation celebrate them or even acknowledge that they exist?

• Oppression is a personal and a political issue, it is *not* neutral (see Kearney, 1996).

• If you wish to be more active in understanding and counteracting oppression you will have to familiarise yourself with some of the political issues involved. This will take time and patience, since you may well find yourself excluded from some groups and sources of information because you will be understandably seen as one of the oppressing group. It is important to accept and work with this perception. This requires some empathy, effort and willingness to risk an uncomfortable shift in self-awareness, plus a determination to learn and change on your part.

If, like me, you are male, white, and able-bodied, then you are one of the most powerful creatures on the planet. It would be easy to say that I didn't ask to be born a man, white, etc. and this evades the issue. Although I didn't ask for anything, I have used this power every day of my life and continue to, most often even without knowing it. The way our society works is that the sort of power invested in white, middle-class, able-bodied men is the sort of power that thrives by taking power away from others. In other words it is a power used to oppress others. Until I find out how this works for me on a day-to-day basis I will continue to oppress others without even realising it. For my part I feel behoven to do something about my part in it all; not blaming myself, but only if I take responsibility for my part in the world can I change it.

None of these suggestions is going to change the world overnight, but they do give you some power in your own sphere of influence. The process of change in your sphere of influence starts with yourself and then stretches out to include your family, friends and colleagues.

'It is our belief that, to some extent, all individuals are racist, sexist, and classist.

In a setting such as this, some of these will become explicit. It is our hope that everyone will be understanding, respecting, empathic and non-judgemental.

In a setting such as this we should all be allowed to make mistakes.'

Joyce Thompson, 1985

Counselling and Helping Attitudes and Skills

5

In Chapter 2 we saw how the different counselling approaches are based upon different principles and to some extent on different values. The foundations of each approach *do* affect the theory and practice of each approach just like the foundations of a building dictate the shape, height and building materials permitted in the final structure.

The practice of counselling is shaped by the founding principles of each approach and you may remember from Chapter 2 that Carl Rogers proposed that his 'core conditions' of empathy, congruence and unconditional positive regard had to be held as attitudes. It would not be enough, as far as Rogers was concerned, for these conditions to be just learned as skills and acted out in a mechanical way. That would make the whole act of helping false, a horrendous caricature of real human caring, wherein the helper was, at worst, merely pretending to care, or at best not really believing in the effectiveness of their actions. The client is bound to detect this incongruence in the helper and may not trust the helper or feel safe with them.

Person-centred counsellors use the terms 'principled' and 'instrumental' to talk about the differences between using the core conditions. In 1990 Barry Grant used these terms to mean:

- *Principled* means where something is held as a principle, is part of your belief-system and set of values. You *are* this thing, you do not have to *put it on* or *act it out*. You express these values as a natural part of being you because they are held at your core.

- *Instrumental* means *using* something as an instrument or tool in order to achieve a given end.

So in terms of the core conditions, 'principled' empathy, congruence and UPR would mean that you hold these human qualities as core values in your life, i.e. you believe that being empathic, genuine and regarding people positively is the right way to be for you. You would not be being empathic, or genuine in order to get a given effect. As a helper, you would be relying on the client's actualising tendency to help them, once your helping qualities of empathy, congruence and UPR were provided.

On the other hand, 'instrumental' empathy, genuineness and UPR means that you would be using human qualities these like tools for helping, but you would not necessarily hold them as core values. You would, for example, be *using* genuineness as a tool to get the client to trust you and 'open up'. You would be *using* empathy to get the client to explain their problem or explore it themselves. You may or may not be doing this because you believed that this helping system was effective.

Person-centred therapists would take a principled approach to the holding (and expression) of the core conditions as values, human qualities and attitudes in life. In 1980 Carl Rogers called this a 'way of being'. There can be no clearer indication of what lies at the heart of helping in a person-centred way — a set of genuinely held core values, not the application of the core conditions as a set of *techniques* or tools.

Not all approaches to helping take this view. Other approaches may, to different degrees, incorporate Rogers' core conditions (or something very similar) into their helping framework. These approaches may talk about the importance of the helping relationship or 'therapeutic alliance'. Cognitive, behavioural, psychodynamic and integrative approaches generally *use* a selection of the core conditions *instrumentally* as tools to further the theoretical aims of the approach in question.

So, for example, a cognitive counsellor will use empathy as a tool to get an accurate understanding of the client's thought processes so that the therapist can suggest the most helpful ways of overcoming debilitating or self-defeating thoughts. In this approach, in order to be effective, the counsellor does not have to be empathic as a 'way of being'.

An eclectic or integrative counsellor will *use* any or all of the core conditions *as tools* if they believe the client will be helped by applying them in this instrumental way. The next client seen by an eclectic counsellor may have a different set of tools applied to their problem.

Chapter 3 on *The Importance of Self-Development* had sections on personal values and counselling values. The importance of these sections should now be obvious. It is clear that, in order to be person-centred, you would need to feel comfortable holding the values of empathy, genuineness and UPR as 'good things to be'. Of course, holding these values (as many of us do) would not mean that you *must* be person-centred in your helping style. You could just as easily hold these values and decide, after careful scrutiny of the theories, that a behavioural or cognitive style of helping makes more sense to you.

Many readers will wish to remain volunteers using basic helping. Those wishing to progress to training as a counsellor will find Chapter 13 useful when we will take a little time to look at the importance of making the right decision about what sort of counsellor you want to train to become.

COUNSELLING AND BASIC HELPING SKILLS
Most people now look upon counselling as a skilled activity practised by trained people acting in a 'professional' way, i.e. according to a set of standards. It has not always been the case. Indeed when I first started as a volunteer counsellor in 1973 I spent a lot of time defending the skills of counselling (as I understood them then) from the assertions of others that counselling was variously: 'Just chatting'; 'Just listening' or 'Just being someone's friend'. I seem to remember that such put-downs always had the double barb that firstly, counselling is what people do anyway ('chatting, listening or being a friend') and secondly, that it was 'just' or 'simply' that and nothing else. It was not something I had to learn, could benefit by practice at, or would get better at by receiving constructive feedback from others. In other words it was not a skill.

> '**Skill:** an acquired higher-order activity to perform complex . . . acts smoothly and precisely.'
> Longman Dictionary of Psychology and Psychiatry (1984).

The idea that human beings use skills to manage relationships is not a new one. This view gained considerable popularity in the 1970s when the notion of social skills seemed to be cropping up everywhere. Social skills was the term used to indicate that the business of being a social being — having to live a life in the presence of others, in parallel to others and interwoven in the lives of others — was indeed a matter of skill. The idea that social skills were important in everyday life soon became accepted and since a skill can be learned and improved with practice, social skills training was set up to help develop the particular type of social skills necessary to have a good marriage, be a good salesperson, be an effective manager, etc.

The idea that helping in general, and counselling

or therapy in particular, could be looked at as a set of components which could be learned was made popular by Carl Rogers when he wrote about the 'core conditions'. (Mentioned briefly in Chapter 2.) Nowadays it is accepted that counselling is skilled and that practice makes better, if not perfect. Most training courses spend a lot of time getting trainees to practise their counselling skills. The question is:

'What are counselling skills?'

This question is closely related to the work covered in Chapter 1: ***What is Counselling?*** In the search for possible definitions of counselling we compared it to other helping roles we are familiar with. So to answer the question 'What are Counselling Skills?' I would ask you to consider other helping roles alongside counselling, e.g. the same ones as in Chapter 1.

Parent	Friend	Doctor

DOCTOR

GOOD AT EXPLAINING MEDICAL THINGS IN EVERY-DAY LANGUAGE

ACTIVE LISTENING

KEEPING PROFESSIONAL DISTANCE

CREATE A SAFE ENVIRON-MENT TO TALK ABOUT PRIVATE THINGS (CONFIDENTIAL)

✍ ....

FRIEND

OFFERS PROTECTION

COMPLETE DEPENDABILITY, HONESTY AND LOYALTY

GENUINE (NEVER CALLS YOU NAMES BEHIND YOUR BACK)

IS ON YOUR SIDE

ACTIVE LISTENING

✍ ....

PARENT

ACTIVE LISTENING

EVEN-HANDED AND FAIR WITH DISCIPLINE

SUPPORTIVE

GIVING UNCONDITIONAL LOVE (NON-JUDGEMENTAL)

UNSELFISH & GENEROUS

ABSOLUTE TRUSTWORTHINESS

✍ ....

COUNSELLOR

ACTIVE LISTENING

GENUINE

NON-JUDGEMENTAL

CONFIDENTIAL

EQUAL (ON THE SAME LEVEL AS YOU)

SUPPORTIVE

✍ ....

The flipcharts on the previous page show a selection of ideas about the kind of helping skills needed in different roles (similar to those we saw in Chapter 1) and it is clear that some common helping skills are emerging. Are your ideas similar or very different? How much do you agree with the list of counselling skills on the flipchart? When you see this symbol:

✍ MAKE A NOTE OF YOUR ANSWERS ↓ EXAMPLES

In Chapter 2, I looked at where the ideas behind modern counselling approaches have come from and it is useful to ask *ourselves* where *our* ideas have come from. What has influenced your ideas on counselling skills? Have your ideas about *counselling skills* come from:

- Personal experience of being counselled?
- The beliefs of friends and family?
- What you've read in the papers or seen on TV?
- Someone you know who is a counsellor?
- Books about counselling or psychology?
- Other books, e.g. novels or spiritual writings?

It is not realistic to expect to be properly trained in the use of counselling skills on a course lasting less than around 100 hours, but it is realistic to expect to raise your awareness to what counselling skills are and to have a go at trying them out to see how it feels. It is in this spirit that I offer the following sections:
- To help you identify the skills you already have.
- To back up any skills training you may be doing.
- To help you further develop your repertoire of counselling skills.
- To give some more detail on the skills you might be encouraged to practise.
- To show a range of skills which you may not be able to cover due to time constraints.

CARL ROGERS AND GERARD EGAN

In Chapter 2 I looked at the origins of theory in counselling, briefly touching upon the work of Carl Rogers and just mentioning the work of Gerard Egan. My own practice has been influenced most heavily by the ideas of Carl Rogers; I describe myself as a Person-Centred Counsellor and I am a member of the British Association for the Person-Centred Approach. At the same time I acknowledge the important influence of the ideas of Egan in developing basic helping skills practice, especially in the voluntary sector in the UK.

Both Rogers and Egan were responsible for developing the idea that counselling was a skilled process, and most would agree that Egan incorporates Rogers' ideas into his framework for understanding the process of helping. Most training courses now emphasise the development of skills as an important, indeed essential, element in training to be a counsellor. At an introductory level we must be content with the basic underlying principles.

THE WORK OF CARL ROGERS

You may remember from Chapter 2 that Carl Rogers developed his ideas in the 1950s, continuing to refine them until his death in 1987. He proposed that the helper or counsellor needs to provide the right conditions before the natural, positive, self-healing tendency within the client is activated or enhanced. Rogers suggested that the 'right' conditions involved the complete absence of threat to the client. He went on to elaborate his ideas in 1957 and proposed that the six conditions necessary in a helping relationship were:

- that the helper makes psychological contact with the person to be helped

- that the client is vulnerable or anxious

- that the helper is congruent or genuine

- that the helper experiences unconditional positive regard or non-judgemental warmth or acceptance towards the client

- that the helper experiences empathy

- that the client receives the empathy, UPR and genuineness of the helper

Rogers originally described these conditions in psychological terminology. For a while it became accepted to condense the six into the three 'core conditions' (empathy, UPR and congruence) and these form the basis for many skills-approaches to counselling, even though Rogers himself was keen to emphasise the important role of the *whole relationship* in the helping process. He did not see counselling as just assembling a set of skills; rather he believed that counsellors must incorporate the core conditions into their ways of being as people. Becoming a counsellor does indeed involve a deal of personal change for the counsellor-in-training, but now we will identify some basic counselling skills that emerge from the core conditions. Firstly a closer look at the core conditions themselves.

In recent years, person-centred theorists and practitioners have preferred to remind all counsellors (whatever approach they use) that Rogers did indeed write about *six* conditions. Moreover that the conditions of psychological contact (condition 1) and the successful communication of the conditions to the client (condition 6) were vital parts of successful helping.

PSYCHOLOGICAL CONTACT

Just because you are in the same room and looking at the person you are trying to help doesn't necessarily mean that you are in psychological contact with them. Interestingly, if you are offering help on the telephone, you will already know how important it is to keep checking that the person on the other end of the phone is still 'there'. Telephone helpers get used to saying sensitively: 'Are you still there?', or 'I can hear you breathing' during silences. In face-to-face helping it might not occur to you that you will have to *deliberately attend* to making contact with your client.

The key question is: *How do you know you have good psychological contact with someone?*

The answer is, to some extent, obvious. We all know when we are 'getting through' to someone. They are responsive to what we say or do in a quick

and appropriate manner. Looking at us, smiling, talking, etc. In normal conversation we can detect quite easily when this contact is missing. We have colloquial phrases like 'away with the birds' and 'on another planet' to describe it. In a basic helping context, however, there might be more silence or less eye contact, so 'natural' checking that you have good contact is more difficult. You might have to deliberately check that, for example, you have been 'received and understood' so-to-speak by saying things like 'is that right?', 'did I understand you correctly?', etc.

It might be difficult to maintain psychological contact with
- someone who is extremely tired or exhausted
- someone who has taken drugs, prescribed or otherwise. Some prescription drugs can have a marked effect on concentration and ability to 'stay with it', especially psychiatric medication.
- someone who is drunk
- someone who has taken an overdose
- someone who is extremely agitated or anxious
- someone who is suffering from what psychiatrists call *dissociation*, or someone who is having a *psychotic episode* and has lost contact with our shared reality

As someone offering basic helping, depending upon your situation, you will be able to respond in one of a number of ways:

- there may be agency policy to help deal with someone who is drunk or under the influence of drugs

- if you suspect that someone has taken an overdose of something, or is so drunk that they become unconscious, get medical help immediately

- there may be agency policy to help deal with people who are having a psychotic episode or experiencing dissociation

- if none of the above apply, you will have to quickly assess the situation to work out:
  - how comfortable you are that you have the personal qualities and skills to see this through
  - if you decide to help, stay calm and make sure you and the person you are trying to help are safe
  - there is evidence from the work of the American psychologist Garry Prouty that slow, extremely basic reflections such as 'we are sitting in the counselling centre', 'you are smiling but not saying anything' and repeating what the client says word-for-word are helpful (See Prouty, Van Werde and Pörtner, 2002).

Don't worry if you don't feel able to do this, just sitting calmly and quietly with them until they are able to make good psychological contact in their own time is probably the best basic helping you can offer.

In summary, then:
- don't take psychological contact for granted. Check and think about doing something about it.
- if you have not got good psychological contact with the person you are trying to help, see what your agency or workplace policy says you should do.

Remember — you cannot really help someone who is not in contact, so simply waiting until they feel able to make contact under their own steam is best if you are at all unsure.

EMPATHY

This is trying to see the world of another person from their point of view. It involves trying to understand their world, their meanings, their life. It has been described as walking in someone else's shoes, understanding how they feel and think — listening to both the 'words' and the 'music'. The emphasis is on not only understanding, but also on doing this gently and sensitively, then communicating this to the other person. Not trampling around their world of personal images and meanings without any care.

Being empathic is:
1. Listening sensitively.
2. Trying to make sense of what you hear.
3. Understanding the other person's experiences *in their own terms*.
4. Checking to see if you've got the meaning right with all its subtleties.

Carl Rogers describes empathy as the ability to sense the client's world *as if* it were your own, without losing the 'as if' quality. He placed particular emphasis on being able accurately and sensitively to understand the client's *feelings* without getting them muddled up with your own. He makes it clear that we cannot actually put ourselves into the world of others, we can never experience the same things as others. Even if we have a similar experience, we will not have felt exactly the same about it.

A good example is bereavement. I can remember when my dad died quite clearly. I was 18 years old and it was three weeks before my A-level exams. I was sure that the pain and loss I felt could not be experienced by anyone else, not even my brother. I knew that his relationship with Dad had been very different from mine (he was 14 at the time). The experience of the loss of a parent, close relative or friend is different for everyone. Some people may feel relief or a sense of freedom if their relationship with their parent was restrictive or burdensome. Such responses can be very difficult to cope with if they accompanied by a sense of pain and grief at the loss.

It might be tempting to think 'Ah yes, that happened to me too. I know exactly how you feel.' And believe that you may have experienced the same feelings as the person you are trying to help. This is called *identification* and is not empathy. In fact it makes empathy more difficult because your own feelings keep getting in the way of your efforts to understand the other person accurately.

I remember feeling very angry with someone who, on the day of my dad's funeral, came up to me and said 'I know how you feel, I was in a prisoner of war camp. You've got to be strong and look after your mother.' In that one phrase they showed me that although they were trying their best to help, they had got it wrong. They just didn't understand how I felt and they hadn't made any effort to. What I wanted (but I didn't know what it was called then) was empathy. Some reaching out to understand or gain insight into my feelings, thoughts and attitudes.

Of course what may have been stopping this person from empathising with me was the fact that they were grieving for my father too. Their own feelings were getting in the way of their efforts to understand me. Not only were they grieving for my father but, by their words of 'comfort' to me, it seems likely that my father's death had reminded them of the pain they felt at the loss of their friends in the prisoner of war camp some 30 years before. Not to mention the other terrible ordeals they had to endure then.

This tangle of emotions is not limited to those who have suffered in POW camps. We all have tangles like this just waiting to get activated! This is why self-awareness is so important if we are to try and help others in a straightforward and effective way.

CONGRUENCE OR GENUINENESS

This involves the helper being open to his or her own feelings as much as possible. It means being my real self — without front or facade, without acting like an 'expert'. Carl Rogers often described it as being 'transparently real' and implicit in the core condition of genuineness is the challenge to us to be ourselves; fallible, vulnerable, imperfect, not knowing any of the answers, etc.

This goes against some of the training we might have received in the so-called 'helping professions' which advises us to keep a professional distance, bluff it out, pretend we know what we're doing (even if we don't) and close ranks. Some of this behaviour *might* be useful when trying to help as a nurse, teacher or doctor (although I must say I'm

not too sure about this), but it is definitely not part of a counselling way of helping.

Rogers describes genuineness from the client's point of view:

'It has been found that personal change is facilitated when the psychotherapist is what he *is*, when in the relationship with his client he is genuine and without "front" or facade, openly being the feelings and attitudes which are at that moment flowing *in* him.'
On Becoming a Person, p. 61.

This doesn't mean to say that the helper lets her feelings gush out in an uncontrolled torrent all of the time. It means that the helper should first of all not deny or avoid, but be aware of her feelings and then not be afraid of expressing them if appropriate.

From the helper's point of view Rogers writes:

'I have come to recognise that being trustworthy does not demand that I be rigidly consistent but that I be dependably real. The term "congruent" is one that I have used to describe the way I would like to be. By this I mean that whatever feeling or attitude I am experiencing would be matched by my awareness of that attitude. When this is true, then I am a unified or integrated person in that moment, and hence I can be whatever I deeply am.'
On Becoming a Person, p. 50.

This means that the whole person is brought to the activity of helping: feelings, thoughts, attitudes, 'warts and all'. We don't just bring a professional expertise, but all of our humanness. Indeed our expertise *is* our humanness, so if we leave that behind, we will not be effective helpers.

Returning to the example of the person at my father's funeral: they could have been congruent, that is to say, aware of their own feelings of grief and the links back to their POW experiences and said: *'Your father's death has taken me right back to the terrible days in the Prisoner of War camp during the second world war. I lost so many friends there. I'm doubly upset because I was close to your father and now I'm reminded of all those years ago.'*

Then I could have seen this person as real, as a person with their own grieving to resolve. They might then have said: *'I can see how upset you are too, it must be terrible for you today, I know how close you were to your dad.'* This last sentence is empathic and would have been much easier for me to hear after the congruent statement above.

Genuineness, then, is any expression of the helper's capacity to be in touch with his or her feelings, thoughts or even bodily sensations as s/he seeks to understand the client's world of experience.

UNCONDITIONAL POSITIVE REGARD (UPR)

This core condition is also called non-judgemental warmth or acceptance. It means that we must be able to totally accept the person we are trying to help as a worthwhile human being. The helper must be able to believe that each person is worthy, is OK deep down, or 'all right' underneath it all. Seeing someone as worthy does not mean that you have to approve of their behaviour. It simply means that you see them as a human being of equal value.

I rather like the term 'non-judgemental warmth', since it puts the rather neutral non-judgemental bit next to the very positive 'warmth'. It also helps us break down the core conditions into two component elements; firstly the absence, or suspension of judgement and secondly the positive feeling of warmth, and the communication of this warmth to the person you are helping. Many people come for counselling-style helping because they have been damaged by other people's harsh, heavy-handed, unreasonable or unnecessary judgement. It's important that they don't get more of the same from those trying to help mend the hurts.

Carl Rogers writes:
'Can I free him (the client) from the threat of external evaluation? In almost every phase of our lives — at home, at school, at work — we find ourselves under the rewards and punishments of external judgements. "That's good"; "that's naughty." "That's worth an A"; "that's a failure." "That's good counseling"; "that's poor counseling." Such judgements are a part of our lives from infancy to old age.'
On Becoming a Person, p. 54.

You may wonder whether an honest evaluation of another person might not be quite helpful under some circumstances, and I guess you would be right. Helping styles and roles other than a counselling way of helping could legitimately use judgements in their repertoire of skills. Teachers for example will have to make judgements about a student's work or level of achievement. However, even in this setting, it is important to be careful and respectful in the manner in which the judgement is delivered. In Chapter 3 I looked at the role of feedback in personal development and, of course, feedback is a sort of judgement. The difference is that it is not a judgement about the person and their worth, but feedback about their behaviour.

The two core conditions of congruence and UPR do leave us with a dilemma though. There are potential areas of conflict between being non-judgemental and warm whilst simultaneously being genuine. In simple terms the dilemma is this:

What would happen if you were supposed to be helping someone whom you didn't like because, for example, you knew that they were a convicted rapist?

• Should you be genuine (and judgemental) and say that you don't like them.

Or,

• Should you be non-judgemental and be (falsely) warm and accepting towards them.

This sort of dilemma is often highlighted by

introductory courses. It's worthwhile taking a moment to consider how you might resolve this apparent conflict.

Often our worries about not being able to be warm stem from our values or deeply held views. This issue overlaps with personal development, prejudice and the work on personal values we looked at in Chapters 3 and 4. (You might like to remind yourself of the issues we covered.) This illustrates how central self-awareness and personal development are to learning about counselling and how to do it. You may be tempted to think that you could 'hide' your judgemental attitudes from the person you are working with. There will be opportunities during your course to do some active listening practice, it might be useful to ask your partner if they think they could see through any pretence.

Finally, do you think you would be fooled? No matter how desperate for help someone is, they usually still have their 'bullshit detector' switched on. Here are some other possibilities for you to consider. In each case the question is how do you experience the conflict between genuineness and non-judgemental warmth — is it more important to be non-judgemental, more important to be genuine or is there a way to be both at the same time? What would you do if:

- You were asked to help a young woman who had a problem pregnancy and was considering a termination.

- You were sexually attracted to the person you were trying to help.

- The person you are helping tells you that they were violent to their children when they were young.

- The person you are trying to help says that they have thought of killing themselves.

✍ YOU MIGHT LIKE TO MAKE YOUR OWN NOTES AT THIS POINT.

SIX CONDITIONS: NECESSARY AND SUFFICIENT

When Carl Rogers described the six therapeutic conditions in 1957, he also said that they were both necessary and sufficient before helpful change was possible. It is easy to forget that there are *six* conditions. It is vital that you, the helper, make *psychological contact* (condition 1) with the person you are trying to help.

By **necessary** he meant that helpful change will only happen if all three core conditions are present. If one is missing, change will either not happen or if it does happen, it may not be helpful change. As we noted in Chapter 3 there are many types of change, and some of the core conditions may be present to a greater or lesser degree, but only when all three are present will the change be helpful. It could be said, for example, that brainwashing is change — but we would not consider brainwashing to be 'helpful' change. This means that providing a helping relationship can be quite difficult since we have to provide all three core conditions, and they have to be *received* by the person we are trying to help.

By **sufficient** Rogers meant that if all three core conditions are present, then helpful change will take place regardless of any other conditions being met — nothing else is necessary. So if the core conditions are provided by accident or in an unplanned manner, helpful change would still take place. Have you ever felt that someone was a 'natural' listener or helper? Someone that was sought out by others to share their troubles with? Such people can probably provide the core conditions quite instinctively, without thinking about it or being trained as a person-centred helper. The exercise on page 72 asks you to identify people who can provide these core conditions singly. Occasionally we meet someone who can provide all three instinctively and we experience them as naturally respectful and understanding, deeply caring and very helpful.

RECEIVED AND UNDERSTOOD?

Being the most empathic, accepting and genuine

Getting to know the core conditions
(A self-awareness exercise)

Think of each core condition in turn — Empathy, Congruence and Unconditional Positive Regard. For each core condition, think of a person that embodies that core condition. Someone who is the living, breathing personification of that core condition for you. (This should be a real person — someone you know.) Think of a time when you were with this person, perhaps recently, when you 'received' the particular core condition from them.

1. Who is the person — what relationship do you have with them? Write down a brief description of them.

2. What are the qualities of Empathy, Congruence, and UPR that this person conveys?

3. How does it feel to be on the receiving end of each core condition?

EMPATHY IS . . .

WHEN I RECEIVE EMPATHY I FEEL.....

CONGRUENCE IS . . .

WHEN I RECEIVE CONGRUENCE I FEEL........

UPR IS . . .

WHEN I RECEIVE UPR I FEEL........

person in the world is of absolutely no use if the person you are trying to help does not perceive these qualities in you. Just as important as you having or 'being' these qualities is the *transmitting* of them and the *receiving* of them by the client.

There are tests used in research to measure how empathic, non-judgemental, warm and congruent a counsellor is being, but it is really not advisable to use them in basic helping settings. The client's view of the counsellor is very important.

The issue of the client's view of the counsellor has most relevance to us because we really should take note of how others receive our helping efforts. In training, you will probably get feedback. If you *intend* to be empathic and warm, but are *experienced* as being well-meaning, but stiff and impersonal, then you should listen to the feedback and try to change the way you express your helping.

THE WORK OF GERARD EGAN

The next step in learning about basic helping is to see how the core conditions translate into a set of identifiable skills. It isn't enough to just think hard to yourself 'I'm being Empathic, Warm and Genuine' or chant the words like a mantra. The core conditions have to be *experienced by the client* before they are of any use.

Gerard Egan published the first edition of his popular book *The Skilled Helper* in 1975. He added to the ideas of Carl Rogers by taking the work of other psychologists and constructing a theory of helping based on the skills required at different stages in the helpful change process. (Along with others, Egan thinks that the core conditions may be necessary, but are not sufficient — they need some extra elements added to them before helping can be properly effective.)

Many counsellors — those who call themselves 'Person-Centred' — think that Rogers' ideas

were fine as they stood and didn't need anything adding to them — in fact this is my view too. (In short, we think that the core conditions really are necessary and *sufficient*.) However, for the purposes of learning about basic helping in a counselling style, Egan's model of counselling is a very handy way of getting across the idea that certain skills are involved and that you may have to change the way you offer help if you are to improve as a helper.

At this introductory level of training, you will not have enough time to practise the skills in order to become proficient. This takes a different amount of time for each of us, although counselling skills courses take around 120 hours over a year and you may wish to continue your training by enrolling for one when you have completed this training. Most people coming to counselling training already have some of the skills necessary, so it's a case of finding out what your skills are then trying to develop a complete or more rounded repertoire of helping skills. In this book, all we can do is find out what the skills are by briefly identifying them, giving examples and maybe putting them in a context.

Stage I: Building the helping relationship and exploration

In this first stage, the helper is creating a warm trusting relationship with the client, enabling the client to look at or explore whatever they choose. The helper is trying to step into the other person's shoes and look at the world from the client's point of view.

Stage I Skills This first stage incorporates Rogers' core conditions of empathy, congruence and UPR. The specific skills associated with this stage are:

- developing a trusting relationship:
  - making and maintaining contact,
  - structuring,
  - communicating non-judgemental warmth,
  - communicating genuineness.
- active listening and communicating empathy:

The Three-Stage Helping Model

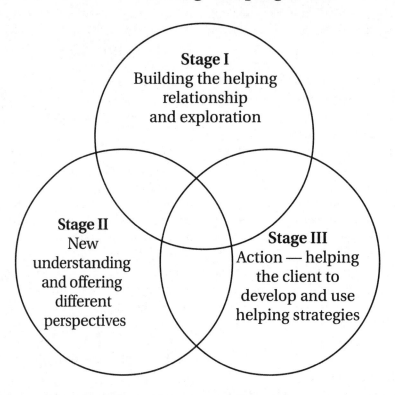

This three-stage helping skills model is derived from the work of Gerard Egan — *The Skilled Helper* (1982). Later editions of the book *The Skilled Helper* describe slightly different versions of the same model, using different terms.

The 1994 edition describes the stages as:
Stage I: Helping clients identify and clarify problem situations.
Stage II: Helping clients create a better future.
Stage III: Getting there — helping clients implement their goals.
The Skilled Helper, pp. ix–xiii.

• identifying, acknowledging and reflecting thoughts, behaviours and feelings,
• paraphrasing,
• clarifying.

We will look at these Stage I skills in more detail under the heading 'Basic Skills and attitudes for basic helping' on the facing page, where I will explain each skill and give examples.

Stage II Skills In this stage the client is helped to see themselves and their life from new perspectives, taking into consideration alternative information and other viewpoints. This is done using all of Stage I skills, plus:

Linking and integrating individual issues and problems into themes:
• showing deeper understanding and empathy,
• helping the client focus on specific issues.

Challenging the client's views:
- offering new perspectives,
- sharing the helper's experiences and feelings,
- helping the client move on.

Goal-setting:
- helping the client identify what they want to achieve.

Stage III Skills Now the helper is trying to look, with the client, at possible ways of acting in the situation to help resolve the problem. Possible outcomes will be considered and risks assessed. The client will then be helped to evaluate the effectiveness of their new behaviour. This is achieved using all of Stage I and II skills, plus:

Helping the client move on to considering action.

Developing and choosing action plans:
- brainstorming
- creative thinking
- problem-solving
- decision-making
- planning

Evaluating consequences of actions:
- recording events, e.g. diary-keeping
- evaluation
- reviewing plans

As the client progresses through the stages proposed by Egan, the emphasis shifts from the client's point of view and their world to a more objective perspective and finally action in and on the client's world to cause change. This may seem far removed from Carl Rogers' ideas of the innate self-healing process. Egan expresses his understanding of the client's ability to direct their own helping process by having the helper as a co-worker, making suggestions or offering ways of tackling issues which the client can use or not as *they* choose.

Rogerian Person-Centred counsellors let the client discover their own new perspectives and make their own action plans by helping them activate their own self-healing process. The counsellor does this by providing the core conditions almost exclusively through Stage I skills.

BASIC HELPING

This extensive range of skills that are used in counselling takes a long time to properly develop, as we shall see in Chapter 13. In this book we can do only a little more than list the skills.

In Chapter 1, I used the phrases 'basic helping' and 'helping in a counselling way' to describe the basic counselling-style helping that uses a counselling approach, but not a full range of properly developed counselling skills. Basic helping does not use the professional or ethical framework that counsellors use either, but those using this basic helping in a counselling way will have at least considered the positive effects of, for example, the boundaries of helping relationships, (see Chapter 1).

BASIC SKILLS AND ATTITUDES FOR BASIC HELPING

There are some skills fundamental to the basic helping process that you might like to practise as part of your own helping. These are the Stage I Skills listed above. You will probably spend an hour or two on your introductory course finding out how difficult it actually is, even though the skills themselves sound quite simple. The ingredients for skills training are repeated practice, evaluation and feedback (we look at feedback in a few places in this book). If your course doesn't give any, or sufficient, time to practise your helping skills you might want to set up a situation in which you can get these ingredients. You may, for example, get together with colleagues from your course, or try it out with friends in your own time. You will need at least an hour — I would recommend two.

The most difficult ingredient to get right in such informal 'training' arrangements is feedback. In Chapter 3, I looked at feedback in a little more detail in the context of personal development.

In a skills training setting it is just as important to be accurate in your observations and honest in your feedback. Since the core conditions have to be communicated to the client, it is the client or, as is sometimes the case in skills training, the person in the client role, whose feedback is most valuable. It is common practice to have a third person acting as an observer who can give the counsellor/helper feedback from a more objective position seeing as they were not on the receiving end of the skills.

Feedback in training is essential, then. It is most useful if it comes from two sources: firstly the client or person being helped or listened to, and secondly a 'neutral' observer. You might want to be reassured that you are looking for the right things when you observe and give feedback. In which case it will help to ask your tutor for assistance.

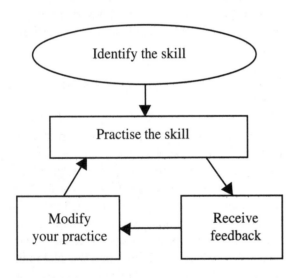

SKILLS OR ATTITUDES — A REMINDER

Just because we are looking at these qualities as skills, doesn't mean that you should not continue to strive to develop them as attitudes. If you find yourself drawn to a person-centred approach in your helping, you will be trying to integrate these *qualities* into your *self*. If you are drawn to a cognitive/behavioural approach in your helping you will be trying to integrate these *skills* into your *repertoire*.

DEVELOPING STAGE I SKILLS

DEVELOPING A TRUSTING RELATIONSHIP
1. Making and maintaining contact
2. Structuring

Every relationship happens in a series of episodes, that is, the times the people concerned actually meet and make contact (this could, of course, be on the phone or by letter, but we will only concern ourselves with face-to-face meetings here). A relationship begins with the first meeting or episode and the first 'task' in the first episode is to work out what kind or type of relationship it is going to be. This happens pretty quickly and will depend upon the setting, the roles that the people are in, their expectations and the first things that are said. It is called '*structuring*':

(College classroom)
> '*Hello, my name is Pete Sanders and I'll be teaching you GCSE maths this year.*'

(Telephone)
> '*Hello, Samaritans, can I help?*'

(Student services in college)
> '*Hello, my name is Pete, I'm a counsellor here. You must be Sandra. I don't know why you've come to the counselling service, but I'll do my best to help in whatever way I can. Would you like to tell me what's concerning you?*'

(Street)
> '*Excuse me, could you tell me how to get to the station?*'

(Bank)
> '*Don't make a noise or raise the alarm. This is a gun under my coat. Now give me the money! MOVE!*'

Some of these are helping relationships and some are not. We can tell because of the setting, the roles, the expectations of the situation or by what is said. How would you make contact in a way that indicates you are offering help?

After you've made contact in a helping relationship, the next task is to maintain that contact. This is done by doing certain things (non-verbal communication) and saying certain things or making noises (you don't have to actually say words). What are the methods of maintaining contact that you use?

> VERBAL METHODS
>
> SAYING 'YES' 'I SEE'
>
> 'PLEASE GO ON'
>
> 'RIGHT' 'UH-HUH' MMMM'
>
> ✍ ....
>
>
> NON-VERBAL METHODS
>
> LOOKING AT THE PERSON
>
> SMILING
>
> NODDING   MAKING EYE CONTACT
>
> LEANING FORWARD IN YOUR CHAIR
>
> ✍ ....

Once again, a flipchart from our imaginary group shows some possible answers. Do you have any to add?

The things we do and say to keep in contact with another person come quite naturally to most of us. In a helping relationship, however, we want to communicate warmth, genuineness and empathy even in the way we say 'I see'. Whether we are successful can only be determined by asking for feedback.

DEVELOPING A TRUSTING RELATIONSHIP
3. *Communicating non-judgemental warmth*
4. *Communicating genuineness*

Both verbal and non-verbal methods of communication figure strongly in this next section too. Communicating non-judgemental warmth and genuineness is as much about *what you do* as *what and how you say* something. Most of us that are attracted to a counselling way of helping tend to be less judgemental than average, but it can still be a difficult task. It's obvious that if you're striving to be non-judgemental in a counselling way, you don't say:

> *'Don't you know that having an abortion is killing another human being and is only done by bad, evil people?'*

However, many of us do have strong feelings about abortion and may well feel something similar. The question is how do you accept someone who is behaving in what you feel is an unacceptable way? It is necessary firstly to separate the person and their intrinsic worth as a human being from their behaviour, which may be unacceptable. Then secondly be aware of your own values and prejudices and be willing to suspend them and withhold judgement for the time being as the person you are helping strives to change. Of course they may not change in a way in which you think is sensible. Skills specific to being accepting are:

Be specific, avoid generalising:
> Say: 'It sounds as though it was really painful for you when your father died.'
> Don't say: 'Everyone feels bad when someone close to them dies, it's only natural.'

Don't debate things — you're not having a discussion, you're trying to help:
> Say: 'So you think it would be best if you went to the Clinic for advice on contraception.'
> Don't say: 'I wouldn't go to the clinic, the best place to go is your GP, they know your medical history.'

Don't push the person you are trying to help too far or too fast — accept their pace:

> Say: 'It seems as though you don't want to go any further with this at the moment.'
>
> Don't say: 'You've spent a long time talking about this topic, don't you think it is time you moved on to what's really upsetting you.'

Don't make guesses or interpretations — you're no expert on the client's troubles:

> Say: 'So you think that the time your boss overlooked you for promotion was the start of this low patch.'
>
> Don't say: 'Well, you say your boss is responsible, but it sounds as though it's more likely to be the fact that your mother died last year.'

Each one of the 'Don't say' responses above is non-accepting or judgemental in some way. For example:

> *'Everyone feels bad when someone close to them dies, it's only natural.'*

This sounds caring and possibly helpful, but the hidden judgemental message is something like:

> *'Your hurt isn't specially bad because this sort of thing happens to everybody.'*

It might be useful to try to identify the 'hidden judgements' behind the other responses and you may know of some other ways of being judgemental which helpers might wish to avoid.

ACTIVE LISTENING AND COMMUNICATING EMPATHY

1. Identifying, acknowledging and reflecting thoughts, behaviours and feelings

Active listening is one of the key ingredients in any helping relationship. It is impossible to be helpful if you are not actively listening. Active listening means that you have to attend to all of the signals given off by a person — not only the sounds, but using your sight to pick up the non-verbal

signals. It should really be called 'active attention' because we are trying to actively pay the most detailed and special attention to the other person using all our senses.

The purpose of this active listening is to pay attention to, and try to understand, the thoughts, feelings and behaviour of the other person. How do we do this? If you were the helper, what would you be paying attention to in the speech and behaviour of the other person?

> ACTIVE LISTENING – WHAT WE PAY ATTENTION TO IN THE PERSON WE ARE HELPING
>
> VOICE QUALITY – SOFT, HARD, CONFIDENT, TIMID, STRONG, WEAK, ETC.
>
> BREATHING – DEEP, SHALLOW, SOBBING, SNATCHED, RELAXED, ETC.
>
> FACIAL EXPRESSION – RELAXED, TENSE, AFRAID, HAPPY, DISGUST, ETC.
>
> WHETHER THEY ARE TALKING OR SILENT.
>
> THE 'STORY' THEY ARE TELLING.
>
> ✍ ....

On the flipchart above, our imaginary group have come up with some suggestions to start off. How do their ideas compare with your own? The list is not complete by any means.

There are three stages to the skill of active listening (the arrows indicate the flow of information):

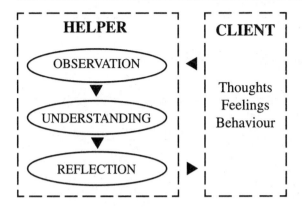

After paying close attention to the other person, comes understanding the meaning of what you are seeing and hearing. In order to do this you need to have achieved some degree of self-awareness. We find it easier to understand another person if we:

• Suspend our judgement of the other person

• Put our own feelings and experiences to one side while we are trying to understand theirs

• Try to put ourselves in their shoes and see the world from their point of view

The final test to see if we do really understand the world of meanings of the other person in all its subtlety, is to check with them. We do this by *reflection, paraphrasing and clarifying*. Reflection is the basic skill and at its most simple involves reflecting the content of the other person's utterances back to them. The purpose is to give the message :

> *'I am listening carefully to what you're saying and I am trying to understand. I will demonstrate this to you by letting you know that I heard what you just said. Did I get it right?'*

The ability to give good reflections without sounding like a parrot is a matter of practice until the activity becomes natural to *you*.

ACTIVE LISTENING AND COMMUNICATING EMPATHY
2. *Paraphrasing*
3. *Clarifying*

Paraphrasing and clarifying come hot on the heels of reflection and constitute the three basic skills of the core condition of empathy. When used together they become a powerful method of communicating your care and attention for the person you are trying to help.

Paraphrasing: is summarising in a few words what the speaker is saying. Depending upon the circumstances, it may be best to use the client's own words or use your own words. It is a matter of judgement to know how best to paraphrase depending upon the situation. In order to paraphrase effectively we need a reasonable vocabulary, especially when it comes to putting feelings into words. For this reason, I have included the 'feelings vocabulary' activity on page 80.

Clarifying: is not quite as obvious as it sounds. It doesn't mean that you clarify the client's muddled thinking, or can see more sense in the client's world than they can. Both of these are rather arrogant positions to be in and would probably be experienced by them as very unaccepting and superior. Rather, it means seeking clarification of your own understanding of the client's world. This can have a number of helpful effects:

1. The client will feel that you're trying really hard to understand.
2. You will get a better, more accurate understanding of the client's world.
3. The client may come to understand themselves better as a consequence of having to explain something in more detail, or in a different way to you.
4. Sometimes when a client is in a muddle or fog, you may pick this up by feeling muddled yourself. If you ask for clarification *for yourself*, it can help your client clarify their own thoughts and feelings.

Developing a 'Feelings Vocabulary'

Because some of us may not be used to being very expressive where feelings are concerned, we may not have a very large vocabulary of words which we use to describe feelings. It can be very useful to build up the vocabulary of feelings words we use. This is a brainstorming activity for small groups, but you can start it off yourself and then ask your friends to make contributions. Simply think of all the feeling words you know and write them down. You may find that some of the words are alternatives, or indicating a subtle difference in feeling. You could try to group them together under headings if you find it helpful. Then, start using them more often to help you get some 'colour' and richness into your descriptions of feelings.

Angry	Sad	Happy	Hurt	Afraid
annoyed	unhappy	elated	upset	scared
enraged	gloomy	cheery	broken	hesitant
cross	choked up	glad	suffering	insecure
sulky	sullen	festive	crushed	panicky
irate	flat	merry	tortured	terrified
belligerent	mournful	jubilant	heartbroken	shaky
✍	✍	✍	✍	✍ ....

Words about intimacy	Words about interest	Other feeling words
loving	curious	envious
tender	fascinated	jealous
close	inquisitive	bored
sexual	attentive	bold
in-tune	enthusiastic	proud
seductive	absorbed	excited
✍	✍	✍ ....

You may find it useful to look at your feelings vocabulary when observing skills practice.

That completes the expanded list of Stage I skills, and as I suggested earlier, it is not appropriate to elaborate the skills associated with Stages II and III any further. There will be hardly any time to practise skills on an introductory course, this activity is given priority on Certificate and Counselling Skills courses. You may, however, wish to use what course time you do get profitably, in which case the following suggestions may be useful if followed with your tutor's more detailed instructions.

PRACTISING AND INTEGRATING STAGE I SKILLS

It's one thing separating out the Stage I counselling skills for the purposes of illustrating each one; it's quite another to put them back together into a natural piece of real-life helping. I have been at pains to point out that an Introduction to Counselling course does not prepare or qualify anyone to do any counselling or use counselling skills other than inform the natural basic helping we all do as colleagues, friends and relatives.

If you do want to practise these helping skills with a colleague, friend or course participant, start off by taking one skill at a time. When you have practised one at a time, you may like to try putting them together in twos and threes. It may help to try them in the order found in this chapter, since this is roughly the order in which the skills are found in an actual relationship.

Never forget that, when practising skills in this way, your prime aim is to learn something. Don't get carried away and begin believing that it is a real helping session. You must make sure that you and your friend feel safe enough to talk and listen freely. Make sure you set some ground rules before you start:

- Are you going to make up a story and play the part of someone else or are you going to be yourselves, talking about your own real issues?

- If you are going to talk about real issues, is the practice session confidential?

- Practice is no good without feedback — how are you going to get it?

- It might help to list the skills on a piece of paper and then check them off at the end to indicate those that were appropriately present in the practice session.

I do not recommend 'practising' counselling skills on unsuspecting friends and relatives. Never *use* others as unconsenting guinea-pigs. It is neither ethical nor respectful, so is automatically an unacceptable and invalid way of improving your skills. You will find, however, that quite naturally your interpersonal behaviour will change, probably without you realising it. Others may notice and comment. If they do, it might be worth asking them what they think the changes are and whether they think it is an improvement. All feedback is useful!

IMPORTANT REMINDER

Finally, remember that the elements of empathy, genuineness and respect, whilst we can break them down into smaller *micro skills* they are not just techniques. They are qualities, attitudes to being with and helping people. They are the fundamentals of good human helping relationships not a series of disembodied techniques, so remember that, following the chapter on *The Importance of Self-Development* it is imperative that we integrate these skills into our very selves. If your approach to basic helping is based on good human relationships, then you will have to integrate these qualities into your whole person. This will mean changing the way you are, not just the way you do things.

'So where might we find information about the human condition which appealed to people's sense of what it is to be human rather than the psychology and psychiatry of diagnosis, drug trials and involuntary treatment? How can we find out about the lived experience of service users, what they want and what they don't? . . . A further challenge for the pseudo-scientific community of psychiatry would be embrace the common place wisdom of philosophy, literature and poetry.'

Guy Holmes: *This is Madness Too*, (Newnes, Holmes, and Dunn, 1999) p. 4.

'Science is essentially half an education. Not only does it produce wooden dancers, it puts little to no demands on the individual to know themselves or to develop social skills . . . or to have any respect for the world of feelings other than to reduce them to biological or cognitive underpinnings.'

Peter Chadwick: *Personality as Art*, p. 162.

What to do When You Reach Your Limits

6

REFERRALS AND RECOMMENDATIONS

When we are helping others in a counselling way, these helping relationships can begin and end in different ways. One particular beginning and ending event in helping that happens — whether you are a counsellor, using counselling skills or helping in a counselling way — is sometimes called *referral*. This is when one agency or professional sends a client or patient to another agency or professional for help, treatment or service.

Some trainers in counselling will be wondering why there is a chapter on referrals in a book aimed at basic introductory courses. The answer is that such handing on of people seeking help doesn't only happen in professional settings. In non-professional settings I have come to call these 'handings-on' *recommendations* rather than referrals in order to distinguish between professional links between helpers (such as a GP referring you to a specialist at the local hospital) and non-professional ones. Since I wrote the first edition of this book an increasing amount of helping is done through voluntary agencies and these voluntary agencies are staffed with well-trained volunteers. Many such voluntary organisations are used by statutory agencies for expert advice and help. For example, Childline is acknowledged as a leading agency in work with child abuse. As a consequence, professional referrals increasingly happen in voluntary settings, when one agency will pass on a client to another agency, so I will use the terms together where appropriate in this chapter.

Professional referrals are nearly always followed up and checked by the person making the referral.

This wouldn't necessarily happen with a recommendation. Also, the person making the referral (e.g. your GP) will get a report back from the person she has referred you to (the hospital specialist will send some notes back to your GP).

• You don't have to be a professional counsellor in order for another helper or agency to *recommend* a client to you for helping. (You will probably not be expected to make any report back on the client.)

•Similarly you may be trying to help a friend or a colleague at work with a problem and think that it might be better if someone else helps them rather than you. You would *recommend* that they go to their GP or Social Services for example.

It doesn't matter whether you are a professional or a volunteer, qualified or unqualified, making and receiving recommendations should be done with the utmost care and consideration for the person you are helping.

Receiving a referral or recommendation is when:
• Someone is recommended to see you for helping/counselling by the helper/counsellor they are currently seeing.

• A person comes to see you after deciding themselves that you are the helper/counsellor that they want to see. (This is called *self-referral*.)

Making a referral or recommendation is when:
- You feel that the person you are helping/counselling would be better helped by another helper/counsellor.

- Your client feels that they want help/counselling from someone other than you.

There are many reasons why we have to pass people on from one helper to another and all of the reasons are to do with *limits* of one sort or another. Here is a list of some of the limits involved (there may be some of your own that I haven't thought of). When you see this symbol:

✍ MAKE A NOTE OF YOUR OWN, ADDITIONAL IDEAS:

- Limits of the situation:
   legal limits
   service/agency limits
   of counselling itself
   time/timetable limits
   ✍ ....

- My personal limits:
   confidence limits
   emotional limits
   ✍ ....

- The limits of my competence:
   no expertise in specialist area
   skills limits
   qualification limits
   ✍ ....

- The limits of the person I am helping/counselling:
   lack of confidence in me
   doesn't like me
   wanting a different style of helping
   wanting a different type of helper, e.g. male, female, gay, black, white, etc.
   ✍ ....

It's possible in our enthusiasm for helping people that we try to help everyone, in every situation, all of the time, regardless of their problem. This way of working is always dangerous. It's obvious that no one can do this, but it's easy to get seduced into thinking that we can.
- Sometimes it happens *because the people we are trying to help expect it of us.*

- Sometimes it happens *because we expect it of ourselves.*

- Sometimes it happens *because our boss tells us that we must do it* — or at least suggests that it's the done thing if you want to get on.

It's dangerous to work beyond our limits because:
- Beyond our limits we cannot be of any help, we will probably *do damage to the person we are trying to help.*

- Beyond our limits we will put stress on ourselves and probably *do damage to ourselves.*

- Beyond our limits we will be seen as acting irresponsibly and *do damage to the reputation of helping or counselling or the agency we work for.*

In order to avoid working beyond our limits we need to understand where those limits are. It will be a little early in your learning about counselling for most of you reading this book to think too deeply about what your limits might be, but it's important to know that as helpers of any kind we must know our limits and stay within them.

We will look at each of these sets of limits in a little more detail, but before we do it's important to remember that with referrals and recommendations, as with everything else in a counselling way of helping:
- each situation is different,
   - each client unique,
      - each requires special consideration leading to its *own* solution.

We will tackle the problem of understanding limits by asking some questions. By now you will realise that the questions we ask in training in counselling do not always have fixed right or wrong answers. They're much more interesting than that — there's room for opinion, discussion and disagreement. These questions are no exception. Remember, when you see this symbol:

✍ MAKE A NOTE OF YOUR ANSWERS + EXAMPLES

Understanding the limits of the situation

• Are there any legal requirements which mean that I cannot help this person?

Examples: it may be illegal to offer certain kinds of help to children — e.g. issue contraceptives or advice about family planning. It is currently illegal to help someone to commit suicide.

✍ ....

• Does my agency have a policy which prevents me from helping this person?

Examples: An alcohol counselling service may not help someone unless they stay 'dry'. A women's counselling centre may not help male clients or people who have undergone a gender reassignment operation from male to female. In some settings (teaching or residential social work), it may be inappropriate for the helper to be alone with the person needing help.

✍ ....

• Counselling cannot help everyone in every situation. Am I trying to use a counselling way of helping in a situation in which it cannot be effective?

Example: Counselling is ineffective in solving 'concrete' problems like being homeless or having no money because you're unemployed or being denied a service because you're disabled or being refused admission because you're black. (Counselling can help to make people feel stronger, less trodden down and more worthwhile as a person, but can't get you a house, a job or human rights.)

✍ ....

• Do I have enough time to help this person effectively?

Examples: Someone may want help when it's inconvenient — during your lunch hour or five minutes before you're due to go off duty or when all appointments for the week are filled. What would you do in these situations?

✍ ....

• Do I have the right physical resources to offer a safe helping environment?

Example: Sometimes there isn't an appropriate space available for helping of a confidential or private nature. 'Safe' also means safe for the helper, so on other occasions agency policy or common sense may mean that you would not work on your own in a building with a client.

✍ ....

Understanding my personal limits

• What 'tender spots' do I have emotionally? (There is more on self-awareness in Chapter 3.)

Examples: Some people say that they could not work with, for example, rapists or abusers. You may feel very emotionally sensitive to certain situations after recent upsets, e.g. bereavement.

✍ ....

• How confident in my helping abilities and skills am I?

Examples: I might be overconfident in my ability to help someone because I've been told by my friends that I'd make a brilliant counsellor or, I might be frightened of trying to help someone in case I mess it up, even though I have the necessary skills.

✍ ....

Understanding the limits of my competence

• Does this person need help in a specialist area that I know little or nothing about?

Examples: Clients might need medical attention, welfare rights information or help from a specialist counsellor, e.g. drug rehabilitation counsellor.

 ....

• How far do my helping skills go?

Examples: It would not be appropriate to try to help distressed or disturbed people with only a smattering of rudimentary skills. Counselling is a skilled and ethical profession requiring lengthy training. If you think your skills are not up to it — you're almost certainly right. Get ready to refer your client on.

Your client may need what Steve Williams (1993) calls 'formal' help. By this he means help provided by statutory services such as the health service, social services, etc. How will you know if your client needs this kind of help?

 ....

• What do my qualifications permit me to do?

Examples: Obviously only doctors can make a medical diagnosis, but you'd be surprised the number of times clients expect you to either be a doctor or be able to give them medical advice, like how many tablets to take or why their baby is crying. Clients may ask for all kinds of advice from helpers. If you give advice you're not qualified to and something goes wrong, you or your agency may be liable.

 ....

Lack of qualifications should not stop you from helping within your limits. The best sort of helping you can offer is *accurate active listening*. This will be a novel experience for many people seeking help — to be sensitively listened to is deeply comforting. It will also have the added benefit of assisting you to make the decision as to whether your client needs any more highly qualified help.

What is formal help?

'When using the term "formal" I am talking about the whole pattern of statutory services that are available to help individuals whose emotional distress is so pronounced that they would seriously stretch the resources of any counsellor.'

Steve Williams: *An Incomplete Guide to Referral Issues for Counsellors*, p. 44.

If you are helping in a counselling way you may be either on your own — helping in your family, community or at work, or working — paid or voluntary — for a service or agency. It is important to know that your helping should not extend to very disturbed people without some kind of backup. An agency or service can provide this backup in the form of support from a more experienced person or medical advice from a doctor on hand. If you are on your own, there's no need to feel completely isolated. GPs, social workers or in an emergency the Accident and Emergency (A&E) department of your local hospital (which used to be called 'Casualty') are all there to help and support you if you are trying to help a relative or friend. Do not try to 'go it alone', professional counsellors have backup *and use it*. So everyone who is helping in a counselling way should be ready to pass the person they are helping on to those more skilled, qualified or able to help.

How do you know if the person you are helping needs formal help?

Persistent symptoms: I may have symptoms such as physical sensations, breathlessness or pains, sleep disturbances or eating problems which persist more than a week or so, these are common symptoms of grief or anxiety. Talking the problem through will help and the symptoms should ease after a short time. If the symptoms persist or get worse, get yourself backup and me some professional help — my GP is best.

Unusual or **extreme** symptoms: hearing voices in my head, thinking that someone is controlling my thoughts, seeing things that aren't there are all unusual symptoms which you are not equipped to deal with and must be drawn to the attention of my GP. Extreme depression (e.g. thinking that I am responsible for all evil in the world) or fear which makes it impossible for me to go out of my house also mean that I should see my doctor. If you notice that I am harming myself by cutting or burning myself or if I threaten to kill myself, again, I should be encouraged to see my doctor.

What to do
Ask me if it's alright if you contact my doctor or social worker. Ask me if I want you to come along to give me moral support. You could encourage me to go and then check up to see if I kept the appointment. Don't take control and act for me without checking unless my behaviour is likely to cause harm to myself and or others. Making this decision is not as easy as it might seem so the most important thing to do is *get support and backup for yourself.*

Understanding my client's limits
The next type of limit also needs some active listening from you. Your task is to understand why your client wants to be referred on, since sometimes a client themselves will identify the need for referral. The questions that follow do not require answers from your point of view. They might, however, give you some idea of the reasons that clients wish to be referred on to another helper. Make a note of any reasons you come up with yourself.

• Does my client lack confidence in my ability?

 ....

• Does this client dislike me?
There is no rule that says we must be able to be liked by all of our clients. Some people just don't hit it off from the moment they
meet. Such instant dislike would inevitably get in the way of the client being able to receive help from you.

 ....

• Does this client require a different style of helping?
Your way of helping, whether it's your own personal style or the counselling approach that you use, may not suit the person you are helping. They might find it too laid-back or maybe too intrusive.

 ....

• Does the person you are helping want a different type of helper?

 ....

WHEN NOT TO MAKE A REFERRAL OR RECOMMENDATION

In his book *An Incomplete Guide to Referral Issues for Counsellors*, Steve Williams pointed out that whenever we consider referring a client on to another helper we must make sure we know *when not to make a referral*. By this he means that we should carefully consider our motives for making or receiving a referral or recommendation. What possibly questionable motives could there be?

- You don't like a client very much and you would rather refer them on because you cannot bring yourself to say so.

- A client's problem is awkward to handle, so you would rather refer them to another helper than try to work with the awkward problem.

- A client is inconvenient, so you would rather refer them on than bear the inconvenience.

✍ YOU MIGHT LIKE TO WRITE DOWN ANY MORE MOTIVES THAT COULD BE BEHIND YOUR OWN REFERRALS.

As we learned in Chapter 5, one of the 'core' conditions of a counselling way of helping is *genuineness* or *congruence*. This core condition requires us to be open about our feelings and reasons for doing things. It might be better to be honest and open about our feelings towards the person we are trying to help, rather than trying to avoid the feelings by off-loading the client to someone else. See Chapter 8 on **Support and Supervision in Counselling** for more help with this.

MAKING A REFERRAL OR RECOMMENDATION: HOW TO DO IT

Having looked at the 'whys and why-nots' of making referrals, the question is, how do you do it? Most people would think that it's just a matter of passing your client on and that the process should be simple and obvious. Even if this is the case (I don't think it is quite that simple), *basic helping in a counselling way is often about understanding and refining the art of the obvious.*

Steve Williams (1993) suggests a checklist for counsellors which I have adapted for use by anyone using basic helping or counselling skills. As soon as the possibility of making a referral or recommendation occurs to you, go through the checklist to explore what action you feel it would be appropriate to take:

- Has anything been said about referral yet?
  - Either by me or my client? (*It is unusual and inadvisable to consider making a referral without the permission of your client. Seek further support and advice if this is not the case.*)

- Who has identified the need for referral?
  - My client (or the person I am helping)?
  - Me?
  - My supervisor or line manager?
  - Someone else?

- What is the purpose of the referral?
  - To get properly qualified help.
  - To get more expert help.
  - So that I don't go beyond my limits.
  - A different type of helper is wanted.
  - A different style of helping is wanted.
  - Any other purposes . . . ?

- Do I have enough information about possible referral agencies?
  - If not, do I know how to go about getting it?

- What do I want to say to my client?
  - Going in to a meeting with a client you have decided to refer requires preparation. Don't fly by the seat of your pants.

- What backup or support do I need for this referral or recommendation?
  - Can your supervisor or line manager help? Some agencies have medical advisors who might assist volunteers.

✍ YOU MIGHT LIKE TO WRITE DOWN ANY MORE CHECKLIST IDEAS THAT MIGHT AID YOUR OWN REFERRALS.

At the heart of each onward referral lie the following aims:

- To pass the person on as though they were a precious gift rather than an awkward bundle.

- To pass the person on so that their life and experience is added to rather than taken away from.

- To make sure the person understands that the 'passing on' that I'm doing is not a rejection of them, but my best attempt to help them meet their needs better.

- To make sure that the person knows that even though they are being referred on now, they will be welcome to seek help from me or the agency I am working for at any point in the future, at which point I will again do my best to help them meet their needs.

✍ YOU MIGHT LIKE TO WRITE DOWN ANY MORE AIMS YOU MIGHT HAVE FOR YOUR OWN REFERRALS.

RECEIVING REFERRALS AND RECOMMENDATIONS

It can be a great feeling to be asked to help someone. They may come along themselves (called a 'self-referral') or someone else may suggest that they come to see you. It can be flattering to think that someone thinks you might be able to help. It's easy to get caught up in the good feelings and say 'Yes of course I can!' before you've considered the implications.

There are several situations in which it is entirely appropriate to offer help to another person and do the best you can. Elsewhere in this book I look at how having a rudimentary awareness of basic helping in a counselling way can make you a better parent, neighbour, friend, colleague or citizen. It would be a sad day if we all had to go away and think about it before we responded as a fellow human being to the distress of others. Being called upon to offer basic helping as an ordinary human being is a wonderful opportunity for us to feel fulfilled as a person.

However, if someone asks you for help because they know you have been on a basic counselling introduction or skills course is a different matter. If your *only* training is this introductory course then you will have to think very hard before offering help *since you are not qualified to offer help.* You must make sure that the person asking for help understands that you are not a qualified counsellor. You must also bear in mind that you might be too close to someone to help them effectively. If, for example, your son or daughter asks for help, it's probably best that you be their Mum or Dad, rather than try out your basic helping skills on them.

If your employer has sent you on this introductory course and expects you to go back to your workplace and act as 'the counsellor', you may have a problem. You should point out to your employer that you are not qualified to counsel people and the tutor on your introductory course will support you with that explanation. If in any doubt contact BACP who will be able to clearly explain the ramifications of the situation to your employer.

If you are working as a volunteer or in a service where you do take referrals to help people in a counselling way, you must be sure you can figure out if the person being referred to you falls within the range you can help. If you work as a volunteer in a drug project — is their problem a drug problem? Again, regardless of the expectations of the managers of the service, you must not work beyond the limits of your competence or qualification. Get more information and support from BACP if you are in doubt.

If you are a qualified teacher, nurse, social worker or support worker, the situation is somewhat different. (We will look at these contexts for basic helping in Chapter 9 in more detail.) Your qualifications and experience will mean that you will be expected to receive referrals within your professional competence in the normal line of your work. This still doesn't mean that you can claim to be a fully-qualified counsellor unless you have gained a diploma-level qualification (see Chapter 13).

Regardless of the setting in which you are offering help, some special considerations might apply.

- Are you prepared to see clients who are sent to you against their will? Sometimes this is a normal part of your helping work if you are, for example, a tutor in a school or college — students may be sent to you because they are not attending their course — yet you may still wish to use a counselling way of helping.

- You will have to be clear about how much information you pass back to the person making a referral. In other words, if a tutor has suggested to a student that they come to you for help, what will you do if the tutor wants to know how the student got on? It is at times such as these that differentiating between a referral and a recommendation is useful.

Finally, we must be prepared to say 'No I am not able to help you'. This can be difficult because we all like to think we can help others, but we must not get out of our depth. If this should happen, both the helper and the person we are trying to help will suffer. The chances of you taking on too much or getting out of your depth is lessened by getting support and supervision for your helping activities. This is true whether you are an unpaid volunteer or a professional helper, and we will look at this in Chapter 8.

Ethics and Counselling

7

WHY BOTHER WITH ETHICS AT AN INTRODUCTORY LEVEL?

Not for the first time do I find myself having to explain the inclusion in this introductory text of an area of understanding which is seen as the responsibility of higher level training. The purpose of this chapter is twofold; firstly to let readers know of the effort put into the development of ethical frameworks by the counselling profession. We are, of course, all potential clients and the British Association for Counselling and Psychotherapy (BACP) *Ethical Framework for Good Practice in Counselling and Psychotherapy* is there to inform and reassure all members of the public both actual and potential clients who seek the help of counsellors and helpers whether or not they are members of BACP. It can be viewed on their website www.bac.co.uk (and printed for personal use). I strongly recommend you look at it as soon as possible.

Secondly, it is important to cultivate an attitude of responsible helping regardless of the perceived level of the helping activity. We should not subscribe to the view that 'low level', voluntary, community-based or otherwise 'amateur' helping should be seen as beyond morals, not worthy of rules of conduct, or somehow not important enough for ethics.

The question is 'How should the issue of ethical behaviour be interpreted at this level of *basic helping* or *helping in a counselling way*?' We'll never find out unless and until we have a go at identifying the issues, so this chapter is a starting point for beginning helpers and their trainers.

ETHICS — WHAT ARE THEY AND WHAT ARE THEY FOR?

Ethics can be defined as a set of moral principles or rules of conduct. Most people are familiar with the idea of ethics in medical practice; that doctors must keep their patients' details confidential, and must always act to save life, extend life or improve the quality of life. These and other rules of conduct for doctors are enshrined in the 'Hippocratic Oath'.

Our appreciation of medical ethics is sharpened because doctors deal literally with life and death, and it is when life-and-death decisions are made that we seek the support of a good set of rules. That is why there is such vigorous debate over such issues as whether to turn off life-support machines, should terminally ill people be 'assisted' to die or at what age is a human foetus considered 'alive', etc. Many of these ethical decisions have a direct relationship with our values, spiritual beliefs, political views and other deeply held convictions.

The profession of counselling has its own 'rules of conduct' and in the UK they have been in a process of development through the professional body, the British Association for Counselling (then BAC; now BACP) since before the first Code of Ethics and Practice for Counsellors was published in 1984. Equivalent codes are provided by all counselling and psychotherapy bodies in other countries in Europe and North America. Although counselling and helping doesn't concern itself directly with life-and-death decisions in the same way as medicine, there are several ethical dilemmas which counsellors and helpers can find themselves caught up in. This is because counselling concerns itself with damaged, distressed, or otherwise vulnerable people. From my own experience of needing help, I know that in some desperate circumstances I would do almost anything to put an end to my distress. At such moments, the 'rules of conduct' or ethics of the helper, whether they are a doctor, lawyer or counsellor, will go some way to protect my interests as a client.

ETHICS IN COUNSELLING AND HELPING

As I mentioned on the previous page, the British Association for Counselling and Psychotherapy published the *Ethical Framework for Good Practice in Counselling and Psychotherapy* which became active from April 2002 and replaced four older codes of ethics and practice. The old codes covered the work of

- those working as counsellors
- those using counselling skills alongside other professional skills in a helping role other than 'counsellor'
- those who provide supervision and support to counsellors
- those providing training in counselling and counselling skills

The new *Ethical Framework* covers the same areas as the old codes. [Note that the BACP has other information sheets and publications relating to ethical practice. The BACP address can be found at the back of this book.]

Other organisations concerned with counselling and psychotherapy also take a view on ethics and good practice (although BACP is by far the biggest). The United Kingdom Council for Psychotherapy (UKCP) makes statements about ethics and good practice, but rather than publish a national code, it works through its member organisations (see www.psychotherapy.org.uk).

For those counsellors and therapists who do not agree with the professionalisation of helping (see Chapter 12) the Independent Practitioners' Network (IPN), exists to promote and maintain good practice. The IPN also works through its constituent groups. They do have an informative website details of which can be found on page 148. More about IPN can also be found on pages 137 and 138.

Ethics in counselling and helping is very much a matter of 'horses for courses'. Different types and levels of helping activity have different ethical requirements. If we want to understand what ethical considerations we might wish to take into account as beginning helpers offering basic helping in a counselling way, we could start by looking at the ethical framework developed by professional counsellors.

My first suggestion is that you obtain a copy of the BACP *Ethical Framework for Good Practice in Counselling and Psychotherapy*. In addition to helping understand the BACP perspective on ethical issues, it is a useful resource for the future should you or any of your friends or colleagues seek counselling or training. You will know what kind of conduct to expect from counsellors, helping professionals using counselling skills, and trainers.

What topics do you think should be covered in a code of ethics for counsellors? Often, when left to our own devices, we get as far as confidentiality and not wanting to damage clients, then dry up. After many years of continual development, the main issues considered by the BACP in their *Ethical Framework* are divided into:

- values
- principles
- personal moral qualities

You will find that the first and third headings (*values* and *personal moral qualities*) have links with the material covered in Chapters 3, 4 and 6 of this book. This chapter concerns itself with the second heading, *principles*.

The BACP ethical principles (BACP 2001) are:

- Fidelity: honouring the trust placed in the counsellor
- Autonomy: respect for the client's right to be self-governing

- Beneficence: a commitment to promoting the client's well-being
- Non-maleficence: a commitment to avoiding harm to the client
- Justice: the fair and impartial treatment of all clients and the provision of adequate services
- Self-respect: fostering the practitioner's self-knowledge and care for self

It is not appropriate to go into the BACP *Ethical Framework* in further detail here. That is more properly the business of tutors on courses. It is essential that you consider how each of these headings is of relevance to basic helping in a counselling way and relate them to the setting in which the helping takes place. This takes time and is best done in discussion with tutors, agency managers, line managers, and supervisors.

BASIC ETHICS FOR BASIC HELPING

So, where can we make a start to consider appropriately ethical basic helping? The following topics are a starting point to stimulate thinking and debate regarding ethical issues.

Issues of competence:
- Do I have enough training?
- Do I have enough personal and other resources?
- Do I monitor my competence? e.g. through supervision
- What am I doing to stay effective? e.g. further training, support and supervision?

Confidentiality:
- What should limit the confidentiality I offer to clients?

Issues of responsibility:
- What responsibilities do I have towards my clients?
- What are my responsibilities to myself as a counsellor?
- Do I have any responsibilities to other counsellors and other helping professionals?

- What are my responsibilities to the wider community?

Advertising:
- How should I advertise any help that I can offer?

Every time that we offer help to someone, we should consider the way we conduct ourselves. Throughout this book there have been pointers to the issues:
- In Chapter 1 we asked: 'What sort of help are we offering?'

- In Chapter 2 we asked: 'What gives us the idea that our helping will be effective?'

- In Chapter 3 we asked: 'What are our motives for helping?' and 'Will our own feelings and thoughts get in the way?'

- In Chapter 4 we asked: 'Do we have any prejudices which will bias our help?'

- In Chapter 5 we asked: 'How do we improve our helping skills?'

- In Chapter 6 we asked: 'Will we keep within the limits of our expertise?'

- In Chapter 8 we will ask: 'Do we have enough personal support to offer effective help without hurting ourselves or those we are trying to help?'

You may see some similarity between the issues raised in the chapters and those included in the BACP *Ethical Framework*. They might be considered to be the 'core ethical issues' of *competent and responsible helping practice*. The answers arrived at as you work through this book will have a strong personal element because, as I have pointed out, ethics are to some extent based on our personal values and beliefs. There are, however, some common strands to ethical conduct:
- We try to act within the law.

- We respect human rights.
- We respect people's autonomy and ability to control their own destiny.
- We keep promises, contracts or agreements we have made with those we are trying to help, however informal.
- We try to act in a fair and reasonable way.
- When faced with a dilemma we try to do the most good and the least harm.

If there is any central strand which draws together these ethical issues, it is the welfare of the person we are trying to help. Underneath it all, helpers are trying to help someone rather than exploit them; to increase someone's options not narrow them down; to help someone make emancipated autonomous decisions not to manipulate them into doing what we want. We find that these ethical issues also manifest themselves in the kind of basic helping that we might be involved in at an introductory level.

For example, if we were to help a colleague at work, or our next-door neighbour, we should not abdicate ethical or moral responsibility. We should do our best to ensure good ethical conduct:

- How might you behave unethically in the case of helping your colleague at work? Although you are not a trained counsellor, a colleague has come to you for support because his wife has just left him. It was a sudden and unexpected separation and he is distraught. How might you behave unethically?

✍ MAKE A NOTE OF YOUR OWN ANSWERS & EXAMPLES

The greatest danger is that the person you are trying to help is exploited by you either wittingly or unwittingly, for example:

- In your enthusiasm to help, you may help more than you are qualified to:
    e.g. you might give him some of your mother's sleeping tablets to help him sleep.

- You may exploit your colleague for personal gain:
    e.g. you may see an opportunity for promotion and break confidentiality by telling your boss that your colleague's work is suffering.

- Your own problems might get in the way:
    e.g. you may identify very strongly with his problem because of a recent separation of your own. This may lead you to suggest solutions you wish you had tried yourself, rather than ones which might genuinely benefit him in his situation.

- You may have a vested interest in a particular outcome:
    e.g. you believe that families should stay together for the sake of the children and try your best to manipulate a reconciliation against everyone's wishes.

- As he turns to you for comfort, in his distress he muddles care and help with sexual attraction and you have a sexual relationship with him.

Quite clearly these ways of acting will not be in the best interests of the person you are trying to help. There are many more ways of behaving unethically in this situation. You may be working as a volunteer in a helping service already. Do you have a code of conduct? If you think it would be helpful, why not draw up your own set of guidelines for ethical conduct in basic helping.

The question of monitoring the conduct of helpers is partly dealt with in Chapter 8 and again in Chapter 12. Any code of practice must have the power to sanction when it is broken. There is a complaints procedure operated by the BACP for the benefit of clients, supervisees and trainees. Where basic helping is concerned, however, there is no governing body to protect us (some would say, rightly so). Everyone doing basic helping must assume the mantle of responsibility to help in a principled and ethical way.

Support and Supervision in Basic Helping and Counselling

8

SUPPORT

Most of us nowadays are familiar with the idea of support. Many people recognise that human beings need various types of support in order to function effectively. Whether you are a single parent, business executive or volunteer, you will understand the need for support. It is often assumed that counsellors and helpers are the ones that give support, but in this chapter I am looking at the notion of giving support to the helpers. Caring for the carers, in other words. As the parent of a daughter with special needs, I know the value of support for Maggie and myself: e.g. a weekend of respite care for Rosie our daughter, so that we can take a break. Helping other people can be exhausting work, and the helpers need to be restored. It does not seem strange, then, for carers to need support, and we must make sure that when we offer helping in a counselling way, we have the support we need to continue to do a good job.

When you see this symbol:
✍ MAKE A NOTE OF YOUR OWN, ADDITIONAL IDEAS

There are various ways of looking at support:
- *Physical support*: crutches or a plaster cast on a broken limb, holding someone up when they're weak or unwell, using your physical presence as support by going along with someone to the doctor's, for example.

- *Verbal support*: speaking up in agreement with someone, being an advocate for someone unable to state their case.

- *Financial support*: a loan for a business venture, a grant for a charity, social security benefits.

- *Emotional support*: a shoulder to cry on, someone to share your troubles with, someone 'rooting' for you during exams, someone believing in you.

- *Just being there*: we all know what this means, and how incredibly comforting it is to know that someone will be there, on call if needed.

- Other support ✍

We've all received support of some kind or another in our lives, both as children and as adults, at work and at home, and would probably have failed without support at some time.

Why might helpers need support? ✍

We often noticed that we had an argument every time that I had reconciled another couple. The couple had invested their violence in me, and I was investing it in my wife. I have always been aware my workshop provided a place where I could discharge my violence. Working on wood, steel or gold with hammer, saw or file, I could invest the violence which my patients had poured out on me in the consulting room.

Paul Tournier: *The Violence Inside*, p. 71.

BURNOUT

Any person's ability to help in a counselling way needs to be maintained rather like a car needs to be maintained between journeys. The oil and water need checking along with the tyre pressure, and we need to make sure there is enough fuel in the tank. We need to assure ourselves that our car is fit for the journey and will not break down. Helping and counselling are, as I have said in previous chapters, responsible activities for which we need to maintain ourselves in a kind of peak form. The helper equivalent of a car breaking down due to poor maintenance is *burnout*.

Burnout is the word we use to describe the damage we might do to ourselves if we don't get sufficient support. We may also, of course, do damage to our helping relationships and/or the people we are trying to help if we don't get sufficient support. Since counselling takes a lot of effort, concentration and a clear mind, we need to be in peak form to be effective helpers or to do our best counselling. For many people, being satisfied with our present level of effectiveness is not enough, we also want to continuously improve our abilities in counselling and helping.

So as helpers we need to do two things:
- Maintain ourselves to prevent burnout or damage to our clients.

- Develop and improve our helping abilities.

How can we as helpers or counsellors achieve these aims? Support for helpers and counsellors comes in many forms from informal, on-the-spot support to formal supervision required by a professional body. In the same way that the more time and effort you put into maintaining your car, the better and more reliably it runs, the more time and effort spent on establishing and maintaining your self as a helper and counsellor, the better off you will be.

TRAINING AND PROFESSIONAL DEVELOPMENT

You will have taken the first step to becoming a more effective helper by undertaking a basic Introduction to Counselling course. You will be helped to make up your mind about how far you wish to go with training. You will get an idea about the limits of counselling and the helping you can offer at different stages of training.

However far you proceed with training in counselling, you will find that your development as a helper never feels 'complete'. Practising professional counsellors attend training events to update their knowledge or gain new expertise in specialist areas. The BACP magazine *Counselling* carries details of a wide range of training events open to all participants regardless of qualifications. Local 'alternative lifestyle' magazines also carry advertisements for events in your area.

PERSONAL DEVELOPMENT — FUN!

Before we get too serious, do remember that it is essential to have balance in your life. There must be room for the things that you enjoy, from cooking to football. Similarly, don't forget the contemplative or spiritual side of yourself. To be a good helper it goes without saying that you will need to be focused and concentrating on the task, but you will also need to be relaxed, and bring your sense of humour and spiritual connectedness to your helping too.

This is a very small section in the book, but a very important one!

SUPPORT YOU CAN GIVE YOURSELF

There are many contexts in which helping and counselling take place. The one common element in the various settings is *you*. There are some simple things we can all do to support our helping endeavours. The following are some suggested questions you could ask yourself before you start any helping activity:

- Make sure you're fit to help:
  - Are you physically well enough to give good quality help (i.e. not ill)?
  - Have you been drinking or taking drugs?
  - Are you alert or are you feeling tired?

- Prepare yourself to help:
  - Do you have the right amount of time to help?
  - Do you have the right kind of space you need to help? (Do you need it to be private, quiet or confidential?)

- After you've done your helping:
  - How do you feel?
  - What do you need to do before you can continue work or go home? Talk to someone?
  - Have you made any notes that may be necessary?

My rough rule of thumb is — if you're not fit to drive, you're not fit to help anyone properly. By 'fit' I mean physically (e.g. not exhausted) and mentally (e.g. not distracted) up to the task. There is increasing awareness regarding the *responsibility* attached to driving a lethal machine. Although not lethal in the same sense, if a suicidal person comes to help and we appear irritated because we are stressed, or bored because we are tired, the consequences could be tragic.

Similarly after a session helping or counselling you may need to sit for a moment to gather your thoughts or maybe talk to someone before you can carry on or drive home. Remember that counselling and helping take more out of you than you think and you may feel preoccupied with someone else's problems if you don't take a minute or two to recover your sense of who you are, and to separate yourself from them.

BASIC SUPPORT FOR BASIC HELPING

At this stage of training, you will be offering basic help and for this you will need to establish some basic support. It is not necessary to set up formal supervision sessions, although this may be done for you if you work for an agency or service as a volunteer.

There are some simple ways of getting the support

you need to be an effective helper:
- *Debriefing:*

  This is when there is a set time after a critical incident, perhaps at work, for talking the incident through, getting any feelings off your chest. During the debriefing, normal work is suspended whilst the aftermath of the emergency is dealt with. In a helping setting this can be of use after a distressing session with a client, maybe one that has been verbally or physically abusive.

- *Co-worker support:*

  This happens when two helpers agree to pair up to support each other. They may make this a formal relationship where they agree to meet at set times, e.g. once a week. During these support sessions they may talk about the personal and learning issues that have arisen during their helping work that week. It can help if one takes the role of 'supporter' and the other the role of 'person supported'. This can stop the session becoming a general chat.

  Sometimes this co-worker support can be in the form of an agreement to be available in emergencies, e.g. perhaps being willing to be contacted at home on the phone to help someone off-load stress.

- *Support groups:*

  Sometimes, a number of helpers agree to get together to talk over the difficulties of their work. They don't have to come from the same place of work, indeed, sometimes it can be an advantage to talk to someone who is not a work colleague since they can give you a different perspective on a situation because they are not so closely involved.

- *Support network:*

  You may agree to exchange telephone numbers or addresses with a group of helpers. Then we offer 'spot support' if something arises out of our helping work on the spur of the moment. This works well in rural or less well-populated areas where people live a long way apart or where people don't have access to transport.

• *Special training events:*
Many services and agencies run special training events every month or two months where people get together to learn about a new or developing aspect of the helping professions. The discussions afterwards give opportunities for informal support or may help you set up one of the support systems mentioned above. There are several regional BACP branches which run events and meetings on a monthly basis. Contact BACP at their Rugby address for details of activities in your area.

SOME GROUND RULES FOR BASIC SUPPORT

If you are called upon to support another helper, whether they are a colleague and/or a friend, try following these rules. Don't be afraid to offer support; if you intend to be supportive by providing a safe environment, you won't go far wrong.

• Support and helping are very similar. Use what you know about helping in a counselling way to give support to other helpers.

• Use active listening skills to listen carefully to what the other person is saying.

• Don't be afraid if they get upset when they're talking. It's quite natural for helpers themselves to get upset when they need support .

BACKUP

So far I've been talking about support for helpers in terms of how to off-load the feelings we all get when we have to listen to other people's troubles on a regular basis.

There is, however, another kind of support which is invaluable, if not essential. I call it *backup*. You will know what backup is if you work for a service or agency such as The Samaritans. There they have more than one person on duty at most times and each volunteer on duty is backed up by a day leader — someone on call at home or work who can give information, advice, guidance and support to the volunteer if something crops up that's beyond their limits. Samaritans branches usually have backup from a local doctor who can help volunteers if the client has a problem which might have a medical element.

Backup is great if you've got it, but very difficult, if not impossible, to organise if you're working or helping on your own. Perhaps you want to use your counselling-style at home with your family and friends, in your neighbourhood or at work. There's no need to feel completely isolated, since we have looked at ways of getting basic support. It is also possible to *feel* backed up even though you haven't any proper backup. There are plenty of professional helpers such as doctors and social workers who can back up any first-aid helping you might do.

When helping someone, you may decide that it's best if they get help from someone better qualified (see Chapter 6: *What To Do When You Reach Your Limits*) or you might want to help them get some detailed information about their problem. Here's a short list of possible steps to take *with the permission of the person you are helping*:

• Find out who their GP is and how to get in touch.

• Do they have a social worker, home help or health visitor?

• The Citizen's Advice Bureau near you is another source of information, advice and backup.

✍ OTHER SOURCES OF BACKUP IN YOUR AREA.

SUPERVISION FOR PROFESSIONAL COUNSELLORS

As I mentioned above, practising professional

counsellors are required to be supervised by various codes of ethics and practice, e.g. British Association for Counselling and Psychotherapy Code of Ethics and Practice for Counsellors. I decided to look briefly at supervision for counsellors to give readers an idea of the responsibilities involved in being a counsellor and the safeguards in place to ensure that clients get the best quality help.

You may be familiar with the term 'supervisor' when used in other settings. For example a supervisor at work may be your line manager or someone who oversees or checks your work. Sometimes a supervisor is someone who takes overall responsibility for a job or chases the job's progress. Counselling supervision means none of these things.

- As a counsellor your supervisor should not be someone you work with. Your supervisor should not be your line manager.

- Your supervisor should not be someone you are, for example, related or married to.

- When either of the above situations arise, it is called a *dual relationship*, i.e. you have two relationships running alongside each other, a work or friendship alongside a supervision relationship. This can lead to conflicts of interest and when this happens either one or both of the relationships may be compromised.

    It has been accepted practice, though, for experienced counsellors to be in co-supervision with colleagues. This is where two counsellors offer each other supervision, one is the supervisor and the other is the supervisee, then they swap roles. It is still vital that your co-supervisor will put counselling supervision before friendship or comfort when working with a colleague.

    If in doubt, don't do co-supervision.

- Your supervisor should be someone who is a qualified counsellor with some years experience of counselling, although it is not neces-

sary for them to be more experienced than you.

- Your supervisor should be someone who can challenge your comfortable assumptions about your work. This is particularly important when you have a co-supervisory relationship. Your co-supervisor must never feel that they should not challenge you on an aspect of your practice because they are afraid that they might lose you as a friend.

'7. All counsellors psychotherapists, trainers and supervisors are required to have regular and ongoing formal supervision/consultative support for their work . . .
8. Regularly monitoring and reviewing one's work is essential to maintaining good practice. It is important to be open to, and conscientious in considering feedback from colleagues, appraisals and assessments. Responding constructively to feedback helps advance practice.'

BACP: 'Maintaining competent practice' *Ethical Framework for Good Practice in Counselling and Psychotherapy,* (2001).

'It is a breach of the ethical requirement for counsellors to practise without regular counselling supervision/consultative support.
   Counselling supervision/consultative support refers to a formal arrangement which enables counsellors to discuss their counselling regularly with one or more people who have an understanding of counselling and counselling supervision/consultative support. Its purpose is to ensure that efficacy of the counsellor-client relationship. It is a confidential relationship.'

Code of Ethics and Practice for Counsellors, BAC (1992) Amended AGM September 1993, par. B.3.1 & B.3.2.

'[The question] "What ought I to do?" is not equivalent to the question, "What is the consensus of my colleagues about what I do?" ... What makes [a given action] right has nothing to do with the numbers of people who take it to be so. Therefore the fact that professional colleagues have agreed to put a rule in your code does not *make* this the right action.'

Dale Bayerstein: *The functions and limitations of professional codes of ethics.* In House and Totton, 1997, p. 422.

'I don't know what I would do without my individual supervisor. I've worked with him for six years. He has been my sounding board, my guide, my inspiration and mentor. I have often come with quite difficult issues and stressful concerns yet he's been supportive, helpful and astute in his supervising.'

'Sally': *Experiences of Person-Centred Counselling Training,* p. 71.

Counselling Contexts and Connections

9

In the next few chapters I am going to be trying to place counselling as an activity in the world in which we live. There will be some echoes back to Chapter 1: *What is Counselling?*, Chapter 2: *Where Do Ideas in Counselling Come From*, and also the pages in Chapter 3 on personal values and counselling values. As we have seen, counselling is a particular kind of helping, no better or worse than any other kind, but with its own ideas, values, skills, limits and ethics. Where does counselling as a helping activity fit? What is the context in which it operates and what other human activities might counselling be connected to?

A short time ago whilst on holiday I struck up a conversation with a fellow traveller. Upon learning that I was a counsellor, she launched into a monologue, complaining that there were counsellors everywhere nowadays and that when she was young she didn't need counselling. Not even when two of her school friends were killed in a road accident; she and her other friends just got on with their lives. In a similar vein, the principal of a college I worked at fretted about introducing a counselling service because he believed that if the students found out that there was a counsellor available they would start having problems that they would not otherwise have had.

These ideas are not as odd as they might initially seem. Many people wonder why there seems to be such a great need for, and emphasis on, helping nowadays. They also wonder if the help on offer might in some way make us weak or cause us as a society to become dependent upon counselling. There are two questions suggested by this, firstly:

Where has this apparent need for counselling, and the increase in people wanting to be counsellors, 'suddenly' come from?

and secondly:

*What is the **meaning** of helping in the twenty-first century?*

The next two sections will look at some possible answers.

WE DIDN'T NEED COUNSELLORS IN MY DAY SO WHY DO WE NEED THEM NOW?

People who ask this and similar questions are appealing to a remembered notion of how life was once, but looking back into the past through our own experience is a process that is fraught with difficulties. Our memories are notoriously inaccurate and as we develop and change, so does the way we perceive the world. For example, I remember that Burton's Wagon Wheels were much much bigger when I was a child. The chances are that Wagon Wheels are just the same size that they always were, but I have grown relatively bigger. Set against this is the indisputable fact that some aspects of our world *are* changing markedly. How do we sort out the real differences from the imagined ones? For the purposes of this book, I am simply going to leave you with the dilemma, rather than provide any answers.

• What do you think?

My own view is that it is highly likely that there has been a change in the needs of people today compared with the needs of people, say, 40 years ago. The reasons for this are likely to be far from simple, but I offer the following explanations for your consideration, so that you can carry the debate further yourselves:

- Perhaps we keep raising our expectations regarding what constitutes the 'good life'. Nowadays, people are not satisfied unless they have satellite TV, a video recorder and a dishwasher. I can remember my mother thinking she had arrived when we had a refrigerator. As each year goes by we *demand* a better quality of life, and our psychological well-being is part of it. We demand that we are cared for better in all ways — we expect more of doctors and social services, requiring them to be more supportive and sensitive. The 'pull your socks up' approach to care is no longer enough, we demand a more up-to-date model.

- It has been suggested that the old community support systems are breaking down; gone is the extended family and neighbourhoods where everyone knew each other. Partly because of the destructive effect of some town planning, increased mobility, better communications technology, etc. we are unable to access the intimate person-to-person support that was such a strong feature of our social groupings.

- It is possible that, years ago, people just weren't 'tuned-in' to psychological distress as we are today. Soldiers suffering from shell shock were often shot for cowardice in the 1914–18 war.

  By the Second World War it was just about recognised as a condition, but many were still thought to be malingerers. Nowadays we have a much more sophisticated appreciation of psychological suffering, just as our understanding of physical illness has developed.

- Some people believe that at the start of this new millennium there is a general disillusionment in our 'developed' Northern European culture focusing around the failure of technology to make the world perfect. To some extent, people are turning away from technological solutions to psychological distress such as drug

treatments and turning towards more 'natural' treatments such as counselling.

- It could be that our technological culture has separated us from our 'souls' or 'spiritual selves' and that counselling offers the hope of rediscovering or renewing this spiritual connection. A connected idea is that the self-awareness and self-affirmation that is a feature of all counselling approaches serves to fill the spiritual void in modern life.

- Finally, counselling is not solely aimed at 'unhappy' people or the 'worried well'. It is increasingly demanded by people for whom the psychiatric services have failed. Psychiatric treatment is still based on drug treatments and patients are increasingly suspicious of drug treatments as public concern over side effects and addiction to psychoactive drugs grows. Counselling is seen as offering a more gentle, natural way of alleviating the distress of mental illness.

- What are your ideas on this?

  ✍

WHAT IS THE MEANING OF HELPING IN THE 21ST CENTURY?

You have decided to embark on the first stage of learning about counselling — a particular form of helping relationship. It is vital that at an early stage in your learning and development as a helper, you ask yourself what it means to be a helper. There are two important questions to ask.

Firstly:
> *'What does it mean to be a helper **in the twenty-first century**?'*

Secondly:
> *'What does it mean for **me** to be a helper?'*

Ask yourself these questions now and note down your answers. Discuss your answers with other members of your training group to see what variety of responses you get.

If you remember in Chapter 2, I suggested that the people responsible for developing the founding ideas behind modern counselling approaches could not escape the cultures in which they lived. The culture at the time *informed* their thinking one way or another. The same is true of you and me. Our ideas about what helping means to us as individuals cannot be divorced from cultural notions about the meaning of helping.

The following are some ideas about helping that are representative of our modern culture:

- Some people believe that we need to be tough in order to get along in a tough world.
- Along the same lines is the view that only the strong will survive and in the law of the human jungle, the weak go to the wall.
- On the other hand, plenty of people hold another set of views regarding helping; namely that the strong should help the weak, that helping people enables them to live to their maximum capacity and become full and active members of society, that helping can be a co-operative partnership of equals, not the strong bestowing charity or protection on the weak.
- Still others may hold the view that it is the divine will that we help those less fortunate than ourselves and that in doing so we get closer to heaven, nirvana or spiritual completion.
- Another view might be that those suffering misfortune in their lives are doing so because they have been bad, either in this life or a previous one and that the sort of help they need is either spiritual guidance or to be left to learn their lesson.

I have included these sets of ideas because they illustrate an important point about counselling and contemporary life. Counselling as a helping activity impinges upon or shares a boundary with many other values in the modern world. The way we choose to help someone says something about us as people.

- How would you arrange counselling so that it fits into your life, alongside those other elements of your life which are driven by sets of values?

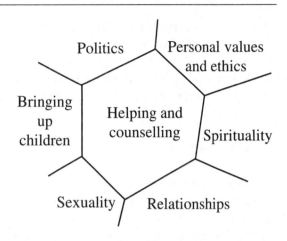

POLITICAL CONTEXTS AND SPIRITUAL CONNECTIONS

Talking about our personal values is often tricky. For some of us it goes too close to the things we are often urged to never talk about at dinner — politics and religion (how do you feel about talking about the other topics in the diagram above?). However, I am going to do just that and I will ask you to do the same.

Helping: how we think about it and what we actually do are not *neutral*. They are shot through with personal, political and spiritual values. As you have been working through this book, and in particular the last section, you may have noticed that most of the things we do in our lives are governed or at least informed by the values we hold. There can be no spiritual or political tradition that does not have something to say about helping and what it means to help another human being. Some readers may believe that counselling is apolitical or has nothing to do with 'soul' or 'spiritual self', but I think there is no disputing the close links over the years, from the work of Jung, Freud, and Rogers, who all acknowledged such connections, through to more contemporary work such as Thorne, 1991 and Kearney, 1996. In Chapter 3 there are short sections looking at personal values and counselling values in which I ask the reader to think about and try to identify links between the two. There are activities presented in these pages to help explore your thoughts and feelings around these issues.

This section is primarily concerned with wider contexts as they affect the person of the helper. Elsewhere (Chapter 12) I look briefly at the meaning of helping and counselling in the twenty-first century for the clients and those seeking help.

MEDICAL CONTEXTS

Counselling and alternative or complimentary medicine

Some recent media coverage of counselling has presented it as part of the 'therapy' boom, or what some believe is a reaction against traditional scientific western medicine: the flight into (or [re]discovery of — depending on your view) alternative healing arts.

There may be some similarities between the social and political position of counselling and alternative medicine therapies. Firstly, some counselling approaches are holistic. They treat humans as integrated working systems; change one element of the system and the whole system is thrown out of balance. Secondly if we look at the types of alternative therapy we can see that

---

Which sorts of help do you think are best for the following people:

1. A homeless person begging on the streets.
   - £5.00 for a good meal.
   - Giving money for a homeless shelter.
   - Saying a prayer for them.
   - A prescription for antidepressants.
   - Trying to change local and national housing policy.
   - Counselling.
   - A kick up the backside.

2. A 70 year-old woman grief-stricken after the death of her husband who is terrified of being taken into a nursing home.
   - Someone to go round to cook her a meal each day.
   - Giving money to the local Help the Aged.
   - A prescription for tranquillisers.
   - Saying a prayer for her and her husband.
   - Trying to change the Government's policy towards pensioners.
   - Counselling.
   - Being told to pull her socks up, what else does she expect at her age.

3. A male colleague at work whose marriage is on the verge of breaking up because he spends too much time at the office.
   - Suggesting that he talk to the vicar at the church he goes to.
   - Counselling.
   - Saying a prayer for him.
   - A stiff drink.
   - Organising other workers to petition management about the unreasonable hours people are expected to work.
   - Telling him that everyone's in the same boat and that if he can't stand the pace to get an easier job.

- Make a note of your responses then discuss them with others in your training group.

- What feelings came up for you when looking at each of the options you were offered?

Your political and spiritual beliefs and your helping approach

• What political beliefs do you hold?

• What spiritual beliefs do you hold?

• How did you come to have these beliefs?

• How do you think these beliefs affect your views on helping?

• How would you behave as a helper if you *fully* acted out your political and spiritual beliefs?

• Are any of the approaches described in this book, or elsewhere, that you have read about or been told about by your tutor, in harmony with your political and spiritual beliefs?

• Make a note of your responses then discuss them with others in your training group.

• What feelings came up for you when looking at each of the options you were offered?

We are taught to expect strong feelings to come up when we talk about these topics. Did that happen for you? Were there strong negative or positive reactions from others when you shared your beliefs?

some alternative therapies are based on 'ancient', 'lost' or ethnic healing systems and some on more recent ideas such as homeopathy. The reason some of these methods are 'alternative' is political. As I said, I don't think it has anything to do with whether they work or not. The medical profession is one of the oldest 'closed shops' in history. Anything that rivals the closed world of medicine is labelled 'quackery' and dismissed as useless, exploitative and dangerous. Because of this, many worthwhile treatments have been withheld for years because they were not within the domain of the medic and many ineffective and dangerous treatments have been peddled by the medical profession in the guise of 'scientific' treatment.

Some 'alternative' medical treatments were, in fact, 'mainstream' until the advent of the NHS. They lost out politically, at least in the UK, when the National Health Service was established and the closed-shop monopoly was handed to the 'scientific' medical physicians. This category would include, primarily, medical herbalism (often local, community practitioners who were disenfranchised thus favouring the new drug companies).

As far as counselling is concerned, the helping approaches described in Chapter 2 do have echoes back to ancient healing systems, since we would admit that the ideas of Freud, Rogers and the rest are probably not new. The theoretical formulations in their present state, however, are only 50–100 years old. Also, the counselling and psychotherapeutic models described in Chapter 2 have all had difficulty in gaining acceptance within the conventional medical system at one time or another but there is evidence that more are accepted today with the inclusion of counselling as a treatment on offer to patients in psychiatric day care and doctors' surgeries.

A large section of the counselling community is busy trying to put (as they say in political circles) 'clear blue water' between alternative medicine and counselling. They suggest that the idea that counselling is part of the alternative therapy boom is largely a media myth. The fear is of the trend in newspapers, magazines and television to cast counselling in the same category as what the media likes to portray as 'quackery', i.e. alternative therapy such as using crystals, aromatherapy, reflexology (massaging the soles of the feet), etc.

Although I spend a little time in Chapter 12 looking at the thorny question of whether or not counselling works, I don't think the current interest in counselling and alternative medicine is to do with whether it works or not (even though the media sometimes try to portray it as such). What does seem to be important is that the media likes to be seen as the readers' or viewers' friend and will make a show of tracking down quacks and charlatans on our behalf. The reporters and editors are so eager to get a good story that accuracy, integrity and, therefore, the real interests of the people they are serving, are either distorted or lost.

- Where, as newcomers to the counselling world, do you stand?
- Do you have a view about alternative medicine?
- Do you think that counselling is associated with the boom in alternative medicine?
- How has media coverage of counselling affected you?

Counsellors in GP practices

Most readers will be aware that counselling is available from a number of GP surgeries in the UK. Some of you will have been referred by your GP to such a counsellor, and that might be why you are reading this book. This provision of counsellors in primary healthcare is relatively recent (gaining ground over the past 15 years) and there are many GP practices without counselling as a treatment option. Sometimes the practice employs its own counsellor(s), sometimes the practice will 'buy in' a service provided by the local psychological services team or another source.

This picture changes year-by-year, as does the type of counselling you might be offered at a GP practice. Ten years ago I believe the majority

of counselling at GP practices would have been person-centred, but there has been a shift in recent years towards cognitive-behavioural therapy. This may be because cognitive-behavioural therapy is thought to be quicker (although there is little or no evidence for this). There is good scientific evidence to show that both person-centred and cognitive behavioural therapy are *equally effective* with a range of problems, and both are better than routine GP care for anxiety and depression.

Counselling and psychiatry

In Chapter 11, I explain what a psychiatrist is and does. The version I give there is the 'official' one. It may help if you read that first if you are unsure about who does what in the helping professions.

Although most readers are taking literally their 'first step' into helping and counselling, I have tried really hard not to protect you from many of the really rather awkward disputes and debates which characterise the helping professions in the twenty-first century. Some of these disputes and debates go back many years. As you read this you must bear in mind that psychiatrists are *primarily* medical practitioners. This bears on the debate in a number of ways, in particular:

- Because psychiatrists are medical practitioners, they use what is known as the *Medical Model of Mental Illness* to describe the full range of human psychological distress and disturbance. Although it is really no more than a system of naming things (e.g. the term 'neurosis', [literally meaning an infection of the nerves] is just a list of symptoms; it actually *explains* nothing), it gives an air of authority to any psychiatric 'diagnosis', when really it is just a set of names with archaic meanings. The medical model of mental illness is a contentious subject. It is supposed to work in the same way as the system for naming physical ills, and was developed at a time when firstly there wasn't any other way of naming distress available and secondly it was developed by doctors, and because of their training (i.e. as specialists in *physical disease)* they genuinely believed that psychological disturbance was rooted in physical causes.

The relationship between counselling as a psychotherapeutic form of helping and psychiatry goes back many years, but I am not going to relate the history of psychiatry here. I will, instead give a few landmarks in the development of the contemporary dispute between therapeutic counselling and psychiatry. There should be a 'Fairness Warning' here, since I would remind you that the following list of landmarks is written by a counsellor, trained in the early seventies, active in the anti-psychiatry movement. I do not apologise for the lack of balance for you will get the other side of the story almost everywhere else you look.

• **1920s** Freud was a physician by training, who until late in his career was shunned by the medical profession.

• **1950s** Carl Rogers used the label 'counselling' for the whole field of non-medical helping for those with psychological disturbance because he was not allowed to use any terms that alluded to psychotherapeutic or psychiatric practice by the American medical profession.

• **1960s** The 'anti-psychiatry' movement was founded, on both sides of the Atlantic, by people who strongly objected to the 'medicalisation' of psychological disturbance and all that comes with it. By this I mean that a whole range of human emotions, distress and disturbance became labelled as 'illness' according to the social mores of the time. In partnership with the law, doctors became (and remain) extremely powerful agents of social control, since you can be locked up and treated against your will for a variety of 'illnesses'.

The following 'medical conditions' were (historically — not necessarily in the 60s!) treatable by force by psychiatrists:
Sexual Deviance: any kind of socially disapproved sexual feelings or practices, including masturbation and being gay, or having an illegitimate child
Drapetomania: The disease causing black slaves to run away(!)

• The anti-psychiatry movement rails against brutal psychiatric treatments such as Electro-Convulsive Therapy and enforced drug treatments, many of which lead to iatrogenic illness (illness caused by a medical treatment). With patients suffering tremors, cramps, mood swings and permanent disability caused by psychiatric treatment (drugs), it soon becomes difficult to tell the effects of the cure from the symptoms of the original complaint.

• The anti-psychiatry movement fails to deliver any alternative treatment methods that seem to 'work' (see Chapter 12), and those offered, e.g. Laing (1969), are subjected to ridicule by psychiatrists. Few, if any, of the alternative treatments for psychological distress are funded by the NHS, and so have to be offered privately.

The American Psychiatric Association produce a diagnostic manual that is used by all American psychiatrists to help diagnose mental illness. It is called the *Diagnostic and Statistical Manual of Mental Disorders,* or DSM for short. It is now in its fourth edition, so you will know what people are referring to when they use the term DSM-IV. It is the 'Bible' for psychiatric diagnoses. If it's in there, it's an 'illness'. If it's not in there, it's not.

You may (or may not) be shocked to know that until 1973 'homosexuality' was in there as an 'illness', in the complete absence of scientific evidence (you would imagine that psychiatry is based on science).

'A notable gay physician, Howard Brown, aptly commented upon the DSM Board vote deleting homosexuality as a diagnosis. He stated, "The board vote made millions of Americans who had officially been ill that morning officially well that afternoon. Never before in history had so many people been cured in so little time."' (Minton, 2002, p. 261.)

- **1970s** Counselling in various forms is established in education and voluntary helping agencies such as the National Marriage Guidance Council (now Relate) and gains rapidly in popularity away from the disapproving gaze of the medical profession. (See next section on 'Educational contexts'.)

- **1980s** From various sources comes the message that counselling is only suitable for helping 'the worried well' or 'normal neurotics' and that the really disturbed people are only safely treated by psychiatrists. This is said even though psychiatric treatment has become only marginally more sophisticated and still causes great suffering with iatrogenic conditions through cavalier over prescribing of drugs.
  - New, non-invasive, treatments for very disturbed people begin to emerge, pioneered by psychologists and counsellors.

- **1990s** Psychiatrists still maintain that some of the most chronic, long-term forms of mental problems cannot be treated. These conditions are evidence that mental 'illness' is rooted in physical causes and can only be corrected by physical (i.e. chemical or electrical) treatments. The best example of this type of disturbance is 'schizophrenia' where the sufferer hears voices.
  - Cognitive psychologists and counsellors mount a concerted effort to demonstrate that much chronic 'schizophrenia' and voice hearing can be relieved at least as much by the sensitive application of new findings and development of new 'talking cures' or psychotherapy, as by drug treatments and Electro-Convulsive Therapy. A self-help action group is formed by voice hearers called 'Hearing Voices'. These people are far from 'mad'; they organise meetings and conferences to discuss treatment options and life in general (some meetings are open to people who *cannot* hear voices.)

- **2000s** Research increasingly shows that counselling approaches are (a) as effective as routine GP care and some drug treatments for anxiety and depression, (b) cognitive and person-centred therapies are equally effective, and (c) the criteria for empirically supported treatment embrace many counselling conditions and skills (even including such apparently esoteric qualities such as empathy). King, et al., 2000; Bohart, 2002; Elliott, et al., in press. [The literature describing these studies is not an easy read for people without a psychology background, but if you enrol for diploma training, you should become familiar with it]

There is still vigorous disagreement in many circles over the 'proper' roles for 'talking cures' like counselling and psychotherapy, and on the other hand physical treatments such as drugs within psychiatry and the helping professions. (It would be foolish to think that this debate is conducted using 'evidence' any more now than it ever has been.) There is, however, real public debate about how best to care for people with enduring serious mental health problems, particularly concerning whether disturbed people should be cared for in the community or in specialist places of safety. You will, I am sure, already have views on this subject.

- Have you received psychiatric care, or do you know anyone who has?
- Have you received counselling, or do you know anyone who has?
- Were these experiences largely positive or negative?
- How has this affected your views on helping?

✍

EDUCATIONAL CONTEXTS

In the 1960s, the ideas of Carl Rogers began to infiltrate education in the United Kingdom.

'I did not have a counsellor; it was only months later I realised how much pain such a person would have saved me, and how much more pain it would have saved my family.'

Brian Keenan, *Daily Mail.*

Counselling Skills for Nurses

In the normal course of a nurse's job (whatever the specialisation), he or she will be 'helping people' in the classic sense. It's why people become nurses. The ability to form good relationships is central to the nursing role. It may even be the case that people get better more quickly from physical illness when they have a good relationship with their carers. However, as with so many jobs, it has traditionally been assumed that the 'working with people' or 'people skills' part of the job is *natural*. It was assumed that everyone could do it just by dint of will, and that it was quite obvious how it should be done. After working through the first eight chapters of this book, I hope you can see that, although some people are naturally good at forming effective relationships, there are some things we can all learn from the world of counselling.

The meaning of illness

People vary in how they respond to illness, whether it be mild or severe. Illness has *emotional* meaning for us — some of us behave as though death is imminent when all we have is the common cold, whilst others are stoical despite great pain and disability. Helping ill people endure and recover from illness is not just a matter of tending to physical needs — psychology plays an important part. *Understanding* the meaning of illness for each patient is the key to good nursing, since some patients exaggerate symptoms whilst others hide them. Being non-judgemental and respectful are also essential to the patient's feeling of well-being. These are the key elements of healing relationships both physical and emotional.

Relatives of ill people

We don't need to be reminded that when someone is ill, the whole family is affected. When the illness is serious or requires lifestyle changes for the patient and their family, nursing takes on a wider supportive function. For example, patients with organ failure awaiting transplants need to adapt their lifestyle, maintain a recovery-oriented way of thinking and feel supported by their families. These expectations (and a natural wish to be supportive) can soon become burdensome and the carers need to sustain themselves and feel supported. When a nurse is the only point of contact, basic helping and counselling skills are the most appropriate qualities on which to base support for patients' families.

Terminal illness

Palliative care is a medical specialisation in its own right; however, general nurses on medical wards and district nurses are the 'front-line' when it comes to routine care and support for people with a terminal illness and their families. However experienced, it is still distressing and draining work. If nurses become inured or hardened to the work, it will show and they will damage their patients and themselves. The self-awareness and self-support qualities of counselling-skills-helping, the ability to be almost infinitely understanding and respectfully protect the patient's dignity can be enhanced through counselling skills training.

If you are a nurse, what areas of *your* work and specific tasks do *you* think would be helped by a better understanding and implementation of counselling skills? ✍

Initially, the idea that university and polytechnic students (away from home for the first time) would find it useful to talk over their problems took hold in a handful of higher education institutions. Amongst the first wave of counselling services in the UK were Keele University, Preston Polytechnic and Portsmouth Polytechnic. These services often were 'generic', that is to say that a student might be helped with a financial problem, changing course or a career choice upon leaving. Indeed, many counselling services grew within or in close association with the careers service.

Postgraduate courses were developed at the Universities of Keele, Swansea, Exeter, Reading and Aston to meet a small but growing need for counsellors in education and the usual course requirement was that applicants be qualified teachers with two years' teaching experience. Again, these courses were often closely associated with careers officers' courses.

In the seventies and eighties, counselling services in higher and further education grew in popularity and became commonplace. It was taken as read that students, whether at the local tech or at Oxbridge, should have someone to go to for a confidential chat. Problems taken to such services ranged from getting the bus fare home through to dealing with a problem pregnancy.

Over this period a few counsellors were appointed to work in schools. A very small number of innovative educational authorities had county-wide schemes to place counsellors in schools, but the majority used the schools' welfare service or educational psychologists in the schools' psychology service, since the only time a pupil was deemed in need of extra help was if they were underachieving academically or disruptive. The overstretched welfare officers and educational psychologists are usually too busy to deal with all but the most serious of cases, so 'everyday' problems from bereavement through to bullying have been left for the form teacher, or pastoral team in most schools.

It is not difficult to argue for counselling in schools. Greater levels awareness regarding the experiences of children in general and the problems of violence and bullying at school, mean that an increasing number of people can see the value of counsellors working independently of the teaching staff in schools. The key here is the *independence* of counsellors. That counsellors can be seen by everyone as different from the teaching staff is both an advantage and a disadvantage. School pupils may disclose more to someone who is believed to be independent of the teachers, but the teaching staff can sometimes view the counsellors with suspicion because they might see them as being on the 'side' of the pupils. Getting the balance right and being experienced with integrity by all groups in a school is part of the challenge of the job — a good school counsellor is a wonderful asset to any school.

Before such provision becomes widely available, counselling in schools would have to be adopted as policy at government level and funding provided.

In the meantime, the BACP has had a thriving interest group 'Counselling in Education' for decades, and you will find details of their activities on the BACP website www.bac.co.uk. Also, some teachers, dissatisfied with the system as it stands, become qualified as counsellors to enable them to take a more skilled, active, specialist role in the pastoral system in schools.

SOCIAL WORK CONTEXTS

The role of social workers as helping agents in our society has been the subject of media criticism in recent years. Social workers are expected to cover a huge range of care functions, from the fair allocation of access to services (deciding who gets what service) through to managing individual cases, carrying out care plans and working in residential settings with children and adolescents. When the system fails to deliver the best care, the social worker is the person at hand who will bear the brunt of the criticism.

Counselling Skills for Teachers

All of us at some time have been pupils, so we know how we personally rate the qualities of a good teacher. My favourite teacher at secondary school treated me like an adult, my least favourite teachers were those that were bullies. I would be very surprised if the qualities of being a good teacher did not include the qualities necessary to make good helping relationships, i.e. empathy, acceptance and genuineness. Of course it is not *simply* a matter of helping skills. Teachers must be good communicators, good motivators and be able to administer fair discipline. These are the professional skills of the teacher, alongside which the skills of good basic helping sit very nicely.

Being a good tutor
In the last years of secondary school, especially when pupils are preparing for work, or further/ higher education, many schools operate a tutorial system. Small groups of pupils will meet daily or weekly for a session where social and personal education is the focus. Tutors will also be available for one-to-one support, and it is primarily in this role that the skills of basic helping come to the fore. Here the adult is less of a teacher and more of a mentor, so respect, understanding and being a good role model are the important qualities.

Helping the bullied and the bullies
Specialist knowledge and skills are only occasionally needed when dealing with the problem of bullying at school. The theories and plans that have been developed to combat bullying draw heavily on basic helping skills. Almost every reader will have some experience of this, either as a victim or a bully, and probably as both. So will the vast majority of teachers. Our personal experience should help develop our sensitivity and awareness of the situation, not cloud our thinking, making us less understanding. Being open, non-judgemental and genuine will enable the teacher to help both the bullies and the victims. Primarily victims need to be believed and bullies need to be understood — this facilitates the next step of resolving the situation, protecting the victim and stopping the bully if necessary.

When home life comes in to school
This is an occasion when the concept of boundaries comes to life. Although we might like to compartmentalise life, events at home will inevitably affect life at school — for both pupils and teachers. It is often the form teacher who notices something first and sensitive intervention, with the qualities of basic helping early on, can prevent the distress being compounded at school. Likewise, if the teacher is to leave their own worries at home, and not visit them upon their pupils, increased self-awareness and an ability to attend to their own needs are essential. Respectful understanding and self-awareness are key helping qualities that help us separate our own emotional baggage from those we are trying to help. Since our experiences at school are a rich source of feelings — good and bad — it is no more than good sense to make sure that we do not bring any leftover feelings to our work.

If you are a teacher, what areas of *your* work and specific tasks do *you* think would be helped by a better understanding and implementation of counselling skills?

At one end of the job, the management and administration of care services may appear to be a mechanical task, but as a parent of a disabled child, I have seen at first hand how decisions regarding funding that affect the quality of life of my family, are made by social workers at some cost to themselves. There is great stress involved in trying to fairly allocate insufficient funds, and there is a high turnover of social workers in some settings.

It would be reassuring to think that counselling skills should be a part of the professional repertoire of social workers who manage and provide care, for example:

- Helping older people as they struggle with a senile partner.
- Supporting a family with a disabled child.
- Working in residential homes with children taken in to local authority care.
- Supporting the same young people when they leave care to live independently.
- Monitoring adoption and foster parents and supporting where necessary.
- Providing respite care and support for carers.

Few would argue that listening, accurate understanding, acceptance and genuineness are essential qualities for such work, yet counselling skills are rarely built in to social work training. It has been the case in the past that it was simply assumed that social workers would be natural helpers, even though the major part of the training involved the administration and legal aspects of the job. Some social workers complete counsellor training as a supplement to their work and go on to offer dedicated counselling services within their team, but this nearly always depends upon funding. Increasingly, social services departments use the voluntary sector to deliver counselling and support to clients.

COMMERCIAL CONTEXTS

Two views of human nature are frequently presented in management texts. These were described by Douglas McGregor in 1970 as *Theory X* and *Theory Y.*

Theory X
- People have a natural dislike for work and will avoid it if they can.
- Therefore people must be controlled, directed, threatened and cajoled to get them to put in enough effort to achieve the organisational objectives.
- People prefer to be directed like this, they dislike and avoid responsibility, have little ambition and want security above all.

Theory Y
- It is as natural for humans to work as it is for us to play or rest.
- People will exercise self-control and self-direction in order to meet organisational objectives to which they are committed.
- People will, under proper conditions, not only accept but seek responsibility.
- The majority of people are imaginative and creative when faced with organisational problems.

You may have worked in organisations which ran as though the managers believed either Theory X or Theory Y. You may also see that these approaches to human nature have some elements in common with some of the ideas that underpin the approaches to helping we looked at in Chapter 2. I think that Theory X is roughly equivalent to a psychoanalytic view of human nature where the assumed anti-social aspects of human nature need containment and direction. Theory Y has more in common with humanistic approaches to helping.

- What do you think?

Management ideas like this become the style, ethos or culture of the company and will to a large extent determine the company attitude towards employee welfare. Welfare officers used to be employed in personnel departments of the vast majority of medium-sized and large companies. It was their job to visit sick employees, take care of the families of deceased employees and even run social activities. My uncle was employed for all of his working life at a car components manufacturers in the midlands and I vividly remember the popular company social club and annual sports days. Company welfare officers have long since gone and personnel departments have been 're-envisioned' as 'human resources management' and employee welfare is now likely to be attended to by one of the many Employee Assistance Programmes.

Employee Assistance Programmes (EAP)

Since the mid-eighties, private companies (EAPs) have provided some of the welfare and assistance services previously provided by welfare and personnel officers, including a range of advice and support, including counselling. EAPs will provide a service tailored to the needs of the client-company and their employees. So, for example, employees may be given a card with the telephone number of the EAP to be called for legal assistance or personal problems. Legal assistance may be delivered via a telephone helpline, and personal problems may be received firstly on the telephone, where a counsellor will assess the situation before attempting to either deal with the problem on the phone or refer the employee to an EAP counsellor close to where they live.

EAPs also offer critical incident debriefing in situations where people require support and counselling, both after major disasters such as train-crashes, and after accidents at work.

Research done with post-office employees in the eighties showed that work-place stress and staff turnover were reduced as were sickness and absence rates, when employees had access to workplace counselling services.

Counsellors employed by EAPs will be fully qualified to diploma level or beyond and will also be accredited or registered with UKRC or UKCP.

COMMUNITY CONTEXTS

Most approaches to psychotherapy go beyond the individual to groups and communities. Almost all of the major theorists found it unsatisfactory to end their theorising at the level of the individual. Freud and psychoanalysts were concerned about political movements in Europe in the 1930s. Skinner wrote a novel *Walden Two* depicting a utopian behaviourist society where all were in charge of their own destiny. Carl Rogers expanded his ideas to large groups and communities, spending the later years of his life working for world peace. Aaron Beck has written extensively on aggression in contemporary society (Beck, 1999).

At the most simple level, regardless of the approach you take, the more people there are with highly developed basic helping qualities, the more caring a society we will have. The values implicit in counselling, from the individual helper up to BACP, are the values of care, mutual understanding and respect, co-operation and sharing. A community based on these values should thrive.

Classical Freudian theory and more contemporary psychodynamic theories take a somewhat darker view of human nature and therefore would expect that the destructive parts of human personality would need containment, or, in community terms, active policing. The qualities of good psychodynamic helping, though, are still seen as good foundations for a healthy community.

Most of the theories of counselling place at least some of the blame for human psychological distress with the community or society so it is sensible that we should look to improving mental health by improving our social and material environment — in short the society in which we live.

- What sort of community would you like to live in?
- What values are the foundation-blocks of this community?
- Are the principles and values of basic helping in a counselling way in accord with this?
- Do you think it is sensible to understand human distress and healing in terms of communities?

Counselling Skills for Social Workers

Nearly all of the tasks involved in social work pivot upon good 'people-skills', but not all social work training pays sufficient attention to the development of such qualities and abilities. The relationship skills at the core of social work practice are practically identical to those presented in this book as basic helping. There are, however, crucial contextual differences between social work and counselling — one of the main differences involves the legal responsibilities of the social worker. Qualified social workers will have no trouble in understanding the concept of confidentiality; however, a counsellor will not have the same statutory duty of care.

Advocacy
One of the key roles for social workers is to act as an advocate for, for example, a child, older person or person with a learning disability who is not able to represent themselves. This role requires sensitivity, empathy, acceptance and courage, as the social worker tries to discern the wishes and needs of their client, and then press the client's case on their behalf. Basic helping skills will help the social worker understand their client (and their needs) better.

Needs assessment
Social workers are frequently called upon to assess what a person or family requires in order to have a reasonable quality of life. A typical scenario would be when a person is disabled, either at birth or by accident or illness. There will be lots of people in the client's life who all have vested interests, family and friends, but the social worker has to take a view that embraces all of these whilst putting the needs of the individual first. My experience as a parent of a child with special needs taught me that, after years of thinking I knew best for my child, I had to admit that the social workers brought a new and challenging view. Basic helping in a counselling way helps everyone avoid being defensive and work towards the best solution.

Crisis intervention
When certain crises hit our lives, social workers are the people who have to pick up the pieces. If a family is made homeless, for example, social workers will have to place the children in care. Rapid responses are needed, but the caring elements of the work must not be overlooked. Confidence in one's basic helping qualities of empathy, acceptance and genuineness will help make a difficult situation as least distressing as possible for all concerned.

Residential care
This challenging sector of social work requires, in effect, being an active helper without respite for hours at a time. Coffee-breaks, mealtimes, 'relaxing' in front of the TV — all become therapeutic possibilities. Having a secure foundation of basic helping qualities, empathy, acceptance, respect and genuineness is the key to survival, let alone good practice. Being able to look after yourself and remain an effective helper requires a high level of self-awareness. An increasing number of social workers in this setting train to the level of counselling skills and beyond in order to better prepare for the rigours of this work.

If you are a social worker, what areas of *your* work and specific tasks do *you* think would be helped by a better understanding and implementation of counselling skills? ✍

Counselling Skills for Managers

A few years ago I would have been laughed at for suggesting that the qualities of good helping would be useful for managers in industry, commerce and the public sector. The 'world of work' may be so-called because we are supposed to believe it is somehow separate or different from our other world at home. It is not, even though we have many unpleasant phrases to describe it: 'cut-throat', 'the rat race' and others just as colourful. There are several areas of management that require the skills and abilities of counselling. If a key function of any manager is to unlock the potential of those that they manage, then the essentially *enabling* qualities of basic helping in a counselling way are nothing short of essential.

Mentoring

Many managers are called upon to either mentor employees new to a job, or manage a mentoring scheme. Mentoring (sometimes called *coaching*) is not simply teaching or instructing. (Most adults have varying memories of teachers and many might not appreciate being cast in the role of 'pupil' especially if they are older than you.) The ability to build a good enabling relationship is at the heart of mentoring — being non-judgemental, respectful, empathic and genuine combine with being a good motivator and educator. Both the workplace competencies *and* the personal needs of the mentored person are developed in this process. Starting from the point of view that the person being mentored has potential, the task is to help them discover this and use it for themselves and the company to live a more fulfilling life at work and at home.

Bullying at work

Recently identified as a major problem in some workplaces, bullying at work (including harassment) is no easier to prevent and resolve than bullying at school. Recently highlighted in the media, bullying and harassment at work can be a major cause of unhappiness and stress at work, as well as leading to poor work performance. Although some specialist training will be required, there is no doubt that the skills of basic helping will serve you well when trying to understand the *people* involved, rather than simply seeing it as another problem to be solved.

Stress and burnout

As the pace of life in general, and the world of work in particular, increases, we are all more susceptible to stress, overload, or just simply 'the pressures of life'. Some workplaces expect employees to work over and above their paid hours in the mistaken belief that an overworked stressed-out employee is more efficient than a happy, relaxed one. The line manager is often the person best able to spot individuals vulnerable to stress, either because of work schedules or personal worries. Knowing your employees well and having a good relationship is the start. Listening, respectfully valuing them as people and genuinely caring for their welfare completes the picture. Stress, though debilitating, can be reduced if the causes are attended to and the person concerned learns new ways to constructively deal with the ordinary, reasonable stresses of work and home life.

If you are a line manager, what areas of *your* work and specific tasks do *you* think would be helped by a better understanding and implementation of counselling skills? ✍

Counselling Skills for Citizens

I hope it doesn't sound too grandiose to suggest that the qualities of basic helping should be a natural part of good citizenship. In the last years of his life, Carl Rogers devoted much effort to furthering world peace. In fact, he was to be nominated for the Nobel peace prize but he died before he could be told. Rogers believed that the qualities necessary for good therapeutic relationships would apply to a wide range of settings including conflict resolution and the building of communities. He conducted groups in South Africa at the height of apartheid and in Northern Ireland at the height of 'the troubles' — going to the heart of political hotspots. Empathy, UPR and congruence in everyday parlance turn out to be understanding, acceptance and genuineness. Who could argue that these would not be included in a list of the essential characteristics of citizenship?

I am not suggesting that we all dive in to try to resolve conflict or solve local problems in our neighbourhood. I am suggesting, though, that as citizens we all have roles and responsibilities. On the preceding pages I have very briefly looked at where counselling skills might fit in to work. Work, however, is only one part of life. Although communities are dependent upon work, other personal and social factors are just as influential. 'Family' and 'neighbourhood' may appear to be concepts that have passed their sell-by date, but the human needs for love, development, protection and community cannot be neglected. We would do so at our peril.

As partners, parents, friends and neighbours we have connections and responsibilities that would be enhanced by better self-awareness and the qualities of basic helping in a counselling way. That does not mean that we should 'play the counsellor' for all and sundry. Far from it. Children need parents to love them in ways that counsellors never can. Neighbours need to give-and-take, live together in ways that counsellors cannot live with their clients. Respect and understanding for, and valuing of, each other regardless of race, class or creed, are the foundations both of counselling and of healthy communities.

It is clear that neither counselling nor counsellors have all the answers. Counselling theories are flawed and incomplete, and counsellors get things wrong. However, counsellors *do* appreciate the value of being non-judgemental to others and one's self. We could be kinder to ourselves and each other by not being so afraid of failure that it distorts our every natural movement. We could be not be so ready to find someone to blame that it strangles our natural inclinations to get involved and help. It might appear that these projects would need co-ordinated effort in order to succeed. However, action at the level of the individual citizen *does* have an effect, and then these individual actions can be organised.

How will you use the learning you have made in your introduction to counselling? Whatever reasons and objectives you may have had when you started the course, how might you enhance your contribution to society as a citizen?

As a citizen, what areas of *your* life and specific contribution to *your* community do *you* think would be helped by a better understanding and sharing of counselling skills? ✍

Who is Counselling For?

10

For the purposes of this brief chapter, I would like to stand aside from the usual debate about what counselling is. Elsewhere in this book I have looked at some of the information and argument in this debate regarding counselling, counselling skills and psychotherapy. I have contributed to the debate by suggesting that there is another type of informed helping at a level below the counselling skills level which is a valid and honourable *basic helping* activity.

Rather than re-hash that debate yet again, I would rather offer a few illustrations of who seeks and receives counselling in the UK. How they do it and what is likely to happen. It is not intended to be a comprehensive list. As with other parts of this book, it aims to be both informative and a starting point for further exploration; aims that are, I believe, in harmony with an introductory course.

WHY DO PEOPLE SEEK BASIC COUNSELLING-STYLE HELPING?

Many people now accept that talking through problems is beneficial. The word *counselling* comes readily to the lips of anyone seeking such an opportunity to talk and be listened to. A glance at the notice board in your public library or a flick through the front of your telephone directory will give you an insight into the range of local problem-related counselling services available. It may seem all too obvious that counselling is for people with problems.

It may be less obvious that a growing number of people in this country seek counselling as a route to self-improvement. In a similar way to seeking self-improvement through yoga classes, sport, arts and crafts, adult education such as writing for pleasure, people seek self-improvement through counselling. Although this may seem to be a solitary and costly leisure activity, it needn't be. There are several peer-support networks around the country where people get together in pairs and larger groups to offer help and counselling to each other. The most well known of these networks are called *co-counselling communities*.

Embedded within this 'counselling-for-self-improvement' activity is a dimension of counselling and helping that is only recently getting the attention it deserves. That is the spiritual dimension. The search for self-improvement and self-fulfilment inevitably touches upon the spiritual side of humanness. Not only is this spiritual dimension present for the seeker, but also for the helper/counsellor. As William West commented in 1994 at the British Psychological Society Division of Counselling Psychology Conference, forming helping and therapeutic relationships with people five days a week all year is a deeply spiritual process. Many helpers and those seeking help make direct links between helping and spiritual life by doing their helping in a religious context. Counselling fits well into many spiritual traditions. There is more on this subject in Chapter 9 and Chapter 13.

PROBLEM-CENTRED AND CONTEXT-CENTRED HELPING AND COUNSELLING

The term 'counselling' sits quite comfortably alongside information, advice and guidance when it comes to thinking about helping strategies for problems. People in need do not care what the process is called, nor what comes along with it. However, most agencies offering information, advice and guidance will explicitly offer counselling, or acknowledge that counselling skills are used in the delivery of their other helping services.

Perhaps it is because we have a keener sense of the need for support at times of personal crisis and a better understanding of what good helping is. Or perhaps it is because of the breakdown of support systems like the extended family in our society, that there has been an explosion of agencies and services offering support and counselling in the past 20 years. As seekers of help we have become accustomed to looking for, and more often than not finding, help tailored to our specific needs. Some of the critical life events that take us to counselling are listed below with a word or two of explanation.

Bereavement

Bereavement is the one life event which is universally accepted as a time when humans need support. Much work has been published on the grief process, how unresolved grief can lead to more serious damage and how counselling can help. Grief support and counselling is popular as a peer activity through organisations such as Cruse (nationally) and many local organisations. It is a specialism offered by many professional counsellors.

Unresolved grief can lead to much more complicated and long-lasting symptoms, so good support through bereavement is sometimes literally a life-saver and invariably improves the quality of life. The term 'grief and loss' can encompass the reaction to *any* significant loss in a person's life including becoming unemployed, having a limb amputated or separating from your spouse.

Relationships and marriage

The well-deserved reputation for excellent counselling gained by the former National Marriage Guidance Council, now known as Relate, has done much to associate relationship problems

with counselling in the minds of the general public. Many people turn to relationship counselling before the relationship breaks down, whilst some want support after the event.

Gay couples are catered for within Relate, by other specialist gay counselling services and through professional counsellors in private practice. People from ethnic minorities with relationship problems have some, though limited, opportunities to get more culturally sensitive help from specific agencies.

HIV and AIDS

It has for some time been a requirement that all those requesting an HIV test receive 'counselling' before the test and on hearing the results. The quality of the counselling offered was variable and an attempt to address the problem was made in the report of the BAC and Department of Health Joint Project on HIV Counselling by Tim Bond (1990).

The need for counselling and support related to HIV and AIDS is not limited to those that are HIV positive or suffering from an AIDS-related illness. Partners, relatives and friends need support too along with people who worry that they might have been infected.

[At the height of the government drive to publicise the risk of HIV, some people became excessively worried about AIDS or HIV infection, despite being known to be uninfected or at little or no risk; these so-called 'worried well' people took up a lot of time and resources of AIDS advice agencies. This particular health worry simply highlighted a more general type of mental distress where people develop debilitating anxiety that they have a physical illness. They are best catered for through the usual channels of psychological help — clinical psychology or counselling at a specialist service.]

The history of the spread of the HIV infection in the UK and USA is that gay men and IV drug users represent the largest groups of infected people. Although this is, of course, not the picture world-wide.

For this reason, most specialised agencies are oriented towards the needs of these groups. However, a growing number of people not in these groups are needing support — there is an increase in HIV infection in young heterosexuals. In some areas a befriending scheme exists where people that are HIV positive are befriended by a 'buddy'. There are yet few opportunities for black and ethnic minority people to get culturally sensitive help; however, organisations like the Black HIV and AIDS Forum (BHAF) are addressing this issue.

Victim support
Now officially the title of a national, government-funded organisation with local branches, victim support can also mean the help and counselling offered to any victim of crime. There is a growing concern that victims of crime have had their needs neglected and the provision of such schemes attempts to redress that imbalance.

The national organisation offers a set of co-ordinated services for victims of crime and, where *counselling* is offered, the counsellors are fully qualified. Counselling for shock is offered alongside more concrete help with form-filling, insurance claims and other everyday things that need doing after traumatic crime through to support during court appearances. Local schemes do try to meet local demand for minority languages and cultural minorities.

Surviving disasters
Post-traumatic stress disorder, or PTSD, is the term used to describe the very distressing after-effects suffered by people who have survived trauma such as disasters. The events at Hillsborough football ground, the fire at King's Cross Station, the Dunblane tragedy, aircrashes and other disasters have prompted the provision of specific post-trauma counselling.

Post-trauma counselling is specialised work and is offered to a wide range of people including, for example, building society staff after armed robberies and members of the emergency services who witness horrific scenes in the course of duty. Anyone surviving a trauma (car crash, mugging, or witnessing horrific accidents) is vulnerable to PTSD and should be encouraged to seek help, whether or not a specific scheme is offered. Post-trauma counselling is now offered as a specialism by counsellors in private practice and counselling at major incidents is often provided by commercial organisations such as EAPs (see *Counselling at work* on page 121).

Surviving abuse and rape
Rape and abuse are sometimes looked upon as separate issues, but I have put them together here to indicate that the victims and survivors are mostly women who have been subjected to male violence. This reflects the pattern of provision of support, help and counselling which is frequently by women for women. There has been an increase in the attention given to child sexual abuse recently and the national agency Childline is a point of first contact for children.

Much long-term counselling work is done with the adult survivors of such abuse. This is specialist work and the effects of remembering past abuse are frequently very traumatic and debilitating. This group does include men and it is thought by some that the degree to which it affects men has been underestimated. Local organisations, rape crisis centres and women's groups should be able to give initial support and make referrals where necessary. There is limited specialist provision for men or ethnic minority groups.

Sex and sexuality
Sex and sexuality are in fact two different problem areas — 'sexuality' usually refers to sexual orientation, i.e. heterosexual, bisexual, gay, lesbian. Sexuality also covers sexual attraction to children, cross-dressing, wanting to hurt or be hurt by others, having less usual objects of sexual desire such as items of clothing or machinery.

Our culture is not very flexible when it comes to accepting sexuality or sexual practices which differ from the perceived cultural norm of heterosexual sex. The problems that most people have regarding their sexuality arises from this societal or family pressure to 'be normal'. Some sexual practices are illegal, such as paedophilia (sex with children) which may make it difficult for an active paedophile to seek help to change.

There are specialist self-help/support groups both nationally and regionally that offer help for people wanting to explore, come to terms with or change their sexual orientation. A mixture of information, advice, group support and counselling may be available.

'Sex' refers to problems with 'normal' sexual functioning. Popular terms describing these problems are 'impotence' in men (including premature ejaculation) and 'frigidity' in women. The problems include a wide range of incomplete, absent or inappropriate sexual responses and cause great distress and shame to the sufferers. Counselling approaches pioneered in the UK by the then National Marriage Guidance Council (now Relate) are effective in a large proportion of cases. This specialist area requires counsellors with specialist training. Some professional counsellors in private practice offer sexual dysfunction counselling.

Medical conditions

Illness is another crisis point in a person's life where support is needed, not only for the person themselves but also for their family. Many medical conditions have long-term debilitating effects and a wide range of support groups offering a range of services from information, advice, guidance to counselling and befriending have grown out of the need for such support. From arthritis and asthma to tinnitus (noises in the ear) there are organisations offering help, sometimes on a local basis — some employ specialist counsellors.

Some NHS specialist areas employ counsellors. You may find counsellors offering support and advice to patients before, during and after diagnostic procedures and treatment for:

- amputees
- prospective parents who may be worried about their chances of having an abnormal child
- infertility and associated treatments
- sterilisation and vasectomy
- terminal illness

Palliative care and the hospice movement

Palliative care is the term used for treatment to help make people with terminal illnesses more comfortable. The hospice movement was at the forefront of palliative care in the UK and counselling is frequently provided for the patients and their relatives. Psychological support in the form of counselling is less frequently available for relatives who want to care for the patient at home.

Having recently cared for my Mother at home as she died I found little or no structured provision to support me and my family. Our GP and District Nurse were, however, wonderful and a few words of comfort from them went a long way. I worry about the single person wanting to do the best for their child, parent, husband or wife. A little appropriate emotional support would be invaluable at such a distressing time.

Suicide and despair

Probably the most famous telephone helping agency, *The Samaritans* was set up to listen to people who were so desperate that they may consider taking their own life. Samaritans branches offer listening and befriending and are reluctant to call their basic helping 'counselling'. Undoubtedly, many Samaritans volunteers are proficient in the use of counselling skills. Volunteers are trained, but remain anonymous so on-going helping relationships are difficult unless a client is 'befriended' by a more experienced volunteer.

A few Samaritans branches offer minority languages and a service which takes into account local ethnic groups. Samaritans now offer email counselling.

Problem pregnancies

Trained counsellors are widely available to help a

woman make the decision as to whether she wants to terminate a problem pregnancy or not. Counselling at this important decision-point was pioneered by the British Pregnancy Advice Service (BPAS) and is now commonplace in other agencies offering a similar service. Some other agencies are tied to a world view or religious view which makes a prejudgement about the morality of terminations and so the 'counselling' they offer is likely to be less than neutral. Information and advice are available in addition to counselling.

Counsellors are trained by mainstream agencies like BPAS and do an excellent job often under great pressure of time. Some limited after-event support is available, but a client may have to go elsewhere for this. Information and sometimes help is available in minority languages, but there are powerful cultural issues in the area of pregnancy and women's rights.

Counselling at work
An increasing number of employers are offering help, support and counselling through the workplace. Whether the problem is work-related or of a more personal nature, employers are beginning to realise the cost-effectiveness of counselling since research suggests that, when counselling is provided, fewer days are lost due to sickness and stress. The current trend is to offer Employee Assistance Programmes (EAPs) rather than permanent on-site counsellors. These give different levels of service to different grades of employee. Most start with telephone support to be followed by face-to-face counselling only if absolutely necessary.

Counselling at your GP surgery
An increasing number of GPs employ counsellors in their surgeries to offer help with a wide range of problems from bereavement through to eating disorders and drug dependency.

Some surgeries may have help and information in minority languages. The counsellors should be well qualified and available on an appointment-only

basis. Ask your GP for information.

Counselling in education
Colleges and Universities have been providing counselling for students for many years. It is often provided under the heading 'student services', 'student support' or 'advice and guidance'. Information and advice, as well as counselling for a wide range of academic, financial and personal problems, is usually available. It is usual for the service to be offered to both full- and part-time students.

Counsellors are usually well qualified and available on an appointment basis, with some limited provision for emergencies. Limited effort is made to provide a culture-sensitive service and information in minority languages, even though higher education institutions attract overseas students in number.

Counselling in schools is less available. Some education authorities have policies to provide schools' counsellors but this tends to be the exception rather than the rule. The recent attention paid to violence and bullying in schools still hasn't led to a significant increase in the number of counsellors in schools.

Counselling and religion
The word 'counsel' does have religious associations and many people seek help from their church or community elders when life presents them with crises. Bereavement is a time when people naturally turn to priests for support and guidance.

People resident in the UK belong to many religions and it is not the case that counselling values are shared by all cultures and all faiths. The help offered by priests and elders may not be in harmony with the counselling values espoused in this book.

Basic helping and counselling skills on the telephone
A number of agencies offering basic helping and

counselling do so via the telephone — either exclusively or as a part of their service. There are several benefits to such provision, particularly if you are serving a client group who have difficulty attending a centre for face-to-face interviews, e.g. people with mobility problems, older people, children or single parents who cannot get out of the house. Many of the counselling and helping skills are the same, but there are some important differences and for readers who work, or wish to work, in a telephone agency, there are some resources listed on page 148.

Basic helping and counselling skills by email and on the internet

In recent years there has been significant growth in the provision of counselling and helping services by email (e.g. Samaritans) and on the internet. Email counselling is often used in educational establishments as a supplement to face-to-face services. Internet counselling and internet therapy is a specialist service and is mostly offered by American companies and groups of practitioners.

BACP has published documents and guidelines for anyone wanting to get involved with email and internet counselling. Visit their website: www.bac.co.uk

Support and self-help for women, lesbians, gays, bisexuals, disabled people, ethnic minorities, young people

Several groups of people band together as self-help groups with political leanings because they experience society's attitudes towards them as oppressive. They may have a view that the particular problems experienced by individuals in the groups are better explained and solved by looking at the issues of oppression first or alongside the problems of the individual.

There is sometimes a culture clash between counselling approaches and political approaches, since some people believe that it is the oppressive system that should change, not the individuals within it. Counselling skills are nearly always used by people in such groups but may not be explicitly acknowledged.

For further information about any application of counselling in the UK you should find the following publication useful: *Counselling and Psychotherapy Resources Directory*, published by BACP. It is updated annually and should be available from your college or local library. Copies can be bought direct from BACP. It contains contact numbers for all national and local counselling organisations, including specialist groups, ethnic minorities, etc. along with individual counsellors and other useful information. BACP also publish information on training courses.

After completing an introductory course in counselling, you might be able to recommend counselling opportunities to relatives, friends and colleagues in need of help. This would, of course, include pointing them in the right direction for well-qualified help, be it Relate, Childline or non-counselling helping in the local women's group. It would not be appropriate to offer help yourself in any capacity other than a relative, friend or colleague.

If you would like to volunteer: First find out the names of the organisations that work in the area of your interest. Contact their national or local address, which you will find in the *Counselling and Psychotherapy Resources Directory* (see above). You will probably have to undergo training by the organisation concerned. Finally, check that you can make the time commitment required.

Most voluntary organisations, with a few exceptions, for example Relate, do not provide training to a professional level. The best you can expect will be good counselling skills training. You will have to go to a college or private training organisation to get training to professional level, acceptable to, for example BACP, for accreditation. (See pages 126, 135–6 and 141.)

Who Does What in Helping? 11
Psychology, Counselling and Psychotherapy

Many people are puzzled by the confusingly complicated array of professionals offering services in the general field of psychological therapies, and it's growing by the day. The British Psychological Society created the Division of Counselling Psychology to add to the more traditional clinical and educational psychologists, so the choice is now between:

- Counsellor
- Psychotherapist
- Counselling Psychologist
- Educational Psychologist
- Clinical Psychologist
- Psychiatrist

What do they all do and who should we go to see or refer our clients to, and under what circumstances?

Starting at the bottom of the list I will give a brief summary of the training and qualifications necessary, the type of clients seen and the type of treatment used for each of the professional groups above. One final word of caution: there will be differences within each professional group so all that I can attempt is a general set of guidelines for understanding this area. There will be exceptions to these general rules, and I hope the information stays current long enough to be useful.

Psychiatrist. It might have been sufficient a few years ago to say that a psychiatrist is a doctor who specialises in the treatment of mental illness and leave it at that. In recent years the medical profession has had to become more accountable and we want to know more about the qualifications and responsibilities of medical practitioners.

After qualifying as a doctor and gaining experience in general medicine and surgery, specialisation is the next step for medical students. Psychiatry is one of several specialisms such as general practice, gynaecology, paediatrics, etc. It involves some years spent in full-time specialised psychiatry training. Look out for the following letters signifying higher qualifications in psychiatry:

DPM (Diploma in Psychiatric Medicine)
MRCPsych (Member of the Royal College of Psychiatrists)
FRCPsych (Fellow of the Royal College of Psychiatrists)
DM or MD (doctoral thesis) in a psychiatric subject

However, any qualified doctor can call him- or herself a psychiatrist if they undertake treatment of psychiatric patients, even if they have no specialist training at all.

The vast majority of psychiatrists work in NHS settings and will have patients referred to them by GPs or other healthcare professionals. Some psychiatrists will see fee-paying patients privately, though there will be little difference in the treatment. Psychiatrists are also usually on call at Accident and Emergency (A&E) departments, so reporting to A&E is a method of self-referral.

The typical caseload of a psychiatrist will include many people experiencing serious mental disturbances of either a temporary or more enduring type. Such serious disturbances often mean that the patient is thought to be a danger to themselves or others (although this is a contentious issue) or is incapable of looking after themselves. There is an increasing tendency to call for the support of a psychiatrist when all other options are exhausted.

The role of the psychiatrist is changing in the UK from someone who delivers treatment, to someone who manages a treatment plan. Their role is also invested with statutory powers such as prescribing drugs and authorising admission to or discharge from hospital.

Treatments used by psychiatrists reflect the medical history and tradition of psychiatry. They are more likely to use 'physical' treatments, e.g. drugs and electroconvulsive therapy (ECT). Only medically qualified persons can prescribe such treatments. Psychiatrists are less likely to use 'talking therapies' themselves (possibly due to lack of time), although they may prescribe psychological treatment via a clinical psychologist or specialist nurse or occasionally a counsellor.

Psychiatric Nurse. This is a different qualification to General Nurse and the different training prepares the Psychiatric Nurse to specialise in the treatment of psychiatric conditions. They will work in psychiatric hospitals, day units and in the community where they will be called a Community Psychiatric Nurse or CPN. CPNs make home visits, make assessments and carry out treatment plans (usually checking that medication has been taken). Sometimes they will give counselling-type support, but are not often trained specifically to do this. Some may have limited training in Cognitive Behavioural Therapy, fewer will have training in Person-centred Therapy, even though evidence suggests that it is as effective.

Psychologist. When used on its own, the title 'psychologist' has little meaning. In order to become a psychologist all that is really needed is a psychology degree (BA or BSc). Psychology is the study of the normal mental life and behaviour, mainly of human beings, but also of some animals where their behaviour can throw light on human behaviour. Being a psychologist in no way qualifies

or prepares a person to offer help to those with any form of mental distress or disturbance.

Chartered Psychologist. Is someone who has a first degree in psychology, a further qualification or period of supervised training in a practical area of psychology, such as clinical, educational or counselling psychology, and been judged fit to practise psychology without supervision. Chartered Psychologists are members of the British Psychological Society (BPS) and abide by their own Code of Conduct with its attendant complaints procedure. Chartered Psychologists can use the letters *C Psychol* after their name. All Chartered Psychologists and a description of the services they offer can be found in the Register of Chartered Psychologists, which can be found in your local public library.

Chartered Counselling Psychologist. Is a Chartered Psychologist specialising in counselling psychology and a member of the Division of Counselling Psychology. They will have a Diploma in Counselling Psychology or have equivalent certified qualifications and experience. Counselling Psychologists can work in a variety of settings including the NHS (in your local psychological services unit) and private practice and will, according to the BPS, work with adults, groups, students and young people, families and couples, the elderly, in health and medical settings, in work settings and in community settings. Counselling psychologists will work using a range of counselling skills and methods that are informed by psychological knowledge and research.

Counselling Psychology is the most recent addition to the list of specialisms offered by BPS Chartered Psychologists and there is an increasing number of practising Counselling Psychologists around at the time of writing. A number are in private practice, and full details can be obtained from the BPS or from the Directory of Chartered Psychologists. Because of the relatively small number, you are less likely to be referred to one (rather than a Clinical Psychologist — see below) by your GP or anyone else. You would probably have to specifically ask or look for one yourself.

Chartered Clinical Psychologist. Clinical psychologists traditionally work in medical or mental health settings. They may have a further specialisation, e.g. in child clinical psychology. They practise a number of psychological assessments and treatment techniques such as psychological testing, behavioural therapies and helping people rehabilitate after brain injury or disease. Many use counselling-type relationship skills alongside the psychological therapies, but not all do. Their clients or patients are likely to be suffering from an acute or enduring mental illness, such as panic attacks, phobias, obsessive disorders, schizophrenia-like conditions, depression, etc.

Clinical psychologists have their own health service structure through which their services are delivered, usually managed by a District Clinical Psychologist. Referral to the clinical psychologist will be from your GP, Psychiatrist or other health service specialist. You may ask for a referral if you think a clinical psychologist would help, or you could find one that takes private clients in your locality.

Chartered Educational Psychologist. Psychologists working in educational settings or specialising in psychology related to education and children are called educational psychologists. They work mainly with children and adolescents up to the age of 19 and receive most referrals via the education system or parents. Their clients will be wanting help with a range of social and emotional problems which may manifest themselves through school, or academic and intellectual problems such as dyslexia and special learning needs.

Educational psychologists offer a range of assessments and treatments including counselling approaches, but also behavioural therapies, e.g. for bed-wetting, and learning programmes or resource management for children with special learning needs. If a child is having problems at school, then the educational psychologist will probably use psychological testing to help diagnose the problem before applying specific treatments. They will also work with children in emotional difficulties, including court work if the child needs to be put in a place of safety.

Educational psychologists are usually employed by Local Education Authorities (LEA) and can be accessed through schools or directly by looking up the LEA or Schools' Psychological Service in the phone book. You can also have private consultations if you wish by finding a local Educational Psychologist in private practice.

Psychotherapist. To some extent the difference between psychotherapists and counsellors is as artificial as the difference between psychotherapy and counselling (see Chapter 12). It is not uncommon to find two people with identical qualifications and client caseloads, one of whom calls themselves a counsellor, whilst the other calls themselves a psychotherapist. By a similar token you may find the same person calling themselves both a counsellor and a psychotherapist (and sometimes a counselling psychologist too).

Laying aside any such problems of definition, the United Kingdom Council for Psychotherapy (UKCP) is a professional body looking after the interests of psychotherapists and psychotherapy. It monitors standards of training, has a code of conduct and a register of practitioners. The UKCP works alongside other organisations such as BACP in the development of standards in therapeutic helping.

Since the BAC changed its name to BAC*P* (for *psychotherapy*), the public would be forgiven for being even more confused. I'm afraid that I can offer no words of comfort here, except to say that I give a little more time to this issue in Chapter 12.

Psychotherapists work in a range of healthcare settings and in private practice. They employ a range of therapeutic techniques for helping clients.

There are many different 'schools' or approaches in psychotherapy, but any competent therapist will explain the basis of the techniques that they use should you wish to know. There are specialisms within psychotherapy including child and family therapists, art and drama therapists.

If you feel that a psychotherapist can help, you should contact the UKCP for access to the register, or contact BACP for information or ask your GP to refer you.

Counsellor. Some years ago a friend of mine wrote a short article for a student magazine defining psychology. His conclusion was: 'Psychology is what psychologists do'. It might seem flippant to start with the statement: 'Counsellors are people who do counselling', but I fear it's going to be the closest I can get in a single statement. (See Chapter 1.)

There is no single route to being a counsellor, and there are many specialisms within counselling: bereavement counsellor, drugs counsellor, student counsellor, HIV/AIDS counsellor, etc. One distinguishing feature which may be helpful is that many counsellors are professional, that is they earn their living as a counsellor. This will usually indicate a degree of training and experience above that usually associated with being a volunteer or someone using counselling skills, *but not always.*

Minimum qualifications would be a Diploma in Counselling or equivalent. The BACP accredits Diploma courses which come up to agreed minimum criteria. Such courses will say 'BACP Accredited Course'.

Many counsellors will be members of BACP (therefore subject to the BACP Code of Ethics and Practice) and some will be BACP Accredited Counsellors (see below and Chapter 13).

If you want to choose a counsellor working in private practice, there are helpful guidelines in the *Counselling and Psychotherapy Resources Directory* or look on the BACP website and follow the links to find a counsellor (www.bac.co.uk). Word-of-mouth recommendation is often the best guide. A job well done is often the best way of choosing someone alongside checking out their qualifications and membership of a professional body. Do not apologise for being choosy.

You can also check with the UK Register of Counsellors (UKRC) to see if a particular counsellor is on the Register. Counsellors can become registered if they are Accredited (see above). For more details on the UKRC read the last section of Chapter 13.

BACP Accredited Counsellor. (Also called Registerd Practitioner) Being Accredited means that the counsellor has a certain level of training and experience that has been scrutinised by the BACP. (A minimum of 450 hours training plus 450 hours supervised counselling practice over three years, plus the ability to reflect upon that practice by submitting written work and demonstrating a commitment to personal development and ongoing supervision.) At the time of writing, approximately 30% of the 21,000 BACP members is accredited (both figures change constantly, so check with BACP if you require accurate information) and BACP continue to work hard to make the accreditation scheme more accessible without lowering standards. They are eligible for entry in the (United Kingdom Register of Counsellors) UKRC. If one is not conveniently located near you, the next best solution is a counsellor who is a member of BACP or a similar professional body so that their practice is governed by a code of ethics and practice.

Contact addresses for the British Association for Counselling and Psychotherapy, the British Psychological Society and United Kingdom Council for Psychotherapy can be found on page 148.

Some Questions for Counselling in the 21st Century

Counselling as we know it today arrived from the USA in the mid-sixties and was taken up by people working in educational settings. The last 30 years have seen great developments in counselling in the UK and now in the early 21st Century we have the United Kingdom Register of Counsellors and a national professional body (BACP) with over 21,000 members. For most of you reading this, you will just be beginning your exploration of counselling. It may seem to you that the counselling 'industry' is well established in the spectrum of helping professions.

As I explained in Chapter 2, the ideas behind counselling and psychotherapy are at best 100 years old and many are more recent than that. In addition, the ideas themselves are probably re-inventions of much older ones. In Chapter 9 I looked at the relatively safe and incident-free history of counselling, compared with, for example, psychiatry. Now I suggest we pause, both to take stock, and to answer some of the questions put forward by the critics of counselling, and to consider some of the important debates within the 'profession'.

As I have written elsewhere in this book, for many readers, this introductory course, or this book, will be your only contact with a counselling way of helping. You will go back to your families, communities or jobs with a set of ideas about counselling and I am determined that you should take with you as accurate a view of contemporary counselling as possible. You will be better able to help your friends, family, colleagues and clients locate and gain access to the best counselling-style

help only if you think that it is based on honesty and integrity, for self- and community enhancement; not motivated by greed, self-aggrandisement or the need to meet the helper's needs above those of the client.

The counselling community is in a constant state of self-questioning and self-development. The activity of counselling requires that individual counsellors constantly monitor their practice through supervision to ensure that they do not place their own needs over the needs of their clients. This monitoring also happens quite naturally in the wider community of counsellors. There is always someone ready to do the supervisor's job and challenge accepted norms within the counselling 'industry' in case we get driven by self-interest. This is done at large gatherings and conferences, through the pages of journals, etc. Issues such as the effectiveness of counselling, the cost of counselling and the availability of counselling are of central concern to counsellors. The following questions are frequently raised in the media by journalists, and counsellors, both locally and nationally, also debate these issues constantly.

With so many people involved in counselling it is easy for any representative organisation to become distanced and out-of-touch with the needs of the community of counsellors and helpers. Everyone involved in counselling needs to be vigilant, responsive and vocal regarding important issues in the helping professions. There are critical voices within the profession — e.g. not everyone thinks that professionalisation is a good idea — and I hope I have represented some of these in this chapter.

IS COUNSELLING A NEW RELIGION?

This is a fascinating question, since it reveals how much our culture has lost its soul — some say to consumerism, some to global capitalism, others to technology and science. The question is often asked nowadays as if to imply that 'religions' are a bad thing. One, I believe intentional, implication behind the question is that anything non-scientific is untested, unproven and therefore not to be trusted. A further implication is that anything even inadvertently filling the niche of a 'religion' in our society should be treated with at least suspicion, since it might appear to be seeking to replace traditional or 'true' religion (e.g. Islam or Christianity) in our souls, hearts and minds. So, I would argue that what is a fascinating question is sometimes asked with the dishonourable intention to discredit counselling and to do so with a hidden anti-spiritual, 'technology is trustworthy' sub-text.

On the other hand, there is a fascinating sociological debate to be had regarding the place of religion and counselling in our increasingly secular society. Paul Halmos elegantly and learnedly explores this notion in his book *The Faith of the Counsellors* (1969).

In the next few paragraphs I will review some of the possible ways in which counselling and religion or spiritual traditions appear to be similar. I am not suggesting that counselling either is or is not supplanting traditional religions, but the similarities are worth looking at and debating.

Some people argue that counselling is, amongst other things, filling a void that has developed in contemporary life. The evidence is that thousands of people turn to counsellors every day and are satisfied enough to return each week. It has been suggested that people only seek and return to counsellors because they are so desperate and they have nowhere else to go. And there, I suggest, is the void. In a civilisation which puts men on the moon, we seem unable to provide a place for people when they are desperate. Every spiritual tradition has something to say about helping others, extending love to others, whether they are your

If   by Roy Harper

If it was right to be believing,
and write his name in blood
and then I met him when I died,
well I'd have it out with god.
But if it means degrading scenes
and sanctioning crusades,
I'd know we couldn't stand man to man
without feeling afraid.

If it was wrong for not believing
in fairytale facade
and then I met him when I died,
well I'd apologise to god.
But if it meant I went down on my knees
well where's the spirit gone
where's the love you're all talking of
when you can't stand man to man?
Man to man
When you can't stand man to man.

I find it hard to believe
in these 'gospels' that I've heard
the forked tongue of the bible belt
the ayatollah's word.
I don't believe most anything
spoken by anyone
as hell's fanatic paranoids
fire heaven's loaded gun.

If it was right to be believing,
then it must be in this
that difference is beautiful
and living it is bliss
there are no teams
there is no side
that life on earth is done
by living the love you're only talking of
by standing man to man.

neighbour or not. If there is a void, partly created by the turning away from religious beliefs, then counselling seems ready-made to step into it.

We can debate whether the media causes or reflects

trends in society, but either way we do not have far to look for confirmation of the parlous state we are in. I find turning on the television a thoroughly disheartening experience — apparently it is entertaining to be assaulted by 'the weakest link' and 'dog eat dog'. I despair. The values of counselling and helping could not be more diametrically opposed to these sentiments.

A further feature of helping in a counselling way is the fact that all approaches involve some element of self-evaluation or contemplation. Counselling provides a time and space in which the centre of attention is *you,* a time for reflection on life and your part in it. This contemplation and self-awareness development does have many resonances with meditation and similar spiritual practices. One strong theme in spiritual traditions is the idea of self-improvement; this is, of course, the *main* theme in counselling. Perhaps counsellors do fulfil the role of secular spiritual guides for those disconnected from, or without any sense of, their spiritual selves, whether that disconnection is by choice or not. Brian Thorne has written extensively and persuasively on this topic from a Christian position (Thorne, 1991, 1998), and I am sure such views are not restricted to one spiritual, religious, or even secular viewpoint.

Again, counselling finds itself at odds with contemporary culture which denigrates the internal world, requiring us to get on-message, live fast, aspire to nothing greater than wearing designer labels and to buy before we think. We live in a world 'Where straight teeth in your mouth are more important than the words that come out of it' (Franti 1992).

'The victims of this world, are advertised on posters
A beach and a pretty girl, if you just drink their potion ...'

The Levellers, *Fifteen Years.*

'Television, the drug of the nation
Breeding ignorance and feeding radiation ...

... TV is the reason why less than ten per-cent of our Nation reads books daily
Why most people think Central America means Kansas
Socialism means unamerican and Apartheid is a new headache remedy ...

... TV is it the reflector or the director?
Does it imitate us or do we imitate it?
Because a child watches 1500 murders be-fore he's twelve years old
and we wonder how we've created a Jason generation that learns to laugh rather than abhor the horror ...'

Disposable Heroes of Hiphoprisy, *Television, the drug of the nation.* Lyrics by M. Franti.

Many people have noted that there is, without doubt, a flavour of the confessional in some counselling situations. People come to counselling to unburden themselves. This unburdening is not *necessarily* because they believe they have sinned in a religious sense or done something wrong in a legal sense, but it can often be because they feel the weight of assumed guilt or having failed to meet either their own or others' high expectations. In an increasingly secular world it could be that counsellors are seen as offering a safe place for people to confess and heal themselves.

It appears that, as this new century begins, many people are turning towards spiritual life in our culture at the same time as turning away from organised religion. If it is a common feature of human life that we seek a spiritual connection, it does not seem so surprising that people will use whatever is handy to make the connection they desire. Whilst counselling would appear to fit the bill in a number of ways, we must not lose sight of the fact that counselling is not offered *primarily* as

Some research findings on the effectiveness of counselling

I have selected some studies that cover a range of counselling and life settings. The full references are in the back of the book and may be available from a good city-centre public library or your local University library.

• Jewel published a report of evaluative study counselling in general practice in 1992. Counselling led to a reduction or cessation of prescribed drugs (such as tranquillisers and antidepressants) in between 20 & 50% of patients taking such drugs.
• Shapiro and Barkham (1993), in a large study of clients attending counselling at Relate, found that over 80% of the clients had most or 'almost all' of their needs met and that 97% were 'mostly' or 'very' satisfied.
• In 1983 Lockhart found that criminal behaviour in boys in care was reduced after around 20 Person-Centred counselling sessions, and that these positive changes were still evident after 2.5 years.
• McLennen in 1991 discovered that students in higher education benefited more from counselling in a counselling service than they did from informal discussions with fellow students.
• In 2000, Professor Michael King, based at the Royal Free and University College Medical School in London, conducted a large £0.5 million study directly comparing three treatments in primary care: Person-Centred Counselling, Cognitive Behaviour Therapy and routine general practitioner care. The patients were suffering from depression and mixed anxiety and depression. Professor King found that
    • Both Person-Centred Therapy and Cognitive Behavioural Therapy obtained significantly better results than 'usual general practitioner care' at the four-month follow-up.
    • There was no difference in therapeutic effectiveness between Person-Centred and Cognitive Behavioural Therapies.
    • Higher patient satisfaction scores were recorded for the psychological therapies than the usual GP care.

For more research evidence, contact BACP who supply lists of research findings on different subjects.
If you are interested in the Person-Centred Approach, BAPCA produce an excellent Briefing Document with research information in it for a small charge. See the contacts list on page 148.

a spiritual activity. It is a helping activity which can be carried to professional levels and may, for some people, have a wider or deeper spiritual meaning, just as people have 'peak' or spiritual experiences when climbing mountains, running marathons or listening to music.

DOES COUNSELLING WORK?
Whenever I hear this question asked I heave a great sigh inside. The question is rather like an iceberg — only one-tenth of it is visible and all of the danger lurks, hidden from view. On the face of it it's a reasonable question; a question we should surely all ask, so what's my problem? In 1990, Berk and Rossi suggested that the initial question *Does counselling work?* has to be immediately followed up with *Compared with what?* In real life, we often offer no help or support to people in distress, so we must compare the effectiveness of counselling with how frequently people feel better without any special, deliberate treatment. Sometimes, in the case of specific forms of disturbance and distress,

we can compare counselling with another more established form of treatment such as drugs.

Most of the time this question is asked, the questioner makes the assumption that the 'scientific method' will yield the answer. It has proved to be extremely difficult (some would say that it has not yet been done) to conduct credible 'scientific' experiments on the outcome of counselling.

The scientific method used in testing the effectiveness of, say, medical treatments is, in principle, quite simple. The researchers arrange for one group of people to receive treatment whilst another group receives none. If the first group get better more quickly or more of them get better than the second group then the treatment 'works'. This approach is fine for physical treatments like drugs, laser beams and surgery. However, when we try to use it on counselling, a number of problems arise.

- Firstly, most science concerns itself with measurable things and counselling, based as it is upon *relationships* and *subjective feelings,* is notoriously difficult to measure.

- Secondly, the whole of a person's life impinges upon their mental state, so even if we treated a series of counselling sessions as though they were pills (i.e. we give the sessions to one group but not another) there is no telling what the people in either group have been doing in between times to make them better or worse.

- Thirdly, the 'treatment' itself, i.e. counselling, is rather variable to say the least. With pills, the dosage can be measured accurately, but how can the 'dosage' in counselling be measured? Are four sessions always twice as good as two, or can some sessions be more powerful than others? By the same token, it is difficult to allow for the variation in the treatment that comes with different counsellors.

As you can begin to appreciate, the whole issue of what works and what doesn't is fraught with complications. I will summarise some of the remaining complications:

- Whenever we ask whether something works, we need to define what we mean by 'works'. You might think that, in counselling or helping terms, we might simply be interested in whether someone feels better. But then we need to ask how long they need to feel better for before we would feel assured that they *really are* better. On the other hand, an employer asking the question might want to

---

ALL PURPOSE LATE TWENTIETH CENTURY CREED   SIMON RAE

I believe in my beliefs.
It's my belief that my beliefs
Are truer far than your beliefs,
And I believe that your beliefs
Are threatening to my beliefs,
So I'm defending my beliefs
And all who hold the same beliefs
Against your dangerous beliefs
And all who share your false beliefs
Or what I think are your beliefs.
And I will die for my beliefs;
And you will die for my beliefs.

And what, in fact, are my beliefs
Beyond the complicating reefs
Of tedious theology
And arid ideology?
The usual: a divine Creator,
Whose love rings earth like the equator;
Justice and the Rule of Law
(And giving hand-outs to the poor);
Respect, of course, for Mother Nature,
Care for every living creature;
And that in the pursuit of Peace
All wars (excepting mine) should cease.

know whether their employee will be able to get back to work next week. Or a teacher will want to know if their star pupil will pass their exams as expected. Unless we work hard to define this term we are never sure that we are talking about the same thing.

• Those counselling approaches which lend themselves to measurement have the appearance of being more scientifically credible, such as cognitive and behavioural approaches. This doesn't mean that they *are* more effective — just that the concepts are simple, instrumental and countable.

• Not all science is good science. We need to be very careful about how the results of scientific experiments are interpreted. Some grave mistakes have been made in recent times where people's lives have been ruined by the too hasty application of what was (often in good faith) thought to be sound science. However, it must be remembered that often, another motive (profit, or a quick-fix) can become tangled up with the honourable desire to help others. Such hellish mixtures have historically led to, for example:
  • the deadly combination of barbiturates used to relieve the stress of everyday life coupled with amphetamines used as stimulants or slimming pills,
  • the over-prescription of benzodiazepines and resulting addictions.

I await with trepidation news of the long-term effects of the enthusiastic prescription of Selective Serotonin Re-uptake Inhibitors (SSRIs, e.g. Prozac) and Ritalin for Attention Deficit Hyperactivity Disorder (ADHD) in children.

We often assume that medical treatments are subjected to scientific analysis before they are used, so it is reasonable to assume that counselling 'treatments' are subjected to the same sort of testing. The truth is that some medical treatments or techniques were never subjected to scientific

testing before they were used (e.g. X-rays and electroconvulsive therapy), so it is not safe to assume that the scientific method is always the benchmark. Expediency, political gain or profit are just as likely to be the guiding rules.

Furthermore, sociologists and psychologists have been developing a different sort of 'science', based not on the measurement of things in terms of numbers, but on an appreciation of the qualities of things. This new way is just as difficult, rigorous and demanding a research method as the more traditional measuring with numbers or 'quantitative' method. The method is able to use the more natural experiences of people (including clients) to tease out how people *experience* counselling rather than trying to condense these complicated human moments into a set of numbers. This turns out to be much more in keeping with the whole ethos of counselling, but medical research does not yet accept the validity of this 'qualitative' approach to science.

• How would you set about finding out if counselling works?
• Would you be satisfied by your own experience, i.e. if you went for counselling yourself and it seemed to make you feel better?
• Discuss this issue with others in your training group.

The questions above undoubtedly have a relevance much wider than counselling. What kind of evidence do *you* require before you believe something? Most people rely heavily upon personal experience, and once they have had an experience, they tend to hold on to it come hell or high water! Do you require 'personal experience' as evidence that counselling works?

So finally I will leave you with what I have come to call the 'Loch Ness Monster Effect'. In the recent Polygram film *Loch Ness* the following dialogue takes place between the sceptical American scientist, John Dempsey played by Ted Danson and a young Scots girl Isabel, played by Kirsty Graham, who has seen and made friends with the monster. Isabel shows John Dempsey a drawing she made of the monster:

Dempsey: *'So this is your Kelpie.'*
Isabel: *'It's my friend.'*
D: *'Are you telling me you actually saw . . .'*
I: *'Aye!'*
D: *'. . . Aye . . .'* (Dempsey laughs.)
I: *'You're laughing at me. You don't believe me. No one does. I shouldn't have drawn it.'*
D: *'No, no, no, I'm not laughing at you, it's just that . . . (Dempsey sighs) . . . I have to see it before I can believe it.'*
I: *'No, Mr Dempsey, you've got to believe it before you can see it.'*

DOES COUNSELLING DO MORE HARM THAN GOOD?

This question raises similar issues to the *Does Counselling Work?* question, since it depends upon how you define the words *harm* and *good,* and secondly, it depends upon whose viewpoint you are taking. I remember reading a tabloid headline many years ago which shouted *'He only wanted to give up smoking, but ended up walking out on his family'.* The story concerned a man who went to see a hypnotherapist with the aim of giving up smoking, but the treatment so changed his personality that he fell in love with his next-door neighbour and left his wife. This headline represents one of a number of commonly-held fears that certain experiences (counselling being one) will change us beyond recognition. Is there really anything to be afraid of? Again, without the space to cover the ground fully on these issues (and whole books are devoted to these subjects), I will give you some discussion starters so that you can debate the issues in your training group, with your friends or just in your head.

Common fears about counselling and change and some answers

• I will change in a way that I cannot control and that people around me, my family and friends, will not be able to keep up with.

• I will uncover things about me that I don't like, things that are better kept under wraps.

• *There's no getting away from the fact that counselling is a form of helping that involves change. At the very least the person being helped is expected to change from feeling generally bad about things to feeling better about things. Such changes don't come in nice neat units because the causes of unhappiness are rarely in nice neat units. There is a chance that there will be more change than you initially bargained for in counselling, but two things should limit the notion of 'runaway' change:*

Firstly there is the skill and professionalism of the helper. (Although you will not be practising counselling at this stage in your training, you will still be expected to behave ethically and properly. The safeguards are there to protect your client.)

Secondly there is the fact that implicit in the workings of the majority of counselling approaches is the notion that the client or person being helped is in control of the rate of change.

• The counsellor might plant ideas and even false memories in my head when I am in a suggestible state.

• When people are desperate and vulnerable they may say things, do things and make decisions that they will regret later.

• Vulnerable people could be exploited by counsellors by getting them to continue to attend for counselling when there really is no need.

• *Codes of Ethics and Practice are there to ensure that counsellors don't exploit their clients when the clients are vulnerable or desperate. Add to this the central notion of all counselling approaches, that the aim is to empower clients to take full control of their lives, and it is difficult to see how a vulnerable person can be harmed, unless the person being helped is a victim of bad practice.*

Most counsellors are trained specifically not to give advice or make suggestions to clients, vulnerable or not.

• Counselling encourages people to look on the dark side of things and *forces* people to look at unpleasant experiences which can easily make people feel worse if they are already depressed.

> • *Helping in a counselling way does not encourage people to talk about anything they don't want to, or to look at anything they don't want to. However, given the opportunity to talk freely without being judged, people do have a tendency to gravitate towards the things that are troubling them. They may have sought help with a particular problem in mind. This may mean that for a while, as they dwell on the unpleasant feelings associated with their problem, they may feel worse than when they started. This can be distressing and any responsible counsellor would explain this. It should pass in a short time, but maybe the person being helped will revisit these negative feelings from time to time during counselling.*

• What have you learned about a counselling way of helping that prevents vulnerable clients from being exploited?

• Make a list and share it with others in your training group.

WHO PROTECTS CLIENTS FROM BAD PRACTICE?

I would like to report that there is a simple answer to this question. In fact there is a vigorous debate within counselling and psychotherapy regarding the best way to protect clients. Some argue for a strong 'profession' of counselling with a comprehensive system of registration backed up with complaints procedures, whilst others argue against this. I will not be able to summarise all of the arguments, but I will try to present the main ones. Then I will explain the role of organisations such as the British Association for Counselling and Psychotherapy, and The United Kingdom Register of Counsellors.

> **For:** A register will bar bad practitioners from harming the public.
>
> **Against:** *A register will have just as many bad*

practitioners on it as not on it. There is no real way to stop all bad practice.

> **For:** A register will be able to operate complaints procedures whereby those successfully complained against would be sanctioned or struck off.
>
> **Against:** *Complaints procedures in the professions are notorious for not protecting the person that makes the complaint, just look at those operated by the Police, Lawyers and the Medical profession. The professionals just close ranks. These systems also favour those with enough money to fund their complaint.*

> **For:** People (including counsellors) should not be trusted to not exploit their clients. We need to have systems to keep these basic human tendencies in check.
>
> **Against:** *Since counselling is a helping method based on the best human qualities, to have monitoring systems based on lack of trust is against the ethos of counselling. We have to have procedures in harmony with this ethos, even if it makes us look (to some) hopelessly optimistic and trusting.*

> **For:** Our modern world demands that customers are placed first and that counsellors as service providers are forced to provide the best service, i.e. by close regulation and penalties for poor practice.
>
> **Against:** *It is precisely because of the breakdown in trust between persons in our society (as evidenced by our increasingly litigious modern world and the tendency to seek financial compensation) that counselling should not become part of the system which eschews resolving conflicts in personal relationships in favour of the courtroom.*

• What arguments can you assemble for or against the regulation of counselling and the registration of counsellors?

• Where do you stand on the subject? [Don't worry

if you think you haven't enough experience of counselling or helping yet. Use your experience as a customer or potential client of counselling.]

• Imagine you are going to a see a counsellor — would you want to be protected? If so, what safeguards would you like to see in place?

✍

• Debate the issue in your training group and amongst your friends. They might be past present or future consumers of counselling or helping services too.

Whatever your view (or mine) might be on these matters, the activity of counselling *is* being subjected to increasing regulation from professional bodies and the non-statutory registration of counsellors has already happened viz the United Kingdom Register of Counsellors.

THE BRITISH ASSOCIATION FOR COUNSELLING AND PSYCHOTHERAPY

The British Association for Counselling and Psychotherapy (BACP) was born in 2000 out of the British Association for Counselling, which in turn was founded in 1977, itself growing from the Standing Conference for the Advancement of Counselling (SCAC). Since then the membership has steadily grown to its present 2002 level of over 21,000. BACP is an organisation that has had to deal with rapid change in the nature of counselling in the UK and there is still some way to go before the whole field of counselling settles down into some stable set of organisational structures. As well as providing a discussion forum for counsellors, the BACP has done its best over the years to provide a regulatory structure in keeping with the ethos of counselling. It developed four codes of ethics and practice backed up by a complaints procedure:
• Code of Ethics and Practice for Counsellors
• Code of Ethics and Practice for Counselling Skills
• Code of Ethics and Practice for the Supervisors of Counsellors
• Code of Ethics and Practice for Trainers in Counselling and Counselling Skills

After much consultation, in 2002 a new *Ethical Framework for Good Practice in Counselling and Psychotherapy* was adopted by BACP in place of the old codes. You will find in Chapter 7 more details of the *Ethical Framework* and how it might inform your basic helping. You can read the document in full on www.bac.co.uk or purchase a printed copy from BACP (see contact page at the end of the book).

In order to join BACP, applicants have to fill in a comprehensive application form and sign a declaration agreeing to abide by the new *Ethical Framework for Good Practice in Counselling and Psychotherapy* and be subject to the disciplinary procedures. These application procedures are now more comprehensive and stringent, preventing casual applications or applications from those using membership simply to attempt to gain status.

If members have a complaint upheld against them, they will be subject to sanctions decided by the panel that hears the complaint. The ultimate sanction is expulsion from the Association and having any special status removed (e.g. Accreditation; see below). This would then affect the individual counsellor's inclusion on the Register (see below).

In addition to the codes, the BACP operates different grades of membership, as follows:

Registered Practitioner: open to current BACP members who have successfully completed at least one BACP Accreditation scheme and who are committed to Continuing Professional Development.

Senior Registered Practitioner: is someone who has held accredited status foe six or more years and continues to maintain their professional and personal development appropriately.

Registered Associate: is for individuals who have successfully completed a BACP Accredited course and also for rejoining lapsed members who have previously achieved BACP Accredited status.

Individual Member: this Grade is for

counsellors, psychotherapists, trainers, counselling psychotherapy supervisors, counselling skills users and graduates or students of non-BACP accredited courses.

Counselling Skills Associate: is for individuals who use counselling skills as adjunct to another primary role.

Student Associate: this grade is for students studying on BACP accredited courses only. Students on non-accredited courses are advised to apply for the grade of Individual Member. A checklist of BACP Accredited courses is available at www.bacp.co.uk.

Fellow: Open on application or nomination to the Management Committee to current individual members with a minimum of five consecutive years' membership, who have gained distinction in counselling or give, or have given, distinctive service to BACP.

The award of Accredited Counsellor, Supervisor or Trainer is conferred on a person only if they can give evidence of a high level of qualifications, a specified minimum amount of experience in supervised practice, a commitment to ongoing professional development and the ability to reflect upon their practice. The evidence presented is thoroughly scrutinised by panels of assessors.

If you, or a friend, relative or colleague are seeking a counsellor, you should bear in mind that only BACP Accredited Counsellors, Supervisors and Trainers, Senior Registered Practitioners and Fellows are allowed to mention membership of BACP in an advertisement. Ordinary Individual or Associate members **must not** mention their membership of BACP in press advertisements, in telephone directories, on business cards, on letterheads plates or plaques, etc. However, members are encouraged to make verbal and written statements to potential clients and in pre-counselling letters and information. These statements should explain that membership of BACP is not a qualification, but does mean that the member abides by the Ethical Framework and is subject to the Complaints Procedure of the BACP.

In addition to all of this, new members also have to have their application countersigned by two witnesses that are either current Individual Members of BACP or a persons of professional standing, e.g. Religious Leader, Justice of the Peace, Solicitor, Bank Manager, General Practitioner, or Chartered Psychologist.

THE UNITED KINGDOM REGISTER OF COUNSELLORS

For the past few years, the BACP, along with other interested organisations, has been working to develop a Register of Counsellors (UKRC) — rather like the Register of Nurses or Doctors. It was 'opened' in 1996 and was officially 'launched' in September 1997. In principle, only those with certain qualifications and experience are allowed on to the Register. Initially, the UK Register will contain counsellors who have already demonstrated the appropriate levels of qualifications and experience by being BACP Accredited Counsellors and will be able to practice as a Registered Counsellor in independent practice or within an organisational setting such as education, the health service or workplace counselling, etc. They will be called *Registered Independent Counsellors*.

Counsellors working for organisations which are able to specify minimum training, supervision and other criteria will also be Registered. These counsellors do not have to meet the BACP Accreditation criteria and they will only be allowed to practise as a Registered Counsellor within that organisational setting. They will be called, for example, *Registered Relate Counsellors*, depending upon the organisation that sponsors them. Only certain organisations meeting the Register's strict criteria will be able to sponsor counsellors.

The UKRC is a *held* register, not a *published* register. This means that you cannot see a copy in a library or buy a copy in a bookshop. The register is held by the Registrar and if a member of the public wishes to check whether a counsellor is on the register or not, it takes just one phone call to UKRC.

• Looking back at your answers to the question of how you would wish to be protected if you were a client, having read the above section do you think the BACP and UKRC do enough?

• If not, what else needs to be done?
✍

Further details of the Register and of the services provided by BACP can be obtained by writing to the respective organisations. The addresses are included at the back of this book.

WHO PAYS FOR THE REGULATION OF COUNSELLING?

The BACP and UK Register of Counsellors are funded entirely by membership fees and donations. The BACP is a registered charity and receives no funding from the Government to assist in its activities. Many members of the various committees and workgroups, indeed of the organisation as a whole, are not paid any fees for the work they do, which can amount to the equivalent of many days, or in one or two cases, weeks or months per year. In order to sustain this commitment both the individuals and their employers pay a considerable price. Each area of activity within the organisation, such as publications, accreditation, complaints, etc. has a paid manager.

Membership of a committee or group involves around eight days' attendance at meetings per year, plus around another four to eight days' work at home. Would your employer give you eight days' leave to attend BACP meetings? Would they let you have time off in lieu or would you have to take unpaid leave? If you are self-employed, could you afford to lose eight or more days' pay per year?

The development of the UK Register of counsellors, involving thousands of hours of committee time, has been paid for by counsellors themselves through membership fees and their own donations, whether those be of money or of time. In the year 2000–2001 this amounted to over £1,460,000 (BACP Annual Report Year Ended March 2001).

The average salary of a BACP member will probably be at or below the national average because many BACP members are voluntary counsellors or working part-time or in private practice, which is relatively poorly paid. This directly affects the fees that the Association can set, which then affects the number of employees, the services to members and the general public, and the publicity that the Association can afford. So, the BACP is not able to ask for high fees whereas Doctors, for example (who earn more, on average, than counsellors), can afford to have a much better professional regulatory body in the form of the British Medical Association.

• What views do you have about how professions should be regulated?
    • Who should pay for this?
    • How should it be organised?

• As a beginning helper in terms of counselling skills, do you think you have a place in BACP?
    • What would you want from the organisation?
    ✍

THE INDEPENDENT PRACTITIONERS' NETWORK (IPN)

As I explained earlier in this chapter, not everyone supports the idea of increasing regulation and professionalisation in counselling and psychotherapy. Some eminent academics and practitioners believe it runs counter to the fundamental principles and values of counselling.

The Independent Practitioners' Network (IPN) was formed to organise the voices calling for an alternative to the headlong rush towards what some disparagingly refer to as the 'MacDonaldisation' of therapy.

There are two excellent web resources giving details of the IPN and other alternatives if you want to explore the other side of the argument on registration and professionalism. (These are given on page 148.) To give you an idea of the IPN position, here are a couple of quotes from their information (both can be found on the website):

'The Independent Practitioners Network (previously the Independent Therapists Network) is an alternative structure for validating and monitoring therapists, counsellors, facilitators, and others in the field. It was founded in November 1994. Its central concept is that membership is by peer group: the members of each peer group (of at least five practitioners) stand by each others' work, and also by the work of at least two other member groups to which they are linked. In this way a web of self and mutual responsibility is woven, where loss of confidence in an individual or group will mean that links are withdrawn and their membership will lapse.'

'Principles [of IPN]
1. The Network exists to further and support good and empowering practice which is open about its aims and underlying principles. It seeks to assure those looking for a practitioner that Network members can provide and sustain a suitable environment for the work they offer and are able to communicate clearly their particular form of work to each other and to the public.
2. The Network seeks to develop a culture of openness, mutuality, support and challenge within and between its member groups.
3. Member groups are committed to fostering evaluation and accountability through an on-going process of self- and peer assessment.
4. Each group takes responsibility for resolving problems which may emerge in the practice of its members, including issues raised by clients. It accepts that its membership of the Network stands or falls by how it carries out this responsibility and is, therefore, prepared to have its process examined, supported and challenged by other groups, and to do the same in return.
5. The Network specifically favours diversity and ecological complexity and has no commitment to any particular model of therapy, therapy training, or therapeutic relationship.'

My aim in this chapter has been to attempt to answer some of the common questions asked about counselling. You have discovered that behind each question is a debate — debates that I hope that you can now take part in. These questions and debates concern everyone with an interest in helping and counselling; perhaps you will continue these and other debates about the place of counselling in our society, whether you choose to go further in your training or not.

'The Independent Practitioners Network links together counsellors, therapists, facilitators, educators, and growth-work and allied practitioners in a non-hierarchical organisation.

It's members are groups of at least five practitioners who support and stand by each other's work and who take responsibility for each other's good practice and the good practice of groups in the network.

The Network operates with no hierarchical structure and minimal bureaucracy: people take on leadership and organisational roles as appropriate. It has no commitment to any particular form of therapy, therapeutic training, or therapeutic relationship and specifically favours diversity. It recognises that there are many ways to become a good practitioner, and many forms of good work, and prefers to leave the discrimination of quality to face to face interaction in peer groups.

The structure provides for:
• Self and peer accreditation, and continuous monitoring of members' work.
• An exciting stimulating and creative context for on-going practitioner development.
• The opportunity to deal with difficulties and complaints in an atmosphere of open-ness and willingness to own mistakes.
• Support and encouragement for excellent practice.'

www.ipiper.demon.co.uk/ipnstuff/ipnleaf

What Comes Next?   13

As you come to the end of this course there are several options open to you. Some people will have already decided what their next step is going to be. Others will not be so sure, nor even be sure what the next step *could* be. In Chapter 10, I wrote that some people seek counselling for self-development rather than to resolve a problem or in response to a crisis. So it is with counselling training. Some of you will have started this course with a view to increase your knowledge of helping processes, general understanding and self-awareness. Initially you may not have considered any career as a helper either paid or voluntary.

Similarly, the process of the course will have helped some of you to make the decision that counselling or helping in a counselling way is not for you. For those of you who have made this decision, I hope that you can be an advocate or ambassador for counselling after your experience on the course. By this I mean that you may be able to explain to friends, relatives and colleagues what a counselling way of helping is, that through your own experience you have found it to be helpful, principled, led by a body of knowledge; not just ad hoc. You may be able to point those around you in the right direction for good quality help should they wonder whether they need it, and help them realise that getting help at the right time improves the quality of our lives.

What options are available for those who wish to continue in their training in counselling? Firstly let me say that, in my view, it is perfectly acceptable to pursue training in counselling to the next stage with the sole intention of developing self-awareness and self-improvement. I say this because I firmly believe that counselling skills are no more than good relationship skills and that I would support anyone seeking to improve their relationship skills. These more highly developed skills could then be used in a 'community' sense amongst one's family, friends and colleagues, and I think such 'communities' will be all the better for it.

THE STARTING POINT — AN INTRODUCTION TO COUNSELLING

The structure of counselling training varies slightly between the organisations offering training. There are usually three stages or levels, starting with basic introductory courses of between ten and 30 hours spread over a weekend or several weeks of two to three hours per week. There will be little or no formal assessment on such a course. Some are organised as 'taster' courses where you will get the briefest of introductions to different approaches. Some dedicate themselves as an introduction to a single approach. Make sure you ask before you start so that you are choosing the right course for you. Further training can be either full-time or part- time.

Although this book is written primarily for this first level, some colleges and institutes start at the next level and incorporate this text into their reading at the beginning of the certificate or intermediate or 'skills' level of training.

PART-TIME TRAINING

The next level of course is often called 'Certificate'; 'intermediate' level; or 'Counselling Skills' level. Such courses are around 100–150 hours spread over one academic year (around nine months). Certificate courses use a range of written and practical assessment, though at this stage of training, the emphasis is usually on skills rather than academic criteria.

The aim of these courses is to continue development of theory, self-awareness and counselling skills and attitudes for those wishing to train as counsellors, whilst providing a genuine stopping-off point for those wishing to train only in the use of counselling skills, but no further. So a certificate course would be of use to:

1. Teachers, nurses, social workers, youth workers, other helping professionals, police officers, managers, indeed, anyone who is aiming to use counselling skills alongside their already established professional skills.
2. Those wanting to proceed to professional training (Diploma in Counselling and beyond) in order to be a counsellor.
3. Volunteers for advice and counselling agencies who want to continue development of their counselling skills beyond that offered by their basic agency training.
4. Anyone wanting to continue a 'counselling training' route to personal improvement and to use their counselling skills in the community, without any firm intention to become a paid or 'professional' counsellor.

Completion of a certificate course does not qualify someone to practise as a counsellor nor apply for a job as a counsellor under most circumstances. Certificates only qualify someone to use counselling skills.

DIPLOMA IN COUNSELLING — PROFESSIONAL LEVEL TRAINING

A Diploma in Counselling is the professional practitioner level course. Diploma courses are of around 300–500 hours duration spread over one or two years. BACP state in their Accreditation of Counsellor Training Courses booklet that a course should be a minimum of 400 hours staff contact. Contact BACP for an updated list of BACP Accredited Courses (visit the website www.bac.co.uk).

Diploma level courses should also require students to practise with bona-fide clients and have this work assessed in some way (often via audio-taped sessions). This practice is also supervised, either by course staff or external supervisors depending on the structure of the course. The trend is to separate the teaching function from the supervisory function and many now see this as best practice, so it is most likely that you will have a supervisor independent of the course. Sometimes the cost of supervision is extra to the cost of the course.

Assessment at Diploma level is rigorous and more academic than on skills courses. Here a balance between skills, academic understanding and personal development is sought so that a well-balanced practitioner is produced. Anyone applying for a Diploma in Counselling should realise that this level of training is demanding (and exciting and rewarding) and should set aside time during their week outside course contact time to see clients, for supervision, for reading and to complete assignments. A frequently heard comment from trainees is that their training has taken over their life.

If you are considering continuing your training as a *person-centred* counsellor, there is a helpful book that is a collection of real-life accounts of the experience of training from the student's point of view. It might help you make the right decision: *Experiences of Person-Centred Counselling Training* by Laura Buchanan and Rick Hughes.

On completion of your diploma, you can practise as a counsellor and apply for jobs as a counsellor.

FULL-TIME TRAINING

A very few institutions offer full-time counsellor training and will take applicants who have completed an introductory course or have equivalent experience. Full-time courses are usually of one year's duration and are eligible for BACP Accreditation.

MASTERS COURSES IN COUNSELLING

There is now a number of higher degree courses in counselling studies. The first level of higher degree is the Masters — the majority of courses are two years part-time. The emphasis is predominantly academic and often a research project or lengthy dissertation has to be completed. These courses are post-practitioner level and usually require a Diploma or equivalent as an entry qualification. Some courses also require two years' experience as a practitioner.

PhD IN COUNSELLING

The next level of higher degree course is PhD or doctorate. On successful completion of such a course you can call yourself 'Doctor . . . '. Study at this level is extremely demanding. Only a very few people are accepted and a significant number of those accepted do not complete the qualification. Some courses are taught (i.e. comprise lectures and seminars) and will have very lengthy dissertations as the major assessment. Others are research-based and again require very lengthy writing. Both types take several years (five or six years minimum) to complete and they require a huge investment of time and effort.

BACP ACCREDITED COUNSELLORS, ETC.

The BACP has a grade of membership called Registered Practitioner (Accredited Counsellor) which means that the qualifications and experience of the counsellor meet certain criteria, importantly including 450 hours training.

[*You should ensure your training hours meet this criterion. Some courses and training programmes do not add up to 450 hours contact time with the right skills/theory balance.* If in doubt check with BACP.]

Supervisors and trainers can also be Accredited. If the member in question has been Accredited (as a counsellor, supervisor or trainer) for six years and completed a substantial number of hours' practice they can become a Senior Registered Practitioner.

Effectively, these are qualifications and permit the counsellor concerned to use these titles. When choosing counsellors or supervisors, you may want to assure yourself that they have an appropriate amount of training and experience.

ATTENTION — REALITY CHECK

Some people enter counsellor training with unrealistic expectations.

They may completely misconstrue the nature of the training process, in which case, although disappointed, they will probably drop out during the intermediate level course or decide not to continue to diploma. This would be considered a success. It would be a failure if such a person continued to diploma level only to become disillusioned then. Diploma level training is financially expensive, personally demanding and very time-consuming. It is frustrating and extremely disappointing to withdraw during the course at that level and it can mean that you feel a failure.

Other people enter training with unrealistic expectations of the life and work of a counsellor. Some people leave well-paid jobs to train as a counsellor only to find that counselling jobs are few and far between and most pay only modest salaries. No-one should enter the world of counselling in the belief that it is a well-paid job. At the time of writing, only a few counselling posts pay on a level with, for example, teaching or nursing. The majority do not come up to these levels.

- Some counsellors are able to obtain part-time (or rarely, full-time) employment in a GP practice.
- When reaching the status of Accredited Counsellor, some are able to get sufficient work with Employee Assistance Programmes (EAPs) to make up a week's work.
- Some are able to generate sufficient work in private practice as a counsellor
- Some work part-time as a counsellor (for example one or two days a week or in the evenings) to supplement or complement another part-time job.

Some people train as a counsellor in order to enhance the job they are already doing, as a nurse or social worker. For example, a nurse in a renal unit may start to offer informal support to patients and relatives. After training as a counsellor this may develop into a formal counselling post for a part of the week if the need for counselling can be demonstrated.

A teacher may choose to specialise in tutorial support work upon completion of a counselling skills course and may be able to make the move to school counsellor after qualifying as a counsellor at diploma level.

The voluntary sector benefits from the over-provision of qualified counsellors since a recently-qualified counsellor will want to continue seeing clients in order to gain BACP Accreditation. One of the best ways of doing this is to work for a voluntary agency. Occasionally, paid posts as co-ordinator of a voluntary service become available and might require a counselling qualification, but are not completely satisfactory since the bulk of the job is desk-bound administration, not face-to-face counselling.

Readers of this book should be aware that they will find precious few jobs advertised in the local (or even national) newspaper that read 'Counsellor Wanted . . .'. Many posts are individually tailored to the person. Once you have gained a diploma in counselling, only a fortunate few make counselling a career without a considerable wait, or lots of effort, or both.

If you are dedicated in your pursuit of a career in counselling and you succeed, the rewards can be great, but probably not in terms of your bank balance.

Endings

14

For some of us, endings of things just come and go along with the rest of everyday life; we are not very sensitive to them. For others, the end of something is an emotional time, a time to celebrate or to mark in some way. In counselling, endings have special meaning since the end of a helping relationship is symbolic of many moments of moving on in our lives.

The end of the course may also be a special time for course participants, perhaps marked by some exercises, at least to help you reflect on the experience of the course and review your learning on it. What do endings mean to you? What words and pictures come up for you?

The flipchart on this page is the last from our imaginary group. How do their responses fit in with your own? The end of the course is the end of the life of the group, the end of the relationships in the group as you knew them. Of course, some relationships may continue beyond the end of the course; you may have made new friends whom you will continue to see after the course or some of you may have decided to continue your training and will meet up with new people on the next course. It is easy to see endings as new beginnings or transitions from one state to another offering new and different opportunities.

How we handle endings on the course may reflect the way we feel about endings in our lives. Some may dread endings and put off thinking about them, others may eagerly look forward to them — impatient to move on to the next thing. You might also have a sense of the timing of endings; do they feel right and natural — has the course come to its natural end? Or does it feel too soon, and that you are unprepared for the end? Are any of these familiar to you? What other endings can you remember, and how did you feel about them? Here are some to get started:

- Last day at school

- Separation from spouse or ending a long-term relationship

- Someone close to you dying

- Moving house

```
                    ENDINGS


    PARTING      DEATH        SORROW

      FINISHED   GONE FOREVER

            NO REGRETS

  'YOU CAN NEVER GO BACK TO THE PAST'

  LOSS     PAIN      GRIEF     SADNESS

  'AS EACH DOOR CLOSES ANOTHER ONE OPENS'

      MOVING ON TO BETTER THINGS

              GOODBYE

        ✍  .......... ............
```

✍ IMPORTANT ENDINGS FOR YOU

These endings may seem to have something in common with the changes we looked at in Chapter 3. Endings *are* change in the sense that they signal a point of change that is inescapable. Some changes are gradual, but an ending or transition has a fixed moment. Sometimes we try to extend the ending by having a false ending before the 'real' one or by putting the ending off or by trying to recreate the way things were before the ending. For example, when someone close to us dies, we might want things to be the way they were — to bring that person back, or if we have a relative who is terminally ill, we begin the grieving process before they die (called anticipatory grieving).

If endings are such strong symbolic events for us, we must be ready to pay them special attention in the helping relationships we have. The people we are helping may have strong feelings about the end of the helping relationship:

- They may feel relief and want to get away from the 'old them' that the helping relationship reminds them of.

- They may want to hang on to the security of the helping relationship because they think they can't cope on their own.

The way we conduct ourselves as helpers in the final stages of a helping relationship will have an effect upon those we are trying to help. We must have an awareness of the meanings that endings have for us and not let our own meanings get in the way of our helping.

The end of the course provides us with an opportunity to experience some feelings about endings, past and present, enabling us to look at our patterns of behaviour.

- How will you end the relationships with the people on your course?

REVIEWING OUR LEARNING

I've deliberately written 'our learning', because, as you may remember, I started this book by saying that it would be better if I could form a relationship through the pages with you, the reader. Now the end of the book is here, I am aware that it is an ending for me. An end to sitting in front of my word processor, a sense of relief and some anxiety because I'm not sure how the book will be received. What have I learned? I like to ask the following simple questions to help review my learning at the end of courses. You could try it too.

- What have I learned about counselling?

- What have I learned about myself?

- What would I add to improve the experience and my learning?

- What would I remove to improve the experience and my learning?

- What will I do differently from now on?

✍ YOU MIGHT LIKE TO MAKE THIS THE FINAL ENTRY IN YOUR JOURNAL.

'This is not the end. It is not even the beginning. But it is, perhaps, the end of the beginning.'

Winston Churchill, November 1942.

Glossary

Active listening Paying close attention to all of the signals (including non-verbal communication) that convey meaning given off by the person being helped.

ADHD (Attention Deficit Hyperactivity Disorder) is a controversial disorder said to be responsible for certain agitated/disruptive behaviour in children. Often treated with the drug *Ritalin*.

Affect The psychiatric and psychological term for any experience of feeling or emotion.

Amphetamines Stimulant drugs (street name 'speed') unscrupulously prescribed as 'slimming' drugs. In the 60s they were prescribed, mainly to women, as 'uppers' to overcome the debilitating effects of the prescription of barbiturates (sleeping pills). Highly addictive.

Antidepressants A class of drugs (see psychoactive drugs and iatrogenic illness) often popularly referred to as 'uppers'. Their main effect is to lift the mood, but there are also 'side' effects which can be distressing. Most often used to control severe depression, but the advent of newer drugs such as Prozac (see below) has led to a popular 'movement' of using mood-altering drugs for general life-enhancement, even when there is little or no evidence of 'illness'.

Anxiety Feeling of unexplained dread or impending disaster often distinguished from fear which is said to be the natural response to a clear and present danger.

Avoidance A defence mechanism in which situations, activities or objects that recall or represent painful events are avoided.

Barbiturates Highly addictive drugs used as anaesthetics and (in the 60s) as sleeping pills. Easy to take lethal overdose.

Befriending The provision of quality support of a 'friendly' nature intended to lessen a person's sense of personal or social isolation.

Behaviour therapy A form of psychotherapy which focuses on modifying faulty or unwanted behaviour rather than basic changes in personality.

Benzodiazepines Addictive minor tranquillizers, e.g. Valium (see tranquillisers).

Boundaries The limits which help define an activity by creating a space within which the activity can take place.

Clarifying Checking by paraphrasing and reflection that the client's meaning has been understood, and seeking the client's agreement with your understanding of what they have been saying.

Client-Centred A way of working in counselling that puts the client at the centre of the activity, and has the belief that the client knows best how to solve their problems. Developed by Carl Rogers; now called Person-Centred.

Cognition A general psychological term for all forms of knowing or thought processes.

Cognitive therapy A psychotherapeutic approach based on the concept that emotional problems are the result of faulty ways of thinking and distorted attitudes towards oneself and others. Most notable contributor is the much-published American psychologist, Aaron T. Beck.

Congruence See Genuineness.

Containment A term from psychodynamic counselling meaning keeping negative or destructive personality traits and forces under control.

Core conditions The essential conditions identified by Carl Rogers without which helpful change cannot take place.

Defence mechanism A psychological strategy employed to protect the individual from unpleasant or harmful forces.

DSM-IV *Diagnostic and Statistical Manual of Mental Disorders,* fourth edition. Published by the American Psychiatric Association, the DSM is a system for diagnosing mental illness. The idea is that everyone making a diagnosis agrees on and uses the same list of symptoms. In some other countries a similar (but not identical) system is used, called the

ICD-10 (*International Classification of Diseases,* tenth edition) and is published by the World Health Organisation.

Eclectic counselling Any counselling theory or practice that incorporates and combines doctrines, findings, ideas and techniques selected from diverse theoretical systems.

Electro-convulsive therapy (ECT) A physical treatment used by psychiatrists for serious and enduring mental health problems. The treatment involves passing an electric current through the head, or sometimes only on one side of the head causing a generalised convulsion similar to an epileptic fit. Patients are anaesthetised and given a muscle relaxant before the shock is administered. Patients' reactions vary, but many report a relief of depression following treatment.

Empathy One of Carl Rogers' core conditions. The ability to sense the client's world *as if* it were your own, without losing the 'as if' quality.

Ethics Moral code or rules of conduct.

Generic General, not specific; a characteristic of, or applicable to, a whole class of things.

Genuineness One of the core conditions. It means being without 'front or facade'; being 'transparent'; being your real self in a helping situation, rather than trying to be the 'expert'. This involves the acknowledgement of your feelings as they arise.

Gestalt therapy A form of psychotherapy first developed by Fritz Perls in which the central focus is on the client's 'here and now' functioning and relationships, as opposed to investigation of past experiences and developmental history.

Hidden meaning Linked to Freud's ideas that actions have unconscious motivations and therefore a meaning that is not available to our conscious mind.

Humanism An outlook or system of thought in which human interests and dignity are valued rather than divine or supernatural matters.

Iatrogenic illness Illness caused by medical treatment, e.g. the 'side' effects of some drugs require further drugs to relieve the patient's symptoms caused by the first prescription of drugs.

ICD-10 *International Classification of Diseases,* tenth edition, published by the World Health Organisation — see also DSM-IV.

Identification The process of associating one's self closely with other persons and assuming their characteristics or views.

Integrative approaches Similar to eclectic approaches, where ideas and/or techniques are

integrated to form a new type of counselling, different from the approaches from which its elements are derived. There are two types of integration; *theoretical integration*, where ideas are blended together; and *technical integration*, where techniques are blended together.

Irrational beliefs Term used in Rational Emotive Behaviour Therapy to mean beliefs that lead a person to have unpleasant feelings and a personally unfulfilling life.

Manipulation Behaviour designed to exploit or control others.

Medical model of mental illness The system of classification of mental distress and disturbance used by western medicine. Originally based on the idea that mental states have a physical cause and that for each 'illness' there is a 'cure'. In this system, if the 'illness' can be diagnosed, then the correct 'treatment' can be applied. Manuals such as the *Diagnostic and Statistical Manual* (DSM) are used to help psychiatrists and others check through lists of symptoms.

Motivation The process of initiating, sustaining and directing psychological or physical activities; the 'reason' for behaviour.

Neurosis Mental 'illness' characterised by a 'normal' human quality, like anxiety, being amplified to unpleasant and debilitating levels. Includes phobias and panic attacks.

Non-directive An approach to counselling and psychotherapy, in which the client leads the way by expressing her own feelings, defining her own problems, interpreting her own behaviour, whilst the therapist sets up a permissive atmosphere and clarifies the client's ideas rather than directs the process. Although credited with developing the approach, Carl Rogers dropped the term in the early 1950s.

Non-interpretative An approach (e.g. Person-Centred) which does not *interpret* the client's behaviour according to a theory. Rather, the client is helped to come to their own understanding.

Non-judgemental warmth See UPR.

Paraphrasing Summarising in few words what a person has just said to check understanding and to convey your attention.

Person-Centred The term chosen by Carl Rogers as the new name for the therapeutic approach he developed and initially called 'Client-Centred'. It is also used rather loosely by some people to indicate any therapeutic or helping approach which is essentially client-led, much to the frustration of

Person-Centred counsellors.

Placebo A treatment that is intended to have no therapeutic effect or power, e.g. sugar-pill with no active ingredients. Used in research as a dummy-treatment.

Projection A defence mechanism in which unacceptable impulses are attributed to others or personal failures are blamed on others.

Prozac An antidepressant drug from the Selective Serotonin Re-uptake Inhibitor (SSRI) class of drugs. It has been called a 'lifestyle drug' because some people advocate taking it even though they may not feel 'depressed', but simply because they want to feel even better than they do already. Recent evidence suggests that there are unpleasant 'side'effects of Prozac and it has been implicated in disturbing violent behaviour.

Psychoactive drugs Drugs which alter mood and mental state.

Psychodynamic General term for approaches to therapy and counselling heavily influenced by the work of Freud, although most such approaches have undergone significant development and owe just as much to the work of other influential figures such as Jung, Klein, etc.

Psychosis Serious mental 'illness' characterised by delusions (irrational beliefs), thought disorders and hallucinations (e.g. 'hearing voices'). Psychoses include schizophrenia, clinical depression and manic-depressive psychosis. The diagnosis and treatment of psychosis is the cause of much controversy in psychiatry and amongst the users of psychiatric services (patients).

Rational Emotive (Behaviour) Therapy (REBT) A therapeutic approach developed by Albert Ellis which concentrates upon the way we determine our feelings and behaviour by irrational thoughts.

Referral The situation where a client or person being helped either moves on to another helper or comes to you from another helper.

Reflection At its most basic this involves reflecting back the other person's utterances as if in a mirror. It is used to convey empathy and as a check of understanding and to convey your undivided attention.

Ritalin A stimulant from the amphetamine family (known also as the 'street' drug, *speed*). Controversially used as chemical treatment for the condition Attention Deficit Hyperactivity Disorder (ADHD).

Schizophrenia A serious and enduring mental 'illness' associated with symptoms of disordered and confused thinking, inappropriate affect, delusions, hallucinations and acute anxiety.

Self-actualisation A humanist idea. According to Abraham Maslow it is the 'full use and exploitation of talents, capacities, potentialities'.

Stimulus In general, any event or situation, internal or external, that elicits a response from a person or organism.

Structuring Establishing the often unspoken 'rules' or boundaries of a relationship. In a helping relationship, this rule-setting or structuring is quite deliberate and may even take the form of some sort of contract.

Supervision The support necessary for all professional counsellors, usually from someone who has a similar background and who has no other relationship with the counsellor.

Symbol Any object, figure or image in our mind that represents something else.

Transactional Analysis (TA) A form of dynamic group or individual therapy originated by Eric Berne, which focuses on characteristic interactions which reveal internal 'ego states' and the 'games people play' in social situations.

Transference Concept used in psychodynamic psychotherapy: the projection upon the therapist of unconscious feelings and wishes originally directed toward important individuals, such as parents, in the client's childhood.

Tranquillisers A type of drug (see psychoactive drugs and iatrogenic illness) which has a mood-flattening effect, often popularly referred to as 'downers' or sedatives. Sometimes referred to in medical literature as either 'major' tranquillisers such as Largactil (*chlorpromazine*) or 'minor' tranquillizers such as Librium and Valium (*diazepam*). Many of these drugs cause serious dependency and all have 'side' effects, some serious and permanently debilitating.

Unconditional positive regard (UPR) Being able to accept the client totally as a worthwhile human being worthy, therefore, of respect; in effect, separating them from their behaviour. And being able to convey that unconditional respect with genuine warmth.

Unconscious According to classical Freudian theory, an *unknowable* part of human personality. That is, my unconscious is unknowable to me. Recently, the term has been weakened to mean 'ordinarily unknowable, but knowable with effort or assistance'.

Contacts and Resources

A WORD ABOUT THE WEB

It is my guess that many readers of this book will be familiar with the World Wide Web and Internet. If you are you will know how to get to the URLs or web addresses included in the details below. There is a huge amount of information available relating to counselling and psychotherapy and it is now probably more convenient to use the Internet than to go to your local library. The websites listed in this book are good starting points if you are wanting information. If you are wanting links to other counselling and therapy webpages, try the sites listed under 'Other Websites' below.

If you do not own a computer and if you are doing an introductory or intermediate course at a college, go to the library or information technology centre and ask the staff to show you how to use the Internet. There may even be a short two-hour course on the subject. Otherwise, I suggest you ask a friend who does own one if they can help you access these addresses.

ORGANISATIONS INVOLVED IN REGULATION AND REPRESENTATION OF COUNSELLORS AND THERAPISTS IN GENERAL

British Association for Counselling and Psychotherapy
1 Regent Place, Rugby, Warwickshire, CV21 2PJ.
0870 443 5252
www.bac.co.uk

United Kingdom Register of Counsellors
1 Regent Place, Rugby, Warwickshire, CV21 2PJ
phone number as for BACP
follow links from BACP website

British Psychological Society
St Andrews House, 48 Princess Road East, Leicester, LE1 7D
0116 254 9568
www.bps.org.uk

United Kingdom Council for Psychotherapy
167–9 Great Portland St., London, W1W 5PF
0207 436 3002
www.psychotherapy.org.uk

Independent Practitioners' Network (IPN)
http://ourworld.compuserve.com/homepages/selfheal/ipn.htm
(The IPN has an excellent Journal — both paper and on-line — called Ipnosis. The online version is free. Visit their site regularly for information.)

OTHER ORGANISATIONS

British Association for the Person Centred Approach (For anyone particularly interested in Person-Centred counselling. They produce an excellent briefing document available from the postal address for a small charge.)
BM BAPCA, London, WC1N 3XX
www.bapca.org.uk

Telephone Helplines Association (THA) as the name suggests; lots of information related to telephone counselling.
0207 651 4321
www.helplines.org

OTHER WEBSITES

• A great general-purpose website for counselling information and links to many other sites:
www.allanturner.co.uk

• An excellent resource for alternative views and issues in therapy:
www.erthworks.co.uk

References

American Psychiatric Association (1994) DSM-IV. Washington, DC: American Psychiatric Association.

Beck, A. T. (1999) *Prisoners of Hate: The cognitive basis of anger, hostility and violence.* New York: HarperCollins.

Berk, R. A. and Rossi, P. H. (1998) *Thinking about Program Evaluation.* Newbury Park: Sage.

Bohart, A., Elliott, R. and Greenberg,L. (2002) Empathy. In J. Norcross (Ed) *Psychotherapy Relationships that Work.* Oxford University Press.

Bond, T. (1990) *HIV Counselling : Report on National Survey and Consultation 1990.* BAC & Dept. Health.

Bristol, C. (1985) *The Magic of Believing.* A Fireside Book published by Simon & Schuster.

British Association for Counselling, *Counselling & Psychotherapy Resources Directory*, (Published annually).

_____ (1985) *Code of Ethics and Practice for Trainers.*

_____ (1988) *Code of Ethics and Practice for the Supervision of Counsellors.*

_____ (1989) *Code of Ethics and Practice for Counselling Skills.*

_____ (1993) *Code of Ethics and Practice for Counsellors.*

_____ (1991) *Definition of Terms in Use with Expansion and Rationale.*

_____ (1990) *The Recognition of Counsellor Training Courses,* Second Edition.

British Psychological Society, *Directory of Chartered Psychologists.* (Published annually).

Buchanan, L. and Hughes, R. (2000) *Experiences of Person-centred Counselling Training.* Ross-on-Wye: PCCS Books.

Chadwick, P. (2001) *Personality as Art: Artistic approaches in psychology.* Ross-on-Wye: PCCS Books.

Coles, A. (1996) From Priesthood to Management Consultancy. In *Counselling.* Vol. 7 No. 3 (August).

Dryden, W. and Spurling, L. eds. (1989) *On Becoming a Psychotherapist.* London: Routledge.

Egan, G., (1982/94) *The Skilled Helper — A Problem-Management Approach to Helping.* Brooks/Cole.

Elliott, R., Greenberg, L. and Lietaer, G. (in press) Research on experiential psychotherapies. In M. Lambert, A. Bergin and S. Garfield (eds) *Handbook of Psychotherapy and Behaviour Change.* New York: Wiley.

Eysenck, H.J. (1953) *Uses and Abuses of Psychology.* Pelican published by Penguin Books Ltd.

Ferguson, M. (1981) *The Aquarian Conspiracy.* Routledge.

Friends, Religious Society of, *Questions & Counsel.* London Yearly Meeting, 1988 No.16.

Gaylin, N. (2001) *Family, Self and Psychotherapy: A person-centred perspective.* Ross-on-Wye: PCCS Books.

Grant, B. (1990) Principled and instrumental nondirectiveness in person-centered and client centered therapy. *Person-Centered Review,* Vol. 5 pp. 77–88.

Green, H. (1972) *I Never Promised You a Rose Garden.* Pan. (1964 Gollancz)

Halmos, P. (1969) *The Faith of the Counsellors.* London: Constable.

Hjeller, L. A. and Ziegler, D. J. (1981) *Personality Theories — Basic Assumptions, Research and Applications,* McGraw-Hill.

Hoban, R. (1975) *Turtle Diary.* Picador/Pan Books.

House, R. and Totton, N. (1997) *Implausible Professions: Arguments for pluralism and autonomy in psychotherapy and counselling.* Ross-on-Wye: PCCS Books.

Newnes, C., Holmes, H. and Dunn, C. (2001) *This is Madness Too: Critical perspectives on mental health services.* Ross-on-Wye: PCCS Books.

Jackson, E.N. (1978) *The Many Faces of Grief.* SCM.

Jewel, T. (1992) *Report of an evaluative study of counselling in general practice.* Cambridgeshire FHSA.

Jung, C. G. (1954) *The Practice of Psychotherapy,* Vol.16 of The Collected Works. London: Routledge & Keegan Paul.

Kearney, A. (1996) *Counselling, Class and Politics.* Manchester: PCCS Books.

King, M., Sibbald, B., Ward, E., Bower, P., Lloyd, M., Gabbay, M. and Byford, S. (2000) Randomised controlled trial of non-directive counselling, cognitive behaviour therapy and usual general practitioner care in the management of depression as well as mixed anxiety and depression in primary care. *Health Technology Assessment, Vol. 4 No.19.*

Laing, R. D. (1969) *Self and Others.* London: Penguin.

Lockhart, W.H. (1983) The outcomes of individual client-centred counselling with young offenders in secure residential care, in *Children of the Troubles,* Harbison, J. (Ed), Stranmillis College Belfast.

Longman Dictionary of Psychology and Psychiatry, (1984), Longman.

McGregor, D. (1970) *The Human Side of Enterprise.* Maidenhead: McGraw Hill.

McLennen, J. (1991) Formal and Informal Counselling Help: Students' Experiences in *The British Journal of Guidance and Counselling,* Vol.19, No.2. 149–59.

Maeder, T. (1989) *Children of Psychiatrists and Other Psychotherapists.* New York: Harper & Row.

Minton, H. L. (2002). *Departing from Deviance.* Chicago: University of Chicago Press.

Nelson-Jones, R. (1993) *Practical Counselling and Helping Skills (3rd edn).* Cassell.

Oakley, A. (1985) *Taking it Like a Woman.* Flamingo (Fontana Paperbacks).

Pasternak, B. (1988) *Doctor Zhivago.* Harper Collins.

Prouty, G., Van Werde, D. and Pörtner, M. (2002) *Pre-Therapy.* Ross-on-Wye: PCCS Books.

Rogers, C. R. (1951) *Client-Centered Therapy.* London: Constable.

Rogers, C. R. (1957) The necessary and sufficient conditions of therapeutic personality change. *Journal of Consulting Psychology, Vol. 21* No. 2, pp. 95–103.

Rogers, C. R. (1961) *On Becoming a Person.* London: Constable.

Rogers, C. R. (1978) *Carl Rogers on Personal Power — Inner strength and its revolutionary impact.* London: Constable.

Rogers, N. (1995) *Emerging Woman — A decade of midlife transitions.* Manchester: PCCS Books.

Russell, J., Dexter, G. and Bond, T. (1992) *Differentiation Between Advice, Guidance, Befriending, Counselling Skills and Counselling.* Advice, Guidance and Counselling Lead Body.

Sanders, P. (1996) *An Incomplete Guide to Using Counselling Skills on the Telephone (2nd edn).* Manchester: PCCS Books.

Secord, P. F. and Backman, C. W. (1974) *Social Psychology.* Tokyo: McGraw-Hill.

Shapiro, D. A., and Barkham, M. (1993) *RELATE: Information Needs Research. Final report to Department of Social Security.* Rugby: Relate Marriage Guidance.

Skinner, B. F. (1966) *Walden Two.* McMillan.

Shlien, J. M. (1994) Untitled and Uneasy. Unpublished paper.

Shlien, J. M. (1996) Embarrassment Anxiety: A literalist theory. In R. Hutterer, G. Pawlowsky, P. Schmid, and R. Stipsits (eds.) *Client-Centered and Experiential Psychotherapy: A paradigm in motion.* Frankfurt: Peter Lang.

Taft, J. (1937) *The Dynamics of Therapy in a Controlled Relationship.* New York: McMillan.

Thorne, B. (1991) *Person-Centred Counselling: Therapeutic and spiritual dimensions.* London: Whurr.

Thorne, B. (1992) Psychotherapy and counselling: The quest for differences. In *Counselling* Vol.3 No.4 (December).

Thorne, B. (1998) *Person-Centred Counselling and Christian Spirituality.* London: Whurr.

Thorne, B. (1999) Psychotherapy and counselling are indistinguishable, in Feltham, C. *Controversies in Counselling and Psychotherapy.* London: Sage.

Tournier, P. (1978) *The Violence Inside.* Tr. Edward Hudson. SCM.

West, M. (1963) *Shoes of the Fisherman.* Heinemann.

West, W. (1994) *A Study of the Relationship Between Counselling/ Psychotherapy and Healing: First findings.* Presentation at the BPS Counselling Psych. Conference.

Williams, S. (1993) *An Incomplete Guide to Referral Issues for Counsellors.* Manchester: PCCS Books.

Williamson, M. (1993) *Return to Love — Reflections on a course in miracles,* Aquarian.

Winnicott, D.W. (1971) *Therapeutic Consultations in Child Psychiatry.* London: Hogarth Press.

Song Lyrics
Björk Gudmundsdottir, Nellee Hooper and Antonio Carlos Jobim: **Human Behaviour**, from the album *'Debut'* by Björk: One Little Indian Records.

David Byrne & Brian Eno: **Once in a Lifetime**, from the album *'Remain in Light'* by Talking Heads: Sire Records.

David Couse: **I am Afraid**, from the album *'I am the Greatest'* by A House: EMI Records.

Michael Franti: **Television, the Drug of the Nation**, from the album *'Hypocrisy is the Greatest Luxury'* by The Disposable Heroes of Hiphoprisy: Island Records.

Roy Harper: **If**, from the album *'Once'* by Roy Harper: Awareness Records.

Robert Smith: **Boys Don't Cry**, from the album *'Staring at the Sea—The Singles'* by The Cure: Fiction Records.

The Levellers: **Fifteen Years**, from the album *'Levelling the Land'*: China Records.

Poems
Simon Rae *All Purpose Late Twentieth Century Creed* first published in 'The Guardian' newspaper.

Benjamin Zephaniah (1995) *White Comedy,* from the book 'Propa Propaganda' published by Bloodaxe Books.

Further Reading

If you do not intend to continue your training in counselling but are still interested in this area:
Richard Nelson-Jones, (1990) *Human Relationship Skills (2nd edition),* Cassell.

If you use counselling skills on the telephone in the course of your job or do telephone helpline work, either paid or as a volunteer:
Pete Sanders, (1996) *An Incomplete Guide for Using Counselling Skills on the Telephone revised 2nd edition,* PCCS Books.

If you are going to continue training on a certificate or counselling skills course:
Frankland, A. and Sanders, P. (1995) *Next Steps in Counselling — A Students' Companion for Certificate and Counselling Skills Courses,* PCCS Books.

If you are continuing your training or you want help with your assignments:
Sanders, P. (1998) *Step in to* Study *Counselling — A Students' Guide to Learning Counselling and Tackling Course Assignments 2nd edition,* PCCS Books.

If you want to read more about specific counselling approaches (these are certificate-diploma level books, but quite easy to read, so don't be put off):
Gerard Egan's approach: Culley, S. (1990) *Integrative Counselling in Action,* Sage.
Carl Rogers' approach: Merry, T. (1999) *Learning and Being in Person-Centred Counselling second edition,* PCCS Books.
Albert Ellis' approach: Dryden, W. (1990) *Rational Emotive Counselling in Action,* Sage.
Cognitive approaches: *Cognitive Behavioural Counselling in Action*
Psychodynamic approaches: Jacobs, M. (1988) *Psychodynamic Counselling in Action,* Sage.

If you are thinking about continuing your training to diploma-level in the person-centred approach, the following book will help you decide:
Buchanan, L. and Hughes, R. (2000) *Experiences of Person-Centred Counselling Training: A compendium of case studies to assist prospective applicants.* PCCS Books.

Index

Main topics only